BREAKING
NEWS

"Not only is Jeremy Thompson a wonderful friend, he is also an outstanding journalist. Jeremy possesses the courage, sensitivity, dedication and tenacity that is needed to make a great reporter, and *Breaking News* is a fascinating account of his life in news."

"A bold and gripping trip through the last four decades of the world's biggest news stories – and some lovely peeks behind the scenes – from the man who defined Breaking News in Britain."

"Jeremy Thompson is one of the great television reporters of his generation. He knows the story, knows how to tell it and knows his audience – as this book shows."

"Jeremy Thompson, one of the world's best journalists and a consummate storyteller, has written a fantastic autobiography."

"Jeremy Thompson's *Breaking News* is a wonderfully told story about the very soul of journalism; about how news gets reported; about the sacrifices serious journalism demands; about paying dues; and about what journalism is supposed to be. It's no wonder that whenever Jeremy's name is mentioned, the word gravitas immediately springs to mind."

"*Breaking News* is so much more than a great memoir. It is history in the making, a masterclass in journalism, and sheer reading pleasure."

JEREMY THOMPSON
BREAKING
NEWS
AN AUTOBIOGRAPHY

Biteback Publishing

This paperback edition published in Great Britain in 2018 by
Biteback Publishing Ltd
Westminster Tower
3 Albert Embankment
London SE1 7SP
Copyright © Jeremy Thompson 2017, 2018

ISBN 978-1-78590-442-4

10 9 8 7 6 5 4 3 2 1

A CIP catalogue record for this book is available from the British Library.

Set in Sabon LT by Adrian McLaughlin

Printed and bound in Great Britain by
CPI Group (UK) Ltd, Croydon CR0 4YY

MIX
Paper from
responsible sources
FSC® C020471
FSC
www.fsc.org

For Lynn, my buddy, my pal and my chum, whose endless love and support made my career and this book possible.

For my sons, James and Adam, in the hope that these words may explain those missing moments.

For my grandchildren, Bella, Sophia, Ewan and Joshua, so that they may be inspired to explore the world.

For my mother, Betty, who believed in me to her last day at the age of ninety-nine.

CONTENTS

CHAPTER 1 Grandchildren...1

CHAPTER 2 The Voice..3

CHAPTER 3 Learning the Trade...11

CHAPTER 4 Local Radio..21

CHAPTER 5 Look North and Beyond...31

CHAPTER 6 Yorkshire Ripper...41

CHAPTER 7 Crazy...51

CHAPTER 8 Indian All-rounder..63

CHAPTER 9 Asian Oddities...73

CHAPTER 10 Tiananmen..85

CHAPTER 11 Coup Two...95

CHAPTER 12 First Gulf War...101

CHAPTER 13 Flight Frights..113

CHAPTER 14 Yugoslav War...123

CHAPTER 15 The Mandela Years...133

CHAPTER 16 Cry Freedom...143

CHAPTER 17 Valentine's Day...151

CHAPTER 18 Black Mamba and the Bad Man..................................161

CHAPTER 19 Somalia: Why I Blame Myself
for Black Hawk Down 173

CHAPTER 20 A Bright Sky 185

CHAPTER 21 African Sky 197

CHAPTER 22 Rainbow Nation 209

CHAPTER 23 Rwanda 221

CHAPTER 24 USA: Two Nations Divided 233

CHAPTER 25 Olympics 243

CHAPTER 26 Kosovo 249

CHAPTER 27 Volcanoes and Tsunamis 259

CHAPTER 28 Millennium Times Two 265

CHAPTER 29 9/11 271

CHAPTER 30 It's Not About Me 275

CHAPTER 31 The Day I Met a Murderer 283

CHAPTER 32 Iraq War 2003 293

CHAPTER 33 US Presidents 303

CHAPTER 34 Saints and Sinners 311

CHAPTER 35 Movies 319

CHAPTER 36 War on Terror 323

CHAPTER 37 Mick Deane 333

CHAPTER 38 Royals 339

CHAPTER 39 PMTs: Prime Ministers' Tales 349

CHAPTER 40 Presenters' Tips 359

CHAPTER 41 Back to Africa 365

CHAPTER 42 Trump and Out 369

Awards 377
Index 379

CHAPTER 1

GRANDCHILDREN

They haven't asked yet. But I'm sure it won't be long before my grandchildren want to know.

'So, what did you do at work, granddad?'

'Well kids,' I might say to them.

I went to more than twenty wars, several civil conflicts, a few *coups d'état*, far too many terrorist attacks and at least one genocide. I've been caught up in massacres and gunfights. I've seen natural disasters – floods and tsunamis, hurricanes, tornadoes and monsoons, earthquakes and volcanic eruptions, drought, famine, plague and pestilence. And I've witnessed a few man-made disasters – exploding factories, poison gas clouds, mining accidents and shipwrecks. I've told tales of crimes almost too awful to recount – serial killers, child abductors – and I've even talked to murderers.

'Wow granddad!' they'll probably say. 'That all sounds pretty grim and rather dangerous. Didn't you do anything nice?'

'Well, nice doesn't crop up in news all that often. But, if it's any help, I have covered loads of elections, most of them peaceful,' I'll offer as consolation. 'At least a dozen British ballots, six US presidential votes and a host of leadership showdowns around the world. I've met Presidents, Prime Ministers, princes and paupers. I've talked to despots and desperadoes; tyrants and tinpot dictators; protesters and repressors; gangsters and law enforcers; hostages and hostage-takers.'

'You must have seen some decent sport, granddad?' the youngsters will no doubt ask.

'Sport. That's almost my favourite bit,' I'll reply excitedly. 'I've seen enough great sport for two lifetimes.'

'What were your favourites?' they will demand.

'I hardly know where to start. How about England winning the Ashes; a British and Irish Lions rugby tour; Europe winning the Ryder Cup; football and rugby world cups; five Olympic Games; cricket tours to Australia, India, Pakistan and the West Indies. Then there's Wimbledon, Wembley, Lord's, Twickenham and the Open. And all in the line of duty!'

'Phew, we can see why you liked your job, granddad,' I imagine they will say. 'Anything else?'

'Well, there's always the odd exotic story. You know, the sort of fact-is-stranger-than-fiction tale, like the Cowboy Poetry Festival in the snowy wilds of Nevada; a real prison chain gang in Alabama; a whole community living on a giant rubbish tip in the Philippines; interviewing a letterbox in Leeds; covering the millennium, not once but twice; dwarf-throwing in Australia; and a white male maid in a black household in post-apartheid South Africa.

'Oh, I almost forgot the royals. I did some great tours – live on the Great Wall of China with the Queen, in West Africa and Australia with Charles and Di, into forbidden Laos and Burma with Princess Anne. Diana in Zimbabwe. Then there were royal births, deaths and marriages and the Golden Jubilee.

'And I got to do some great wildlife stories in Africa.' Anyway here are some of the highlights.

CHAPTER 2

THE VOICE

'I'd know that voice anywhere,' boomed a man from across the Heathrow terminal.

'You're the voice of Breaking News.'

The man was a complete stranger, but apparently a big fan of Sky News.

'I recognised your voice before your face,' he told me as he snapped a selfie of me and him. I was only checking in for a flight, but, speaking loudly enough, it seemed to have alerted an admiring viewer.

||||||||||||||||||||

It was a familiar story. I'd never lacked volume. Now, as a television news presenter, I was getting spotted as much for my distinctive voice as for my facial features or my career achievements.

As I was to discover, a hint of a celebrity can be a curious thing in an age of reality TV and the desire to be famous.

I had never sought it. It just crept up on me over many years. I'd started life as a journalist on a local newspaper, with dreams only of making it to Fleet Street, if I was good enough. Back in those days, the late 1960s, they'd barely invented broadcasting. For a newsman there was only the BBC or ITN, and they seemed unattainable for a lad with no connections.

Then local radio started, opening up a route into broadcast news that was hitherto unavailable. Scores of us scrambled through this new portal of opportunity and it transformed our careers. But it didn't propel you into stardom overnight; it was more of a long, steady climb of progression. I spent three years at BBC Radio Sheffield before getting a sniff of telly at BBC *Look North* (Leeds). I was nearly thirty by the time I reached network news, becoming the Beeb's first North of England TV correspondent. And it was another decade before I became a foreign correspondent with ITN.

I set up and ran three foreign bureaux on three different continents (Asia, Africa and North America) for ITN and then Sky, before a boss finally insisted that I become a news presenter. Even then I was a bit reluctant. I'd always loved being a reporter, out on the road, gathering stories at the grass roots. I knew anchoring or presenting or newscasting, call it what you will, would remove me a step or two from the day-to-day frontline of news. But it had its upsides. It gave me a bigger say in the news agenda and allowed me to have a greater impact in shaping the channel's image.

At Sky we ramped up the tempo of rolling news and made 'Breaking News' synonymous with our brand. We told the viewers loud and clear when a story was 'Breaking News'. We plastered it across the screen, adding yellow straplines and pulsing red flashes to let you know it was 'Live!'

It worked. Before long, focus groups told us that Sky was the first channel they'd turn to for breaking news. A lot of viewers were of the opinion that we were the first, the fastest and even the fairest when it came to bringing them a rolling news story. Many people told me, texted me or emailed to let me know that I was the man they associated with the latest big stories. I had become their 'Voice of Breaking News'.

It meant I was recognised more often in countries all around the world where Sky News was broadcast. That could be a help or a hindrance when I was out presenting on location. In places like Israel, Spain and South Africa, people were often more willing to talk to me or give me information because they knew me from TV. In more hostile environments like Syria, Iraq or the former Yugoslavia, however, recognition simply made me more of a target.

In South Africa, where I was based for four years and still have close links and many mates, most people approach me like I'm their good friend. No doubt in their minds whatsoever. Whenever I find myself in Woolworths, the South African equivalent of Marks & Spencer, I've often found myself lurking awkwardly by the ladies' underwear section as my wife stocks up on new bras. Invariably, this is the moment 'women of a certain age' rush up shrieking: 'Oh! Jeremy. You're my best. I watch you every day.' Trapped against the undies, I'm left with no other alternative but to grin gratefully, sign autographs and gurn for selfies.

Some of these rather predatory females have been known to add, with a coy smile playing on their enhanced lips: 'I sometimes watch your programme when I'm in bed.' I try not to think about that.

This strange world of celebrity was a far cry from my earlier days in broadcasting when I could get through life with a degree of anonymity.

In my first few years at Sky we just wanted to get noticed by the viewing public. We felt like we had to prove something to the world. We got the feeling we weren't taken seriously enough by rivals at the BBC and ITN, some of whom were downright patronising towards our 'upstart' channel. But this was a great motivator. The national newspapers weren't much better, never printing our programme schedules and rarely writing about our successes, even when we'd blown the opposition out of the water, which happened more and more during the 1990s.

We were seen as the new kids on the block and expected to earn our stripes. A lot of British viewers were still stuck in an analogue age, slow to switch to satellite.

My wife, Lynn, and I were going out to dinner with her sister, Angela, and her husband David, who live in West Yorkshire. We got a taxi from Liversedge to the restaurant in Elland. After a few minutes the cabbie, whose name was Tariq, turned to me in the back seat and said: 'Eh! I know that voice. Now don't tell me, I'll get there.' For a couple of minutes, Tariq struggled to place me, then he burst out in triumph: 'Got it. You're that Jeremy Thompson, off Sky News.'

He apologised for taking so long, explaining: 'You see, my wife and I are 'aving our 'ouse done up. And we're 'aving to stay at me mam's. And the terrible thing is – she's only got proper telly.' For Tariq and millions of others, 'proper telly' meant terrestrial channels only. He said it was torture, 'Like being stuck on the moon.' He'd got used to the choices on satellite TV and he loved Sky News – it was to take a while for the rest of Britain to catch up with Tariq.

For today's generation, Sky is one of the news channels of choice, though viewers are just as likely to be watching on a laptop or a tablet as they are a conventional TV set.

Many is the time an aspiring young news trainee on work experience has skipped across the newsroom to let me know: 'I want to do what you do.' I'd ask 'So, what do you think I do as a news presenter?' 'Well, you're on TV, that's all that counts,' the ambitious wannabe would reply, following this up with: 'So how long did it take you to get this job?' I'd answer, in all honesty and accuracy: 'Well, about thirty years.' Clearly less than impressed, the youngster would give me a look that said: 'Silly old fart. I'm not waiting that long for a chance at TV and a shot at the big time.' For some, being famous seems more important than checking facts and developing a craft.

Of course, appearances can be deceptive. I still chuckle when I recall the day Lynn brought our youngest granddaughter, Sophia, to Sky to see where her granddad worked. As I sat down at my impressively large desk and the title music signalled the start of *Live at Five*, Sophia, then aged five, looked up at the floor manager and asked, in all innocence: 'Is granddad a rock star?' As you've since discovered,

Soph's granddad can't hold a tune in a bucket, as they say, so that was never going to happen. Being a newsman was as glam as it would ever get – and I wouldn't have swapped my career for anything.

For me, being a newsman was all about telling stories. Journalism was gaining experience, building up knowledge, checking details and sources, understanding the context of stories. This was even more important with breaking news. Live rolling stories give you less time to gather and verify information, so they demand even greater care in filtering what you put out on air. The viewers have tuned in to your channel because they trust you. I was always determined not to let them down. Give them the right stuff, not the guff. The rise of social media has created a dilemma. There's no doubt it can be a fount of information. But it's often unsourced, unfiltered, unmonitored and unchecked. As a journalist, you might have no idea about whether something is a reliable source. My instinct was to avoid the temptation to use it on live TV news.

As you'll discover in these pages, I take the business of news very seriously, even if I take myself slightly less so.

There are times when I feel like a living museum of journalism. I started out on newspapers with a notepad and pencil, dictating copy from red phone boxes, while feeding them with coins. I went through local radio wielding a large tape recorder and cutting quarter-inch tape into stories using razor blades on a metal block. In regional TV, we worked on film, which had to be developed in the 'soup' or processing bath for an hour, before we could edit. I was part of the transition in 1975 from black and white to colour. And we thought that was a historic breakthrough. The weather was composed on a local map using Letraset stick-on sun, rain, clouds, fog or whatever was needed. It was pretty primitive.

Then came another 'great leap forward' – U-matic. This was the first generation of analogue video cassettes. The same size cameras, but with huge recording units so heavy they left scores of sound recordists with droopy shoulders and dodgy backs. ENG or electronic news gathering, as it became known, steadily evolved into cleverer, smarter, slimmer variations. Eventually the cassettes were replaced by memory cards. Then the cameras started to be scaled down. By the end of my career many of the cameramen I worked with were using DSLR cameras, with video function; light and easy to use, great quality and readily hidden in tricky situations.

The way we transmitted the pictures and stories has also changed radically.

From the original fixed point locations, the advent of flyaway satellite dishes in the 1980s gave TV news freedom of movement for the first time. But the flyaways were far from fairy-winged. They were big old lumps – ten to sixteen feet in diameter and weighing a few tons. It took time, money and manpower to move those big silver boxes to the action.

In the summer of 1980, I was travelling through South and Central America, reporting on a trip by the then Foreign Secretary, Lord Carrington. Me and my BBC news crew were still working on film. One day we got a call from the desk in London on a landline (no mobile phones in those days) sending us off to Texas to cover a huge hurricane named Allen, which was threatening the Gulf Coast. We drove down to Corpus Christi in Texas, anxiously watching as 1 million people drove the other way, checked in at the La Quinta Motor Lodge, where they gave us a 'storm discount' price on our room.

We filmed Hurricane Allen in all his destructive glory. But then we had to fly up to New York three and a half hours away to get the film processed at the BBC bureau before it could be edited and fed to London for broadcast. Talk about long-winded!

Nowadays, flyaway dishes are fold up and go. Increasingly we're using live video links via wireless cell phone networks. Devices like Live-U are basically small boxes full of SIM cards that bundle up the data and livestream it back to base. The cameraman just carries it in a light backpack and plugs it into the camera. In areas where there is a good 4G signal, it's revolutionised our ability to present live on the road from almost any location at a moment's notice. I covered most of the Trump election across the US using these portable video live links. We were able to spring into live mode in a matter of minutes.

After the Paris terror attacks of November 2015, a story broke early one morning that police had cornered some of the suspects in a flat in the suburb of Saint-Denis. The links truck I was working with got stuck in bad traffic. So Sky's Europe correspondent Mark Stone swiftly clamped his iPhone to a lighting stand, stuck a pair of earphones in my ears, handed me a microphone and dialled up Sky Centre using a clever little app called Dejero. Within two minutes we were live on air, talking about the siege just down the road. I presented live for more than two hours using just a mobile phone – and few viewers seemed to notice the difference!

It was a far cry from the callow hack in a Cambridgeshire phone box with his two-pence coins. Or my first 'foreign' in 1970 when the paper sent me to Northern Ireland to report on our local regiment who were stationed there.

'Here's a tenner for your expenses and a ticket to Belfast,' growled Eddie the news editor.

'Any advice, boss?' I asked.

'Yes,' he said. 'Sharpen your pencil, take an extra notebook and make sure you've got some change for the phone. Now get out of here before I change my mind!'

It was sophisticated stuff in those days.

The pace of news has gone into overdrive. In the days of one major TV news bulletin a day, a single story could last days if not weeks. Now most angles can be explored and exhausted in a matter of hours. The 6 a.m. lead story might be eclipsed by 6 p.m. The 24-hour cycle devours news. It's a far cry from the era when I disappeared up the Orinoco River for a few days or slipped into Somalia for a week, totally out of contact, until we emerged with a camera full of stories. These days, people want news now.

The picture package, the craft I spent most of my life as a reporter trying to perfect, has been usurped in importance by the live two-way. How a programme looks can upstage its story quality. It is a case of cosmetics over content. Ever-evolving technology has made breaking news more mobile and more immediate. There are few places left on the planet where we can't bring you live pictures. It's allowed TV journalists like me to take viewers closer than ever to the frontline – not just to wars, but to all the big stories of the twentieth and twenty-first centuries. As a presenter, I've seen my role as offering a guiding hand, an objective voice of reason, providing context and authenticity. It's been the great privilege of my job, to witness the makings of history and share them with those who watch.

CHAPTER 3

LEARNING THE TRADE

'You want to be what?' I can still hear my father say.

'You want to be a journalist?' There was a mix of exasperation, disappointment and resignation in his voice.

It wasn't the first time we'd had this conversation. But this time I think he knew I meant it. I didn't blame him for his doubts. I knew where he was coming from. But this was my life now.

||||||||||||||||

You have to understand the background. My dad, Gordon Alfred Thompson, was born in south London in 1911, one of eight children. His father was a watchmaker. Dad had left school at fifteen and began working in 1926 – the start of the Great Slump, a period of economic downturn and hardship. He started out as a clerk in the City offices of the Caledonian Insurance Company. In those tough days of financial crashes, strikes and hardship, employment was in short supply. My father was for ever grateful just to have a job. So years later, as I was leaving school, he drummed into me those same values – the need for a regular job, a decent education and, above all, a pension.

Somewhat reluctantly, I agreed to train as a chartered surveyor, a career Dad found acceptable. I aimed high, applied only to firms with a double-page advertising spread in *Country Life* and ended up with a trainee position at Strutt & Parker, Lofts & Warner property managers, land agents and surveyors, with Mayfair offices at 41 Berkeley Square.

Apart from the correspondence course, it was quite enjoyable. I was assigned to a delightful old partner, Charles Stone, who took me off to survey grand country estates, often accompanied by a decent lunch in a rural pub. And we did our best to sell large town houses in London, mainly to those folk with country estates. The highlight was showing Carlo Ponti and Sophia Loren around a mansion they were thinking of buying on Prince's Gate in Knightsbridge. They seemed an odd match. She was stunning. He was short and stout. They didn't buy the place, despite my best efforts as a salesman. And really my heart just wasn't in chartered surveying.

I had a brief go at the advertising industry, largely because my flatmates worked for agencies and they seemed much better off than me. For a while I wrote copy for Gestetner office machines and Adams butter, but it wasn't really for me.

So I decided to stop messing around and try to get a job as a journalist, which I'd secretly always fancied. I can't tell you exactly why I knew I wanted to be in news, but JFK's assassination had a big impact on me. I was in a history A level class at school on 22 November 1963 when our teacher 'Boff' Nathan broke the news – it suddenly made history exciting and relevant. I read all I could about the events in Dallas and imagined what it must have been like to be there reporting the story. Hence a conversation with my father was needed. By now he'd risen to the rank of highly respected regional manager in his insurance company. He clearly wasn't impressed by the news media. When it came to professions he considered credible, reporters were close to the bottom of the pile.

'Do you realise there's only one working category seen as a worse insurance risk than journalists – and that's jazz musicians.'

He delivered this statement with the sort of finality of reasoning that was meant to put me off reporting for life. Needless to say it didn't. We begged to differ on career paths and I set out to find myself a job as a journalist. I headed for the local library, got out a copy of *Willings Press Guide* and jotted down the names of six regional newspapers in town or cities where I fancied working. I wrote to editors in Bristol, Brighton, Southampton, Plymouth, Oxford and Cambridge. They were all morning or evening papers. I thought I'd aim high and skip the weeklies.

Five replied in the same vein, suggesting I should sign up for Britain's very first media course. It was a one-year diploma in journalism, run by the National Council for the Training of Journalists, at Darlington Technical College. My heart sunk a little. As a southern lad, Darlington sounded a long way from my dream ticket into papers. But I sucked it up, sat an entry paper and won myself a place on the course.

What a far cry from today's training scene. In 1967, there was only one diploma course for journalists in the whole of Britain and it was in Darlington. Today there are at least 100 university degree courses to choose from in the UK, which turn out thousands of budding journalists each year. I always wonder whether there are enough jobs to go around for so many skilled graduates.

Fortunately, the sixth newspaper, *Cambridge Evening News*, invited me for an interview and offered me an indenture – a four-year apprenticeship. So began my life as a journalist. It was a dream come true, though it proved far from glamorous. I soon discovered that the junior junior's job consisted mainly of making tea, tidying the newsroom desktops and writing up news paragraphs.

I soon progressed onto weddings. I was told it was a promotion. But I wasn't so sure. It didn't involve going to churches or registry offices as you might imagine, just slogging away at the back of the newsroom. Brides and grooms, or most likely their mums, were given pro forma to complete, filling in all relevant details of the upcoming wedding. From this often sketchy information, the lowliest journalist in the newsroom was expected to construct a dazzling and exciting report on the matrimonials.

'Hockey club captain bullies off with rugby winger,' one report might read.

'Love blossomed over the billiards table.'

'Hitched after hiking the Quantocks.'

'Round Table man weds square dancer.'

It took a lot of imagination and skill to turn the humdrum lives of 'Sid and Doris Ordinary' into readable copy. And in peak marriage season, I could find myself writing up fifty or more wedding reports every Friday afternoon and well into the evening.

But the real work began early the following Monday, when I had to check out every wedding to make sure it actually took place. Newsrooms were full of fabled stories of weddings that never happened: brides who got cold feet on their way to the altar; grooms who disappeared with the maid of honour; stag parties the night before that left the betrothed incapacitated; punch-ups between the families of the bride and groom; churches evacuated because of gas leaks; sickly vicars and so on.

Not quite the story of the Bartered Bride. But often a comic opera in the making.

So the news editor insisted that every event was carefully checked with either the family, the registrar or the clergy. It was surprising how many marriages didn't end in confetti and three cheers. And that was another story – quite literally. A failed wedding often merited more column inches than a successful one!

Soon I was 'promoted' once again. I was handed the honour of doing 'the calls'. This was a vast list of every decent contact in the area – from priests to parish councillors, club chairmen to W.I. presidents, post office managers and pub landlords, village shopkeepers to allotment secretaries. It was the holy of holies, inscribed on a seemingly endless single sheet of three-ply that emerged from the huge rolls attached to our archaic Olympia typewriters.

Colin Blakeley, now the most senior junior on the paper, presented the calls list to me with great ceremony, then winked and said: 'Good luck with all that!' I soon realised what he meant.

An hour later I was in the *Cambridge News* car park about to climb into my car, clutching the pink contacts list, when the news editor, Eddie Duller, came marching towards me, shouting: 'Oi you, stop right there.'

Pointing at my battered but treasured old Austin A40, Duller demanded: 'What's this shit?'

'My car, boss,' I replied.

'Well, get out and lock it up. What are those?' he said, pointing at my legs.

Slightly confused, I confirmed they were my legs.

'Well, bloody well use them,' said Duller, pushing his black-rimmed specs back onto his nose. 'And use those as well,' he said jabbing towards my eyes. 'Then you might spot a story or two out there. Now bugger off and come back with some news.'

Duller was blunt, but he was right. Walking the highways and byways of Cambridge, taking buses out into the villages, using my eyes and ears, talking to everyone I could find, knocking on doors and asking questions – all this proved an invaluable lesson. I soon learned how to spot stories. My ears pricked up when I heard something new, something different, something changed, something out of place. I soon realised there were news stories everywhere, if you looked hard enough. Before long I was coming back from a day's calls with up to a dozen tales to tell. Not all page leads. But good page fillers – grist to the media mill.

I picked up another good tip off Eddie Duller – in a urinal. I was down the pub one evening near the paper's offices when Duller followed me into the toilet. As we relieved ourselves, he said: 'That's a bloody good story the guy at the bar was telling you. What are you going to do about it?' I snapped into work mode, realising the casual chat I was having over a beer was the basis of a decent yarn. 'I'll write it up, boss,' I told Duller.

'You do that,' he said. 'Just keep your ears open in the pub. You bring me plenty of stories and I'll pay for your beers. OK?' It sounded like a deal to me.

So, from then on, I tried to ensure I never had too many pints in case I forgot a story. I always popped into the loo to jot down notes. I stopped having to pay for too many beers out of my own pocket.

I was learning the trade and loving it. I knew I was meant to be a journalist. But Duller never let us juniors get too carried away. Every now and then when we took our copy up to the news desk, he would read through the carefully typed folios with a deadpan look, and then rip up the paper and throw the pieces in the bin. He didn't need to say much. We just knew it hadn't met his quality threshold. So off we'd troop and have another bash at writing the story, until it finally met the Duller benchmark.

I learned plenty more from the Fleet Street guys, who covered our patch. I soon discovered there were free beers to be had from them too, if we slipped them copies of our best stories. If they liked the yarn, they'd rework it into a national newspaper tale, usually turning our average local offerings into tabloid tapestries. I marvelled at their ability to conjure up tales of the unexpected.

My best mentor was the legendary Michael O'Flaherty, who worked for the *Daily Express*. I still remember how he transformed my rather unpromising story about a row among neighbours over a pet budgie into a blockbuster page lead headlined: 'This is a SOB Story – Save Our Budgerigar.'

O'Flaherty was later famed for being part of one of Fleet Street's great scoops – tracking down the Brazilian hideaway of Great Train Robber Ronnie Biggs. O'Flaherty was the sort of hard-drinking, ace-writing, larger-than-life character, who fired up my imagination and my enthusiasm for the news business. My aim was to make it to Fleet Street to work alongside the real hacks.

I met other aspiring journos who were working for Michael Jeacock, known to one and all as 'Jolly Jack' Jeacock. He ran the local wire agency, the Cambridge News Service. I'd often hang about in his office just to hear him dictate the latest news story down the phone to all the national newspapers, one after another, each piece told in their own individual house style, and all off the top of his head. It was a work of art and craft.

Then Jolly Jack would disappear round to the Farmer's Club for a 'little, light lunch', invariably followed by a bottle of port and a game of cards or dice. He rarely came back to the office, leaving his young sidekicks, such as Zack Hicks, to hold the fort. I'd help out, learning more about filing for the national papers and sometimes earning a bit of extra cash.

But my best early break came when our editor, Keith Whetstone, was looking for a rugby correspondent. As an avid rugby man and ex-player, I pressed my suitability. And when nobody else seemed keen, I got the job. I soon found myself covering Cambridge University rugby, which, in those amateur rugby days, was one of the most prestigious clubs in the land, packed with international players.

Part of the job was to get regular briefings with the team captain. The first year as correspondent it was Martin Green, who went on to become an England coach. The second year it was England star centre John Spencer. They were always generous with their help, though I think they found it unusual talking to a rugby reporter who was even younger than they were as students.

One of the great rituals of university rugby was the announcement of the team for the annual Varsity Match against Oxford at Twickenham. This took place on a Sunday a couple of weeks before the match in St John's College Music Room. The players were dressed in their light blue rugby blazers, some sporting the ties of capped Blues. What I wasn't prepared for was the traditional drink. Black Velvet, a heady blend of Guinness and champagne, mixed in galvanised buckets and poured in pints. It was smooth, glorious and lethal.

It wasn't until I crawled back to the newsroom that evening to compile the story of the freshly announced Varsity team that I realised

I was writing rugby rubbish. I must have fallen asleep. Some hours later, as the sun crept through the windows, our office cleaner shook me awake. Never a good sign when the cleaner's your alarm clock. My bloodied fingers were wedged between the keys of my old Olympia typewriter – testament to my drunken efforts. I quickly scrubbed up and shaped up, and with the aid of copious cups of coffee, completed the story in time for the first edition. I made a note to beware of Black Velvet.

A week and a half later, I was reporting on the Varsity Match from the press box at Twickenham. I couldn't believe my luck. I was nineteen years old, a rugby correspondent and living the dream.

But it was a part-time dream. The rest of my working days were spent covering general news and still included a few weddings. After two years reporting on university rugby, I was assigned to our Ely office to vary my training. Under the tutelage of chief reporter Doug Thorley I was given more responsibility. There were just the two of us and a photographer covering a huge area of fenlands around Ely. I got to write more big stories and more page leads. I also learned some more useful lessons.

One Saturday I was sent to cover a football match at Soham on the windswept fens. Soon after the game started, a brawl broke out between the two sides. When the referee tried to intervene he got punched in the melee. That was enough for him to withdraw his services and declare the match null and void. The ref drove off nursing a black eye, the players drifted home and I raced off to write up a cracking little story that read: 'Ref flattened in Fen free-for-all.' A few days later I discovered my rival reporter from the local weekly hadn't bothered to write a word, telling his editor that the match had been called off so he didn't think it was a story. The lesson: there's always a story.

Talking of sport, I finally got to play rugby again as well as report on it. Ely had a thriving rugby club and I reckoned I could fit in a few games around my work commitments. What I had to figure out was how to file copy at half time and full time for our Saturday sports Blue Edition. And to make sure no one at headquarters found out I was playing and working at the same time.

I largely relied on friends, fans or injured teammates making notes and jotting down scores for me while I was out on the field. At half time I'd quickly scribble 200 words on how the game was going, send the designated 'reporter' off to the nearest phone box armed with a two-pence coin and the number of the copytaker at the *Cambridge News*. At the end of the match, I'd finish my report and dash off in my muddy kit to phone over copy, while the rest of the team were already in the showers.

There were a few hiccups. I couldn't put my name down in the paper as a scorer, as I wasn't really meant to be playing. So I either had to wait on the try line to give someone else a scoring pass or, if I touched down, I'd award the try to a mate who hadn't scored for a while. Prop forwards had never touched down so many tries. On the team sheet in our Friday paper, I was just 'A. N. Other' – week after week. Nobody said anything.

An away match with West Norfolk RFC proved the biggest headache. Their pitch was on remote farmlands out in the Wash, well beyond King's Lynn. Our only travelling supporter was our injured scrum half Billy, a farm lad with a broken leg and a limited grasp of written English. At half time I did the usual, wrote out a report of the first half – in capital letters to make it easier for Billy to read over the phone. Ah, what phone? There were no red kiosks to be seen. And the nearest sign of life was a farmhouse nearly a mile away. Anyway, game lad that he was, Billy set off on his crutches, over fences and stiles and hay bales. It was well into the second half by the time he reached the farmhouse and began negotiating the use of their phone. He barely made it back by full time. Then it was my turn to finish off my match report.

I got away with it all for nearly a season. Until I ran out for a home match in Ely and was confronted by none other than my editor Keith

Whetstone. I'd forgotten he was a selector for the Cambridgeshire county side and had come along to run his eye over some of the talent in our team.

'What the hell do you think you're doing?' he blustered, clearly taken aback to see me in my Ely rugby kit.

'Well, I'm playing rugby, sir.'

'But you can't,' he said. 'You're supposed to be reporting the match, not playing in it.'

I explained how I'd managed to do both all season without letting down his paper or the team. I followed up by appealing to him as a rugby man: 'Sir, surely you wouldn't want me to let down my teammates.'

He reluctantly agreed and then looked even more surprised when I handed him my notebook and asked if he minded writing a few notes and scores on the match. Good professional journalist and devoted rugby fan that he was, he went along with it. But that wasn't the end of the affair, although it was the end of my rugby career at Ely.

On Monday morning I got called in for a severe bollocking from Eddie Duller, who told me the main reason they were stopping me playing was because it contravened the company's insurance policy. But it didn't stop the editor telling the story of his cheeky rugby-playing reporter at every rugby club dinner in the county.

And it didn't slow down my progress. I was soon assigned to run the district office in Huntingdon. It came with the perk of a flat over the office and a patch of my own. But it was to prove the pinnacle of my career in newspapers.

CHAPTER 4

LOCAL RADIO

Since starting out in journalism, I'd always had my sights set on Fleet Street and a job on the nationals.

Broadcast news never entered my head. Frankly, there wasn't much of it around in the 1960s. The BBC and ITN, that was about it. It didn't sound like a place where I would stand a chance. My generation had always seen it as rather elite, drawing heavily on Oxbridge graduates.

But then the BBC began rolling out local radio as an experiment. Stations opened up in several big cities to meet a new demand for popular music and local news, triggered by the popularity of pirate radio. It was to transform broadcasting, opening up the hitherto narrow and hallowed corridors of Auntie BBC to a wider intake of new talent. Hacks from the hoi polloi, we used to call ourselves: members of the third estate clambering through the fences into the fourth estate.

||||||||||||||||||||

As my four-year apprenticeship at the *Cambridge News* was coming to an end, I got a call from an old mate, Ralph Smith, who'd been a reporter on the *Ely Standard*. He'd joined Radio Nottingham and said he was really enjoying this 'radio lark'. He told me there was a reporter/producer's post going at the recently opened BBC Radio Sheffield and he thought I should put in for it. I was accepted for an interview and stopped off in Nottingham on the way to pick up a few interview tips from Ralph.

The 'Board', as the BBC liked to call it, seemed to go well. I headed back to Huntingdon and waited to hear the outcome. And waited. And waited.

Some three months had passed without a word. I assumed that I hadn't got the job. But just out of interest I called the Beeb's appointments department and was put through to a man called Robin, who'd chaired my interview panel. I told him I was just checking to find out where I'd failed, so I would be better prepared if I applied again.

Robin sounded terribly flustered on the phone: 'Oh God. Aren't you there yet?' he stammered. 'In Sheffield, I mean. You're supposed to have started weeks ago.'

'No, I'm still at the *Cambridge News*. I hadn't heard anything. So I assumed I hadn't got the job,' I explained.

'Oh dear, oh dear, oh dear,' blustered a posh and panicky Robin. 'What a dreadful mess.'

Robin then launched into an unexpected stream of consciousness, telling me far more than I needed to know about how his first wife had died tragically; how, as a middle-aged widower, he'd fallen in love again much to his surprise; how he'd just got married and had been away on a glorious honeymoon and in the marvel of the moment, he'd clearly become very confused – and completely forgotten to tell me that I had got the job at Radio Sheffield. Then he just kept apologising. Robin really was a charming man, the sort of absent-minded, slightly antiquated administrator frequently found in BBC corridors back in those days. It was hard to get cross. I congratulated him on his recent marriage and promised to start work as soon as possible, though I had to give notice to my paper. It was a strange start to my life at the BBC.

Radio Sheffield was based in a grand old house, with fine wooded gardens, in the western suburb of Broomhill. It was a tranquil retreat from the gritty industrial city that had built its reputation on steel. For a Kentish man, who'd spent his life in the south of England, it was a serious eye-opener. This was the north of dark, satanic mills, of great sparking steel works, of coal mines with whirring wheels of pithead gear – the crucible of the industrial revolution. I sometimes found myself looking in wonder at these working monuments of manufacturing – the powerhouses of coal and steel, textiles and shipping. They had a sort of stark beauty like nothing I'd seen down south.

But in the early '70s, revolution was turning into economic evolution. Political confrontation was in the air, as the unions took on the government in a titanic battle of wills. Little did I know at the time that I was reporting on the last pitched battles to save Britain's primary industries. Looking back at those years, it felt like I spent my working life covering strikes. The powerful National Union of Mineworkers voted for its first official strike since 1926 over pay, challenging Ted Heath's Conservative government.

I got to see a lot of coal mines and a lot of miners. As there were only a handful of us local radio reporters we soon became well known on the picket lines. The miners called me 'that southern Jessie'. In other words, an educated kid from the home counties, who looked and sounded well out of place at the pit gates of South Yorkshire.

They loved a wind-up: 'Eh look! It's that southern Jessie. Why don't you run home and tell Ted 'Eath about them nasty Yorkshire miners! He's one of your lot, in't 'e?'

It was a good time and place to learn how to stand up for yourself as a reporter. 'Why don't you tell me what your problem is and why you're standing on a picket line?' I'd say to them, pushing my Uher tape recorder and microphone in their direction. 'Then I'll pass it on to Mr Heath.'

I remember one miner calling me over and saying: 'Ask us where us werks.'

I just about got the drift, so I asked: 'Excuse me, where do you work?'

To which he replied in dialect: 'I werks a'Ticky ontop.'

I hadn't got a clue.

'Ah! you daft 'apeth. Does tha know nowt?' he went on.

'Clearly not,' I said. 'Perhaps you'd be kind enough to enlighten me.'

So he spelled it out, like I was an idiot from another planet – which I probably was to him and his mates.

'I am a surface worker at Hickleton Main Colliery. I werks a'Ticky ontop.' Much merriment ensued. They loved a piss-take on a picket line.

Another little linguistic test for the southern Jessie was discovering what they were mining for – when they weren't on strike that was.

'Coal,' I'd say.

'Nah, coil, tha pillock,' came the correction. 'And in case you're wondering, we go down oil in ground to dig out coil.'

'So,' I dared to venture. 'If you go down an oil in the ground, I'm intrigued to find out what you put in your car engine.'

More rolling of eyes, as the miners continued to educate the alien reporter.

'Grease, of course.'

It was a whole new world I'd become immersed in. Despite the banter on the picket lines, I was learning that industrial action could be ugly, dirty and, at times, violent.

By now I'd met and interviewed Arthur Scargill, the rising star of the Yorkshire NUM, who'd dreamed up a smart new tactic to put pressure on the bosses and the government. They were called 'the flying pickets'. Teams of striking miners were bussed to key targets, like power stations, steel works, ports and coal depots, to shut them down. Other unions were persuaded to join them in solidarity.

Railway workers refused to transport coal, and power station workers refused to handle coal. With coal-powered Britain being strangled, Prime Minister Heath was forced to call a state of emergency. The Battle of Saltley Gate, when 2,000 miners closed a Birmingham coke works, brought the confrontation to a head. The miners accepted a new pay deal and returned to work – but not for long.

By January 1974, the NUM was on strike again and Ted Heath had imposed the three-day week, reducing working hours in order to conserve dwindling fuel stocks. Electricity was restricted to three consecutive days a week.

I remember power cuts, darkened streets, candlelight and cold dinners in a cold winter. It was hard to keep any business going, and this included radio stations. We stayed on air with the help of generators. We often had to edit our stories, cutting and sticking the quarter-inch recording tape by the light of candles and torches. On top of that, the oil crisis in the wake of the latest war in the Middle East meant petrol was rationed. There were endless queues at filling stations and we reporters were obliged to walk to many of our stories. Sheffield's two great football clubs, United and Wednesday, couldn't even use their floodlights. Our elders told us it was just like wartime again, but without the bombs. You couldn't beat a good bit of British stoicism.

It might sound like a gloomy diet of industrial conflict – it certainly was for Ted Heath as PM – but it was also a fascinating time of political and economic upheaval. Heath's slogan 'Who governs Britain?' backfired big time. The answer from the voters came through loud and clear: 'Not you, mate!' A hung parliament saw Harold Wilson back in power.

I spent much of my time going to Camelot, King Arthur's Castle, the nickname for Arthur Scargill's NUM HQ in Barnsley. He certainly liked to hold court, feeding us hacks the news lines he knew would cause tremors in Parliament. Though still only a local official, this red-haired ex-miner was one of the most powerful figures in Britain.

But it wasn't only strikes that made headlines. The first mining accident I covered was a stark reminder of the price these men sometimes paid to produce the nation's coal. At Markham Main in North Derbyshire, eighteen miners were crushed to death when a pit cage crashed to the bottom of the shaft. Watching the grieving families and comrades gather at the pithead made me realise the closeness of these colliery communities, a bond few outsiders would understand.

Sheffield was certainly a varied place to be a radio reporter. It had an impressive city council, where I cut my teeth as an interviewer, quizzing the likes of Ron Ironmonger, Enid Hattersley, Irvine Patnick and David Blunkett, the absurdly young and talented Labour councillor who went on to become Home Secretary.

I had run-ins with local MPs, who constantly challenged the reporting of this upstart local radio station and its newshounds. One Sunday, Dennis Skinner, the recently elected Labour MP for Bolsover, rang in to complain about our reporting of the Clay Cross council scandal. I was manning the news desk alone.

'What's your name then?' he challenged.

'Jeremy,' I answered.

'Jeremy.' He chewed it over a few times, in that sort of tone that suggested he was thinking 'Bloody southern Jessie. What's he doing in my neck of the woods?' Even if he didn't say it.

'Jeremy, Jeremy. What sort of a name is that?' he demanded.

I came back with 'Well, I think Dennis is a very nice name too, if you don't mind me saying, Mr Skinner.' Impertinent, but imperative I thought, if I was to avoid being bullied by him over the phone.

He seemed to back off a bit. And we managed to carry on the conversation in a slightly more civilised tone. I made a vow to myself that day. Don't be browbeaten, especially by MPs.

At Radio Sheffield, we weren't just journalists. We had to be jacks-of-all-trades. Like my great mate, Bob Simpson, who went on to be a top-class correspondent on BBC Radio News, we all had to turn our hands and voices to whatever was required. I not only wrote and read the news, but hosted current affairs programmes, compiled documentaries, acted as a disc jockey, ran quiz shows and presented the Saturday afternoon sports roundup.

When he wasn't reporting, Bob spent much of his time, covered in oil, tinkering with his beloved and temperamental Triumph TR4 on the front drive of the radio station. We were still joking about those good old local radio days when we met up twenty years later in Saddam Hussein's Baghdad as high-flying correspondents covering the First Gulf War.

Back on that radio beat, Sundays were always the biggest challenge. A weekend skeleton staff turned into a single soul by lunchtime. So the duty dog had to ring round contacts, like police, fire and ambulance stations, to gather the news. Then write up the bulletin and read it live on air every hour, while at the same time hosting the Sunday music request show for several hours, and then introduce and play in a pre-recorded chat programme for the rest of the afternoon. By that time you were ready to drop. I wasn't the only one who nodded off at the news desk, only to be woken by frantic phone calls from colleagues to say the station had gone off the air. There was nothing worse than the sound of a tape end flapping round on a turntable, a sure sign that the programme had finished long ago. Time to open the mic and apologise to listeners for a 'slight technical problem'.

BBC local radio was all very new to the listening public, so we often fielded curious calls. As we were the only BBC number in the Sheffield area telephone directory, a lot of people rang up to say their radio or television had broken down and demanded that we rush out to repair it. There were others who called offering to pay us their TV licence fee. Many more just wanted to moan about anything they didn't like on the BBC, whether it was from London, Manchester or Glasgow. We became kind of agony aunts for the whole of Auntie.

At one time we had an acting news editor who hailed from Perth in Scotland, but had a slightly guttural delivery. He liked to read the news bulletins, even though we tried to steer him away from the mic.

One day, as duty newsman, I took a call from an irate Sheffielder who shouted: 'Get that bloody Pakistani off the radio. This is Yorkshire, tha knows. Not Karachi.' My insistence that our newsreader was a very nice Scotsman failed to appease 'Mr Angry of Attercliffe'.

Another discovery in those early days as a broadcaster was that radio studios can have a febrile atmosphere all of their own. It was curious how often they crackled into life, amplifying emotions. How a slight slip of the tongue could escalate into moments of gibberish, or how the hint of a snigger or smirk could send colleagues into near hysteria. A fit of the giggles was a serious working hazard.

This wasn't helped by regular pranks played on those in the studio. One favourite was to set fire to the bottom of a news script as the presenter was trying to read the hourly bulletin live on air. The rest of us would watch in delight as they raced to finish the script before the words were consumed by flames.

There were those who failed to spot the red light was on before crashing into a live studio. Famously, one distracted radio station manager burst in, realised his mistake and blurted out: 'Oh Christ!' As if that wasn't enough, he then spluttered: 'Oh Christ! I've said Christ.' And then, in blind panic, said: 'Oh Christ! I've said Christ AGAIN!' It was to be his last job in radio management.

We also entertained ourselves by winding up our news editor, a splendid chap called Allan Kassell, who was an excellent newsman, but not a gifted broadcaster. When he occasionally read the news, we'd switch the output desk so that he heard his own voice fed back a fraction after he'd read his script. This audio feedback effect on anyone caught in this situation was that their brain quickly became scrambled and their words slurred. You soon sound like you're drunk or talking rubbish. Poor old Allan was especially susceptible; within moments he was spouting utter gobbledygook.

Oh! the joys of local radio. The great thing was you could learn about broadcasting, make mistakes, have fun and make mischief – all without bringing down the government. Local radio and regional television stations were safety valves where bright young broadcasters could let off steam, sharpen their skills and find their voices.

Nowadays, many new journalists, fresh out of media college, bypass the old regional training grounds and head straight into national newsrooms. As I've seen all too often in recent years, errors get amplified in the harsher glare of network news. When you're learning your trade in the big time, there's no hiding place when you fail. I look back gratefully at those early years when I was allowed to cut my reporter's teeth in relative obscurity.

CHAPTER 5

LOOK NORTH AND BEYOND

My career as a television reporter began in a crypt. A cavern beneath an old church in Blackman Lane – the first home of BBC Look North Leeds.

||||||||||||||||||||

Perhaps it was a fitting venue, as in those days, we had to endure countless interviews with the local Leeds celebrity, Jimmy Savile, who was given copious amounts of airtime to promote his various BBC programmes and charities. We always thought he was a bit creepy. Several of the women in the newsroom would call him a pervert and kept a good distance when he was in the studio.

Savile apart, *Look North* was a great place to work. The founding of the BBC English regions had opened up broadcasting to a whole new generation of youngsters. *Look North* was full of talent – journalists, camera operators, producers, directors and editors.

Many of the characters who cut their television teeth in Leeds went on to make a major impact in network TV, including fellow reporters Mike Smartt, who years later set up BBC News Online, and Tim Ewart, now a respected ITN correspondent. There was Peter

Bazalgette, the *Big Brother* pioneer, Stuart Prebble, who worked on *World in Action*, and Mark Byford, who rose to the rank of BBC Deputy Director-General. Nick Barratt and Gerry Troyna, my first floor managers in the studio, made their names directing and producing top network shows.

The place was buzzing with energy and ideas. There couldn't have been a better environment to learn how to be a television reporter. It was a place where I made friends for life, like Christina Sayers, who heroically typed my scripts as I babbled out a stream of consciousness seconds before I dashed on air. And her now husband, Peter Staunton, a producer, later a reporter, who's worked with me for over forty years at the BBC, ITN and Sky. My closest relationships were with the cameramen – Keith Massey, Dave Brierley and Ron Hurrell. They were three great pros who first taught me the power of pictures.

In those early days we worked exclusively on film. The standard camera was an Arriflex, a big, solid and reliable beast that recorded on Commag film. It combined film with an audio strip down the side, known as the stripe. This allowed us to record images and audio together.

Massey favoured an Aaton or Eclair, high-quality cameras that took mute images. They were then synchronised to a separate audio deck, carried by the sound recordist – in Massey's case, his long-time teammate, Ken Evans. The sound and pictures were synced by using a clapper board, so the film editor would know later which pictures went with what sound.

Time and timing were everything. The magazines carried just ten minutes of film. Loading another magazine was a messy business involving the sound recordist, working unsighted, with his hands in a big, black cotton bag threading film onto cogs so that the new stock didn't get exposed to light. They never thanked you for demanding a second mag. It was a big discipline to learn – trying to shoot a whole story in just ten minutes. And that included the pictures, interviews and piece to camera.

How times have changed. In today's digital era camera operators often shoot hours of material, knowing there are no real limits. It's an enormous luxury, though sometimes it can be a problem when the reporter and editor simply don't have enough time to view all the footage before cutting the story.

The biggest lesson I learned was to respect the images. Pictures were always king in television reporting. The words came second. I might be the guy with his face on the screen, but I was left in no doubt by my cameramen that I was just there to sell their pictures!

So in the edit room I saw my role as doing justice to the images. The key was to cut sequences that told the story almost without voice-over. I saw it like a strip cartoon. Look at the pictures and you should be able to gather the gist of the storyline. The reporter's words, usually voiced later, were designed to add value, to give more depth to the story. They were like the captions and the bubbles coming from the mouths in those strip cartoons.

For the majority of my television news career that was the craft I constantly strived to improve on, trying to create the perfect package – the best blend of images, sound and words. In many ways, pure reporting, making those news packages, gave me the greatest satisfaction during my forty-two years in TV news.

The good thing about regional TV was that you got to do everything, from skateboarding ducks to strikes that brought down governments. The absurd, the abnormal, the abstract and the unbelievable – all in a day's work. It was where I got to cover my first big stories that made it onto network news, like the Cod Wars and the miners' strikes. But it was my first disaster that left the biggest impression.

It was my first flight in a helicopter. Exhilarating and intimidating. What lay ahead was downright daunting.

We were literally flying into an inferno. As the chopper rose from an airfield east of Leeds, we could see the black granite sky filled with giant smoke clouds, tinted orange by flames.

Yet we were still over forty miles away.

All we knew was that there'd been a huge explosion at a chemical plant. We headed for a village in North Lincolnshire none of us had heard of. The name of Flixborough would soon become fixed in our memories. As we touched down, Massey, Evans and I headed towards the blast site. It was virtually demolished. I remember vividly walking through corn fields trimmed to a foot-high stubble by the blast waves. The huge car park was just earth. The tarmac had vaporised. Firemen told us everything had been burned to nothing except car tyres, which withstood the intense heat. It was as though the place had been hit by a fuel-air bomb.

We learned that twenty-eight people had been killed, thirty-six badly injured. We filmed rescuers searching for those missing. It was the first time I had seen charred bodies. It was 1 June 1974. I was a rookie reporter. It was the first time I'd found myself heading into a danger zone.

By chance it was a Saturday, with only seventy-two staff on duty. On a weekday there would have been four times that number. The firemen believed a vapour cloud of leaking caprolactam, used in making nylon, had been ignited by a spark. The massive blast at the Nypro plant was the biggest peacetime explosion ever seen in Britain. It stopped the clocks at seven minutes to five at Burton Post Office two miles away. I interviewed kids who'd been blown through their French windows, mums bowled over the garden hedge, and the pub landlord watching *Grandstand* on TV when he was blown out of his armchair with such force his head hit the ceiling.

As the fires blazed over the next two days we stayed on to report the disaster.

Then, another first for me – I was 'bigfooted'. The BBC sent big-time correspondents up from London, who made it abundantly clear that it was now their story. 'OK, regional reps, I hereby serve notice you've been officially bigfooted. So hop along,' one said. Arrogant bastard, I thought. Apparently we'd just been 'holding the fort' until the 'big guns' arrived. I'll never forget how patronised and angry I felt. It was then I vowed to myself I'd make sure I worked hard enough to become a 'top gun'.

Within three years I'd made it to network news, appointed the BBC's first North of England TV correspondent. The title came with a bright blue staff Ford Cortina, fitted with one of the very early mobile phones. It was so big the battery took up most of the boot and the not-in-the-least-bit mobile handset was welded between the two front seats. I soon discovered it got a signal only at the top of hills, so I spent a lot of time driving up Ilkley Moor, the Chevin or the Pennines.

On the west of the Pennines, I was at Oldham General Hospital in July 1978 to report another piece of history – the birth of the first test-tube baby. I interviewed Patrick Steptoe and Robert Edwards, the two doctors who'd pioneered the procedure of artificial insemination through IVF, in vitro fertilisation. They told me with a mixture of relief and delight that baby Louise Brown and her mother were both doing well. Twenty-five years later as a Sky presenter, I was to interview Louise, by then a mum herself.

Although he was to be overshadowed by the Yorkshire Ripper, another West Yorkshire murderer known as the Black Panther had his moment of infamy and gave me a career break. Donald Neilson turned to crime when his builder's business failed. He killed three people in a series of raids on small post offices. Then came his most notorious crime. He kidnapped a seventeen-year-old girl by the name of Lesley Whittle, demanding a ransom from her wealthy family. Her body was found hanging in a drainage shaft at Kidsgrove in Staffordshire. It was uncertain whether Neilson had pushed her off a ledge with a noose round her neck or whether she'd simply choked to death.

His capture had a comic element. He was finally overpowered outside a fish and chip shop in Mansfield after two customers dropped their battered cod and ran out to help two injured police officers who were struggling to arrest the gun-toting Neilson. The trial was held at Oxford Crown Court as it was decided he wouldn't get a fair hearing in Yorkshire.

Although still only a regional reporter at the time, I was given the trial to cover for *Look North* and the BBC's *Nine O'Clock News*. Every evening after the court session I'd drive sixty miles to BBC TV Centre to edit the day's story. It was a taste of the big time, mixing with the star reporters. I even splashed out on a shockingly flash green suit to make my mark on national news. I think it may only have served to distract from my work as a journalist. But the trial did get me network exposure. The Black Panther was sentenced to life in jail. He was a nasty little man, with military delusions of being in the special forces. It turned out he was born Donald Nappey, which may not have helped.

Another high-profile crime was to come my way. Lord Kagan, the man whose company invented the Gannex raincoat, famously worn by his friend, Prime Minister Harold Wilson, had run into trouble for tax evasion. He took evasive action and fled to Israel. A year or so later we got a tip that he was hiding in Paris. I was sent to the French capital with a BBC film crew and a customs and excise officer in tow. We staked out the *Bourse de Paris*, the Paris Stock Exchange, for several days. And sure enough, Kagan who'd been made a life peer by Wilson, eventually emerged from a nearby office. We thought we were being very discreet, but later Kagan's son walked over to check us out, asking in French if we had a light for his cigarette. Without thinking our good old BBC sound recordist, Bill, answered in pure east London: 'Nah, sorry mate, we don't smoke.' A few minutes later Kagan made a run for it, though it was more like a waddle. We filmed the exclusive snatch as our customs man cuffed the fugitive Lord.

There were plenty of sports stories. Leeds United's success was huge. Brian Clough's forty-four days as manager at the club was a highlight. I heard he liked champagne and gave him a bottle at his first press conference. It gave me good access to the football legend until he was sacked. Leeds captain Billy Bremner, an irascible Scotsman, was my first interviewee to stick his hand over the camera lens.

I spent a day in Geoff Boycott's mother's front room at her home in the pit village of Fitzwilliam, trying to persuade him to do a TV interview with me about why he'd pulled out of a tour to Australia. For five hours Boycott paced the parlour wearing a white terry-towelling dressing gown with dried-up shaving foam on his face, while mum, Jane, made endless cups of tea on the cast iron Yorkshire stove. It was bizarre. I thought he'd lost his marbles. And he never did the interview, with me or anyone else.

I managed to cover part of the legendary Botham Test match at Headingley in 1981. But I was rushing back and forth to Liverpool for the Toxteth riots, when long-standing tensions between Merseyside Police and the local black community spilled over. On the last day of the Test, Thatcher sent Michael Heseltine to Liverpool as her trouble-shooter to deal with this outbreak of inner-city violence. We filmed him walking the battered streets of Toxteth as I fed him score lines of England's amazing comeback against Australia.

On my own sporting front, I started playing rugby again. With a few other reprobates, we set up a veterans side at Ilkley Rugby Club, calling ourselves, rather grandly, the Barbarians. We encountered some interesting opponents. At Ribblesdale, a rural retreat around Settle, I propped against a large, red-haired sheep farmer. Two days later I came out in a terrible rash. The doctor said it was sheep rot. It seemed my farming rival liked to carry his sheep draped over his shoulders as he strode across the Dales.

At Castleford, several of our team arrived in their fancy sports cars, about the same time as our opponents clocked off from a morning shift at the nearby colliery. Some ran onto the field still covered in coal dust, muttering: 'Aye, bloody posh gits. We'll show 'em.' It was a class war. About fifteen minutes into the match the bloke I was marking at the back of the line-out said to his mates: 'Eh! look, it's that bloke off the telly. Him off *Look North*. Bet he'd look good with a black eye on Monday.' Naturally, they spent the rest of the match trying to give me one. It kept you quick on your feet.

There was no shortage of whacky stories. There was a plague of ferret tales in those days. Richard Whiteley, presenter on our rival show Yorkshire TV's *Calendar*, was famously bitten on the finger by a ferret during a live studio interview. My *Look North* colleague Ken Cooper came back with an even more throbbing yarn. He'd been filming a ferret-legging champion, who was demonstrating the noble art of keeping a ferret down the trouser leg for as long as possible. Suddenly the man yelped, and dropped his kecks to reveal his pet mammal with its teeth firmly sunk into the end of his penis. Not being a man to fluster easily, he asked Ken to get him a six-inch nail from his garden shed and proceeded to prise open the ferret's jaws and free his manhood. Ken and crew filmed it all, much of the time with their eyes closed. But the editor decided it wasn't fit for public consumption on TV anyway.

One of my favourite stories involved interviewing a letterbox. At the time, a group of British mercenaries had controversially joined up to fight in the Angolan Civil War. We got wind that their recruiting sergeant, an ex-para by the name of John Banks, was hiding out in Leeds. We found his house. Keith Massey rolled the camera and I knocked on the door. No answer for a few minutes. But I was certain I'd seen movement inside. I called out: 'We've come to interview John Banks. Does he live here?' To which a man inside answered: 'No, I don't live here. There's nobody here.' A bit of a schoolboy slip. So I kept talking.

'So if you aren't Mr Banks, who are you?' The reply: 'I don't know. No, I don't know him. He's not here. Go away.' I came back with: 'Well, if you don't know him, how do you know he's not there? And do you know who you are?' With Massey giving me signs to keep it going, a Monty Pythonesque dialogue unfolded over the next few minutes as the indiscreet mercenary dug himself into a hole. It was TV gold dust. We ran the letterbox interview in full that evening. A five-minute chat with a man you couldn't see and who denied his own existence. It taught me a useful lesson. Never quit on a story, however unpromising it looks.

CHAPTER 6

YORKSHIRE RIPPER

When does a killer become a serial killer?

The common definition is a person who murders three or more people, previously unknown to them, usually committed as separate events, with a cooling-off period between each killing.

|||||||||||||||||||||

We had no inkling of what was to come when we got a call-out to some playing fields in the Chapeltown area of Leeds. It was October 1975. A woman's body had been found. Police soon confirmed it was murder. She was named as 28-year-old Wilma McCann. She died within 100 yards of the home she shared with her four young children. In those days the police let us know from the outset she was a prostitute.

There seemed no more to it than that: just a local tragedy in a rundown part of the city.

Three months later the body of another woman was found battered and stabbed on derelict wasteland in a similar part of north Leeds. Emily Jackson was a 42-year-old housewife, mother and part-time prostitute. If the police thought there was a link they weren't telling us.

It was over a year until the murder of Irene Richardson, whose body was discovered by a jogger in Leeds' Roundhay Park, raised the real possibility that the killings could be linked. Detectives were clearly withholding some specific details from the media that suggested a pattern. Reporters got wind that a screwdriver and a hammer had been used on the victims to brutal effect.

Local papers soon came up with the nickname 'The Yorkshire Ripper' and it didn't take long for us television reporters to follow suit. The Ripper suddenly gave the case a brand and an identity. But media attention was short-lived. Tina Atkinson, another young prostitute, was savagely attacked and murdered in Bradford two months later. The sad truth was that, in the 1970s, prostitute killings weren't considered of great public interest.

Shortly afterwards, a murder occurred that was to change the public mood dramatically. The victim was a pretty sixteen-year-old shop assistant called Jayne MacDonald. She was found beaten and stabbed in a children's playground. Police said she was the Ripper's first non-prostitute murder or 'innocent victim', as they described it in their rather unfeeling parlance.

I can remember the chill fear that descended on the region. Until then the public had believed it was only 'working girls' who were at risk. Now there was a feeling that no woman was safe. It quite literally changed the way of life for millions of women across the north of England. Few dared go out alone any more, certainly after dark. From then on, women ventured out only in pairs or in groups. The killing of Jean Jordan a few months later in Manchester merely widened the arc of menace now afflicting the North.

West Yorkshire detectives still seemed convinced the Ripper was a man driven by a hatred of prostitutes. They concluded that Jayne MacDonald's murder was a case of mistaken identity. But the public was less convinced. They saw the Ripper as a monster prowling the streets in search of any vulnerable woman.

About this time I became the BBC's first North of England TV correspondent. For some years, the Beeb had been outgunned on the reporting front by ITN's roving correspondents in the region, Martyn Lewis and then Ken Rees. Finally BBC News in London decided to match them and appoint their own man in the North. For me, it was the ideal step up from a regional newsroom.

High on my agenda were the Ripper murders, but seemingly not on London's. It wasn't long before I was having heated debates with news editors in London. They didn't rate the story.

'This man's already slaughtered six women that we know of,' I remember arguing. 'He's a serial killer.'

The news desk response: 'Yes, but it still feels like a rather regional story, old boy.' How bloody metropolitan!

'Well, how many women does he need to kill before you take this story seriously?' I came back, blazing with indignation. 'If he'd murdered half that number in London you'd be leading the *Nine O'Clock News* with it.'

There was an element of truth in my argument. The old North-South divide still existed. London-based newsmen often took some persuading to take 'provincial' stories seriously. Then came two more murders. Yvonne Pearson in Bradford. And ten days later, eighteen-year-old Helen Rytka, in Huddersfield. Police described both as prostitutes.

I remember filming the timber yard close to Huddersfield Town's football ground where Helen's broken body was found: a bleak January day in a dowdy part of town. She'd been covered with a sheet of asbestos. Her clothes were scattered nearby. It was a grim place and a gruesome way for the life of a young lass to end.

The legend of the Yorkshire Ripper was growing ever larger. And the fear factor on the streets was intensifying. Finally, the BBC news desk in London agreed it was a story of national importance. And I got my first full Ripper report on the evening news.

But the killings didn't stop. Now I was being asked for regular reports.

Then came a seminal moment. On a June morning in 1979, the media was summoned to a news conference at Millgarth Police Station in Leeds. We set up our camera and microphones. I sat in the front row as the man leading the Ripper hunt, Assistant Chief Constable George Oldfield, filed in with his senior offices. They set up a tape machine and told us to listen.

What we heard was a slightly tinny voice with an accent from the North-East, possibly Geordie: 'I'm Jack. I see you're still having no luck catching me. I have the greatest respect for you, George, but Lord! You are no nearer catching me now than four years ago when I started. I reckon your boys are letting you down, George. They can't be much good, can they?'

There was a pause as we took in the startling contents, then a total hubbub as all the reporters in the room tried to shout questions to George Oldfield.

The tape was a tease and a taunt and a challenge to poor old George, who'd aged visibly during this long manhunt. He seemed to take it very personally and, more importantly, very seriously. He said it was a strong lead and they were putting plenty of resources into tracking down the Geordie voice.

In hindsight, it was to be a turning point in the case and one of many errors made by detectives. The Ripper Squad revealed that they'd had three letters claiming to be from the killer, postmarked in Sunderland. The letters had a similar taunting tone. It was enough for the squad to divert vital resources away from West Yorkshire and distract investigators, possibly giving the real Ripper the freedom to keep killing.

The search for 'Wearside Jack', as the man behind the voice and letters became known, was to prove fruitless and, in the end, a complete waste of time. It was to be another twenty-five years before it was revealed as a hoax. In a review of the case, DNA from one of the envelopes led police to an estate in Sunderland and a man named John Humble, who admitted being the hoaxer. He was sentenced to eight years in jail.

What we suspected at the time, and later turned out to be true, was that the Ripper Squad were overwhelmed by the sheer scale of the inquiry and struggling to cope. In the days before computers, everything was manual. Reports, interviews, sightings of suspicious men in red-light areas, tip-offs, information from the public were all catalogued and indexed by hand. At the squad's main base there were more than 1 million index cards, filed in scores of wooden boxes. It emerged much later that the Ripper's name and identity were noted on those cards several times. But nobody had the time or the ability to cross-check the information on all those cards. So his name was to remain a mystery to police for over five years.

The killings continued – in Leeds, Bradford, Halifax and Huddersfield. It was the thirteenth and what turned out to be the Ripper's last known murder that had the most impact for me personally.

Jacqueline Hill was a twenty-year-old English student at Leeds University. She was returning to her residence in Headingley on a wet Monday night in November 1980 when she was killed. Her body was dumped behind the Arndale Centre.

Now this was getting close to home. Lynn and I lived not far up the road. Lynn worked a few streets away. We did our shopping at Safeway in the Arndale Centre. Headingley was where we met pals at local pubs and did our socialising. We had friends who were students at the university. This was our home patch and the Ripper had murdered in our midst.

Lynn and all our female friends now shifted from being frightened to downright terrified. Social events and evenings out all but disappeared as most people we knew opted to stay at home rather than run the risk. The police still seemed no nearer to catching the Ripper and halting his reign of terror. In the end, it needed a stroke of luck and some sharp policing in Sheffield to stop his killing spree.

I was visiting Lynn in hospital, where she was recovering from an appendectomy over the New Year, when I received a tip-off that police might have got the Ripper. I apologised to the patient and raced off to find out more.

Our sources at West Yorkshire Police weren't giving much away. But we could tell from their tone that they were mighty excited about something. We had a feeling this could be it. We reported as strongly as we dared, hinting that Ripper Squad detectives believed they'd made a crucial breakthrough.

Then, on Monday 5 January 1981, the news came that police were about to charge a man called Peter Sutcliffe. We headed for Dewsbury where the magistrates court in the heart of this old mill town was already besieged by crowds. Word had spread fast. I reckoned there were more than 2,000 people spilling across the street. As the white police van drove up to the courthouse around 5 p.m., the public anger was palpable. People were screaming: 'Die, you bastard, die!' And: 'Murdering scum, bring back the gallows!' It felt like a lynch mob. The police had their hands full holding back the crowd as a man covered by a blanket was led into the building.

In court we finally heard his name: Peter William Sutcliffe, of No.6 Garden Lane, Heaton, Bradford. He was charged with murder. He answered only to confirm his name and that he didn't want reporting restrictions lifted. He had black hair, a beard and moustache, just like some of the photofit sketches. We now knew he was a 35-year-old lorry driver.

Earlier I'd got an interview with his boss, William Clark, who told me how everyone at the firm had been interviewed by police, including Sutcliffe. It was the first hint that Sutcliffe was in the police files. In my initial report that night we had shots of his wife, Sonia, going into court and of their home now being guarded by police.

In a news conference afterwards, West Yorkshire Chief Constable Ronald Gregory was so excited he almost had Sutcliffe convicted before a trial, suggesting they'd 'nailed their man'. He left us in no doubt they'd caught the Ripper. But we knew that police in Sheffield had only come across Sutcliffe because he was in a red-light area with a known prostitute. Later they spotted the false plates on his car and found a hammer and screwdriver he'd discarded at the scene.

I asked the Chief Constable: 'Was there an element of luck in his arrest?'

'I think there's always an element of luck that they were there at a particular time,' said Mr Gregory. 'But, of course, the more efficient the men are the more advantage they can take of opportunities which might amount to luck.'

But the Chief Constable would never admit to the many mistakes made by his own force during the long manhunt.

Working with me on the story was a young man who'd just joined the BBC from Leeds University as a graduate news trainee. As soon as I heard his name, Mark Byford, I thought he might be an asset. I already knew his father, Lawrence Byford, from his days as Chief Constable of Lincolnshire. Lawrence had become Regional Inspector of Constabulary and was later to be promoted to the top job, Chief Inspector, just in time to conduct an inquiry into the Yorkshire Ripper case.

Mark had grown up around policemen in West Yorkshire, where his dad had started his career as a beat bobby in Normanton. So there weren't many cops he didn't know. The doors began to open. Through interviews on camera and off-the-record chats, we started to build a picture of Sutcliffe's killing spree across the North, and of the police errors that had allowed his murderous campaign to continue unimpeded. We discovered that police had interviewed Sutcliffe on nine separate occasions, but failed to make any connection. So he had never become a prime suspect. As we suspected, the Ripper Squad's obsession with the hoax tape and letters proved a huge distraction.

Byford and I, under the guidance of Gordon Carr, a veteran BBC executive producer, put together an hour-long documentary of the Ripper murders to run on BBC One at the end of his trial. We even tracked down the cemetery where he had once worked as a gravedigger and where he claimed he'd heard the voice of God sending him on a mission to kill. The film had almost everything we needed to tell the tale. There was just one thing missing – an interview with Sutcliffe's wife, the mysterious Sonia.

On the eve of the trial at the Old Bailey, I made one last effort to talk to Sonia. I discovered she was staying with her parents at their council house in Bradford. They were a curious family. Her parents, the Szurmas were Czech refugees, who'd settled in Bradford after the Second World War. They lived as virtual hermits, making few friends or social contacts. Sonia was no less strange.

To my surprise, when I knocked on the door they let me in. I told Sonia I wanted to interview her so she could tell her side of the story.

I wasn't the only one keen to get the exclusive. I was aware that several national papers were trying to get to her. So my old mate, Peter Staunton, a producer at the BBC and a keen car rally enthusiast, came with me in his souped-up Ford Escort. He was the 'getaway driver'. He parked outside the Szurmas' home and kept the engine revving, so we could whisk Sonia away if she agreed to an interview.

It turned into a long day. The Szurmas barely seemed to inhabit the real world and were naively unaware of the interest in Sonia's story. For hours we sat in their small kitchen beside an old enamel stove that dated back to the '40s as they discussed what she should do. At one stage there was a knock at the door. They didn't answer. An envelope, addressed to Sonia, was pushed through the letterbox. When she opened it there was a cheque for £120,000 from the *News of the World* for an exclusive interview.

Now I had a battle on my hands. I told Sonia that this amounted to blood money and she'd be selling out her husband, Peter, to the tabloids. I asked her if she could trust them. I argued that the BBC was offering no cash, but, as a public broadcaster, we could be relied on to put out her story in her own words.

Sonia was difficult to read. Her moods were unpredictable. One moment she seemed reasonable, the next she'd fly off the handle.

She was remarkably unperturbed that her husband was about to be tried for the Yorkshire Ripper murders.

For a while I thought I'd persuaded Sonia to come with me to a secret location where we could conduct an interview. Outside, I warned Staunton to get ready for a quick getaway to evade the tabloid hacks now ranged outside the Szurmas's house. Then in a flash she changed her mind. She became adamant that she would talk to no one. After six or seven hours of bargaining I came away empty-handed.

That night Sonia climbed out of a rear window of her parent's home, avoiding detection by the media, and made her own way to London to be at her husband's trial.

Sure enough, Sonia was in the packed public gallery as proceedings got under way at the Old Bailey in May 1981. Peter Sutcliffe cut an unlikely figure as he stood in the dock dwarfed by four prison guards. Slightly built with a scraggly black beard, he hardly looked like the monster who had killed thirteen women and terrorised millions more. He had an oddly soft-spoken Yorkshire accent as he pleaded not guilty to all counts on the grounds of diminished responsibility. His counsel explained that four psychiatrists had diagnosed him as a paranoid schizophrenic. The judge, Mr Justice Boreham, rejected the plea and insisted the case should be tried by jury.

The trial in Court One lasted just two weeks. Much of the evidence went uncontested. Yet there was still a daily sense of drama. Some of the most notorious criminals in Britain have passed through the Old Bailey, but few as infamous as the Yorkshire Ripper. Hundreds queued every day for a seat in the small public gallery. Celebrities were often seen. One day the great Arsenal goalkeeper Pat Jennings turned up to watch. A wag on the press benches whispered: 'Apparently, if the jury can't make up their minds, the trial's going to be decided on penalties!' The judge admonished us hacks for sniggering too loudly. But frankly there weren't a lot of laughs during the trial.

As the judge finally convicted Sutcliffe and condemned him to life in jail, I raced outside to write up my story, ready to deliver it live on the BBC early evening news at 5.45 p.m. As usual, I dictated my words to a copy typist in our truck parked nearby. She typed up my script on a narrow roll of paper, which was then fed into the autocue machine fixed to the front of the camera.

It had worked like clockwork every day for a fortnight. But this time, there was a howling wind swirling down Old Bailey, the street on which the legendary courthouse stands. With just a couple of minutes to go before the programme, a gust caught the autocue roll and sent it spiralling and unravelling down the road.

That was my entire script. With the help of the cameraman, soundman, autocue woman and assorted others, we grabbed the typed-up paper roll, now torn to pieces, and tried to reassemble it with sticky tape. The programme was just seconds away. It was no use. I got hold of the first few bits of paper, checked they were in the right order and got ready to go. I asked my team to just keep handing bits of the script, preferably in the right order.

So, looking like a man trying to straighten a twisted toilet roll, I went on air and did my best to get through a ten-minute live read to camera from assorted scraps of script. We just about got away with it. I checked later and nobody in the BBC newsroom noticed anything was wrong. Phew! It was an unnerving way to wrap up the most sensational story I'd ever covered.

Not for the first or last time in my career, I reflected later how a journalist often gained from the misery and misfortune of others. Five years reporting on the Ripper had undoubtedly raised my profile as a TV correspondent.

CHAPTER 7

CRAZY

They all said I was crazy to do it.

Not only was I leaving the BBC for ITN, but moving from hard news into sports news.

I knew it was risky. But I fancied a change and a gamble. I'd always loved sport and this seemed a brilliant opportunity to indulge my passion and see where it took me.

'Just check out where I am at the end of the year,' I challenged my mates with more bravado than certainty. 'Then you'll know who's crazy!'

⸻⸻⸻⸻⸻

As it turned out at the end of that first year – 1982 – I was to be found enjoying a fabulous New Year's Eve party, drinking champagne, lounging in a swimming pool in Vaucluse overlooking Sydney Harbour, just one of the hardships of covering an Ashes Tour to Australia. I'd got lucky again.

The title of ITN Sports Correspondent was a passport to all the great sporting events and venues you could ever dream of – the way into Wembley and Wimbledon, Lord's and The Oval, Twickenham and Murrayfield, St Andrews and Troon, Cheltenham and Aintree. Not forgetting World Cups and Olympic Games.

Funny how it all came about.

I was sitting on the press benches of Teesside Crown Court in Middlesbrough when Brent Sadler from ITN mentioned that they were looking for a new sports correspondent.

Brent and I were covering an intriguing trial at the time.

An eminent Newcastle surgeon named Paul Vickers was being tried for the murder of his sick wife. He was alleged to have killed her with an overdose of her own cancer drugs. The motive was said to be love. The prosecution alleged that he was having an affair with Pamela Collison, a former beauty queen, who was said to have also been 'very close' to a number of Tory MPs.

The comely Miss Collison denied all rumours about her personal life. She tried to sound prim, but it didn't suit her pose. In fact, it was noticeable that she couldn't keep her eyes off the dashing Mr Sadler. I'd say it was nothing short of flirting, as during the trial they kept passing glances and notes that weren't of a strictly legal nature.

As so often in such cases, there were numerous subplots being played out. After counsels' closing arguments, I couldn't help noticing that Dr Vickers's QC Gilbert Grey looked very pleased with himself, even though it seemed like his client was going down. When I challenged him, this Rumpole-like barrister with a twinkle in his eye told me he'd won a bet with the prosecuting counsel, Harry Ognall QC.

'Harry bet me that I couldn't get the word rhododendron into my closing argument,' winked the mischievous Mr Grey.

I flicked back through my notes and sure enough, there it was. In Gilbert's closing argument, he came up with this: 'Members of the jury, I implore you to picture this image. The defendant, the poor benighted Dr Vickers, worried sick about his wife's illness, with the weight of the world upon his shoulders, trudging home, pushing open his garden gate and brushing aside the rhododendrons, as he made his way with heavy heart to his own front door.'

Job done. A tenner passing hands from Harry QC to Gilbert QC.

A quick side bet just to keep their legal brains sharpened. It didn't stop Paul Vickers from being jailed for poisoning his wife.

As soon as I'd filed my court report, I rang ITN and lodged my interest in the vacant post. A month later I was their sports correspondent, starting out on a whole new chapter in my career.

The BBC tried to persuade me to stay. Peter Woon, the recently appointed Editor of Television News, had just begun to use journalists as newscasters, replacing the traditional newsreaders. John Humphrys and John Simpson were the two chosen to pioneer the move. Woon wanted me to be their backup man – the third presenter. And he offered me an extra £1,000 a year.

When I said: 'Thank you, but no. I'm moving to ITN', the mood rapidly changed from warm to icy. Woon really did deliver a threat of 'you'll never work for the BBC again'. He was right. I never did. But out of choice.

So, one week I was BBC North of England correspondent covering the latest floods to submerse parts of poor old York. It was an almost annual event as the River Ouse gushed more than oozed over its banks and filled much of its flood plain. I well remember spending all day in a flat-bottomed army dinghy looking for marooned residents, only to end up filming a story of how our brave troops saved a nanny goat from the upstairs window of an inundated farmhouse.

Just a few weeks later I found myself in a very hot South Africa reporting on the first rebel England cricket tour. It was to prove an explosive story, branded as sanctions busting. The tour had been kept a close secret, most of us finding out about it only when the England players landed in South Africa. The white apartheid government made plenty of political capital out of the tour, claiming it signalled South Africa's return to international cricket.

But by the time I arrived at Berea Park in Pretoria for the first match, the England players, led by Test stars Graham Gooch, Geoff Boycott and John Emburey, were already being dubbed the 'Dirty Dozen' back home.

The tour was a disaster. It was soon clear the England XI was far from a full Test team. The series was one-sided, with the rebels no match for a superior home side, which had been starved of top-class cricket for years. The likes of Graeme Pollock, Barry Richards, Eddie Barlow and Mike Procter wiped the floor with the England team.

The South African government gained some propaganda value and the rebels picked up a decent pay cheque, but they paid a huge price – banned from international cricket for three years. For some, it marked the end of their careers.

Right from the start they seemed curiously naive about the implications of the tour. The cricketers were to prove mighty sensitive when those of us in the travelling UK media group repeatedly asked them about their motives. They seemed to think they were doing nothing wrong and that we'd leave them alone after an early flurry of interest. How wrong they were. The stories we reported were far more about the rebels' impact in England and South Africa than about the matches. Not for the first time, politics eclipsed sport.

In Cape Town, Bob Woolmer did his best to repair some of the damage, taking us out to film at Avendale, a club largely made up of Cape Coloured players, where he had played, coached and tried to promote equality in sport. It was a rare positive story in a tour dogged by racial tensions.

The almost inevitable press/player showdown came in Cape Town. I'd filmed a report explaining how hard it was for non-whites to watch the matches. They weren't allowed in the pavilions or stands and most couldn't afford a ticket anyway. We had shots of faces peering through gaps in the fence for a free glimpse of this now infamous tour. We spoke to several who were strongly against the tour.

Geoff Boycott, a man with whom I'd crossed swords professionally several times when I was based in Yorkshire, summoned me to the England dressing room for a showdown.

He hadn't actually seen my latest report, but said he'd heard from back home in Britain that it was 'racist and full of lies'. He insisted that I'd made out that black South Africans were banned from all their matches. I strongly resented his accusations, which he'd based on hearsay and inaccurate feedback. An argument ensued watched by Gooch and Emburey, who looked rather uncomfortable about the whole thing. They were starting to realise their decision to come to South Africa had not been a great idea. The row ended with Boycott telling me the England squad wouldn't talk to me again. I suggested he kept his nose out of my business.

'I don't tell you how to bat. So don't tell me how to do my job. The day you can prove you're a better journalist than me, you can start writing my stories,' I told him. 'And there's about as much chance of that happening as me opening the batting for England, Geoffrey.'

It was sort of a drawn match.

The Ashes tour to Australia later that year turned out to be a lot less confrontational. For a cricket-loving sports nut, I couldn't have dreamed of a better trip. I was being paid for going Down Under to report on an entire Ashes Test series. And much more.

I teamed up with ITN Sports Producer Mike Nolan, born and bred in Melbourne, but now settled in London. As I often kidded him, he was mainly along as an interpreter for when the locals got too 'Ocker'. We promised each other that we'd work hard, play hard, enjoy ourselves and, above all, prove good value to ITN.

By the end of that trip, we'd filed over seventy stories in seventy-seven days. That included five Test matches and several One Day Internationals. But also everything from a drought at Dubbo in the outback to bush fires, a plague of locusts, an unemployment crisis, the Sydney to Hobart Yacht Race and the start of a Round the World Race. We covered stories about the royals, Australia's best surfer, nicknamed the Seagull, and a dwarf-throwing contest. It was a pretty rich and varied diet. But then I was determined to make sure ITN would find good reason to send me on any future tours.

We still found time to have fun and get up to no good. Well, the England cricketers were doing it, so why shouldn't we? Apart from

Mike Nolan, I found a new mate in cricket photographer Graham Morris. Morro, as he was known throughout the cricketing world, was on his first major tour as a freelance and funding himself on a very tight budget. That meant he quite often ended up sleeping on a sofa in my hotel room and adding his laundry to my ITN bill. In exchange, Graham always kept me amused with his insouciant humour and he always seemed to manage to purloin a motor from the distributors with promises of pictures of their vehicle and a famous cricketer.

Basically we got a free ride as long as we were working in Oz.

It all went well until one night in Brisbane when, emboldened by the local amber nectar, a car full of us hacks persuaded Morro to drive through the sliding glass doors of our hotel and into the lobby. Needless to say, the freebie motor got stuck in the doors and we had to clamber out through the tailgate and over the roof to get into the lobby. Moments later the England captain, Bob Willis, and tour manager, Doug Insole, arrived at the front door and found their entrance blocked. They were not impressed. It cooled team-media relations for several days.

Generally, though, we all got on well. There was an unspoken agreement in those days that 'what went on tour stayed on tour'. In other words, we wouldn't spill the beans on the players' social activities. Like the day we filed copy to the *Daily Mirror* in London on behalf of its fabled cricket correspondent Chris 'Crash' Lander who'd gone walkabout on the Gold Coast with a Sheila.

One episode that would have been all over social media these days and probably led to an inquiry, took place on the rest day of the Adelaide Test. Rest days? Well, in those days they took a day off after the first three days of a Test, so players could refresh themselves ready for the final two-day push.

On this particular rest day, both teams – Australia and England – were invited to relax and 'refresh' themselves at the famous Hill-Smith winery at Yalumba, an hour outside Adelaide. The hosts were most generous. It goes without saying that there was plenty of wine available and many players felt no great need to restrict themselves.

Soon many of them were splashing in the swimming pool. Then someone spotted the overhanging lemon tree. The fruit became ammunition. It wasn't long before the two teams were engaged in a full-scale citrus war. More feisty than zesty, the hostilities on the cricket pitch were easily transferred to the pool. Allan Lamb and Ian Botham, Lamby and Beefy to one and all, were in the thick of it. As were the Aussies, Border, Thomson, Hookes and Marsh. Lamby, the England batsman, picked up Aussie fast bowling legend Dennis Lillee and chucked him into the water. It was an all-round free-for-all. The tree was wrecked, lemons were splattered everywhere, party-goers were drenched and nobody seemed to mind. It was all good sport. And not a word got in the papers.

Nowadays there are no Test rest days, the two teams probably wouldn't socialise, the media certainly wouldn't be invited and the players would be heavily disciplined, maybe even sent home from the tour for bad behaviour. How times change.

Christmas Day in Melbourne on that tour was memorable. A few of us touring journalists decided to lay on a party for the players. I rang up a winery called Seaview and rather cheekily asked if they'd give me some sparkling wine, Aussie champagne to the locals. To my surprise they promised to send round ten cases of their finest, for free.

So on Christmas morning the England squad gathered round the swimming pool at the Melbourne Hilton. Morris and Lander emerged wearing full morning suits and began serving bubbly to the players and team management on silver salvers. With Morro and Crash nothing ever stayed serious for long. So, within minutes, our formally clad waiters were in the pool, trays laden with champagne glasses above their heads, still serving to a cheering audience of England cricketers. It really felt like players and press were all in this Aussie adventure together.

We'll never know if our party made any difference, but next morning England began the fourth Test at the MCG. It was to be the only Test they won on a rather ill-fated tour. And even then it was by the skin of their teeth. Victory by just three runs on a dramatic final morning that ended with the Aussies' last batsman, Jeff Thomson, being dismissed as Tavare and Miller juggled a joint catch off Botham's bowling. Like the rest of my first Ashes tour as a reporter, it was unforgettable.

On another memorable, but far more notorious, England cricket tour – to the West Indies in 1986 – the off-field antics did spill over into print. For the first time, the tabloids had sent out reporters just to dig up non-cricketing stories. Allegations of off-field sex, drugs and rock and roll, or maybe that should be reggae, swirled around the team. As always, Ian Botham, known to his mates as Beefy, seemed to be at the centre of most controversies. At one stage on tour, Beefy, the self-styled Prince of Badness, appointed Crash, Morro and myself as his 'Three Knights of Shame' to advise him on potential media pitfalls and how to stay out of trouble. Unfortunately Beefy wasn't great at listening to our sage advice. So he continued to be bashed up by the tabloid dirt-diggers.

On the field, Beefy and the rest of the England boys were being battered and bruised by the Windies' fearsome fast bowlers. The number one calypso of the day, 'Captain Your Ship is Sinking', couldn't have been more appropriate as David Gower's squad went down almost without trace, beaten 5–0 in the series.

Things were going so badly that on the rest day in Trinidad, Lamby called me over and said: 'JT, I've got to get out of here. I need a break.' So I booked Lamby and myself onto a plane to neighbouring Tobago. We spent the day snorkelling, taking part in the Goat Race festival and drinking rum out of a local policeman's solar topee pith helmet.

At the end of this ill-fated tour, Mark Austin, my BBC counterpart and myself, pooled what cash we had left and hosted a party for the England team at a beach bar in Antigua. Many of the great Windies team joined us and players and media partied till dawn. Some partied a bit too much. Many hours later, radio reporter Dominic Allen was found asleep on a sunbed, still snoring and rapidly turning lobster pink under a broiling midday sun. In the words of the great sports writer Frank Keating: 'Another Bloody day in Paradise.'

Back home, we gave cricket coverage a shake-up too. For some years, ITN had been gathering match footage using a small, three-camera, outside broadcast unit. The BBC had the rights to cover cricket live. But ITN was granted news access, as it was known, of two minutes of highlights per bulletin. And ITN was allowed to put cameras in any major sports grounds to film its own material.

That all changed in the early 1990s. Sports rights became much more competitive with the arrival of Sky. From then on the broadcaster owning the rights wouldn't allow any other channel's cameras inside the stadiums. Only their footage could be used by other TV networks for news access. Owning the rights meant total control.

In the '80s it was still open season. I started working with an ITN cameraman, Derek Seymour, who had such an eye for live sport, I realised we didn't need any other cameras. We devised a system where we could film cricket from one end of the ground and still give ourselves plenty of variety to edit. Each over, Derek would follow the bowler in for a couple of balls, then focus on the batsman and pull out for two more balls, and then keep a wider shot. We then had enough shots to cut together shots or wickets.

To keep down the amount of footage, at the end of each over, Derek and the tape editor would check with me whether they should keep the over or not. If there wasn't much action, Derek would rewind and use that tape again. I'd make careful notes of every scoring shot, each wicket and any other images of interest. Then, when it came to edit, we could put together a package in quick time, often feeding it live into the ITN bulletins.

Derek, who was a decent sportsman himself, never seemed to miss anything important. He had an extraordinary instinct for where the ball would go. In fact, he became such a legend of reliability that BBC producers would quite often pop round for a copy of a crucial shot that their ten-camera outside broadcasting unit had missed.

We tried to make our reports distinctive and different. And to have a bit of fun with them. After all, it was only cricket. At one England match, the irrepressible Ian Botham turned up sporting a shocking new haircut, with blond streaks and highlights. In typical style, Beefy went on to score a swashbuckling half-century capturing all the headlines. So I asked the tape editor, Duncan Jones, to start our piece with a close-up of Botham's hairdo. Then to cut together all his boundaries in rapid succession and leave me room for an ITN sign-off. Nothing else in the package.

My opening line was succinct: 'Like Botham's barber, we've just picked out the highlights.'

Then we simply ran shots of all his fours and sixes, with great natural sound of bat on ball and crowds going crazy. And I signed off: 'Jeremy Thompson, ITN, Headingley.' Stick to that old TV news adage: if the pictures are good enough, give them room to breathe and let them tell the story.

The cricket was good, the football less so.

Although 1982 was a World Cup year, it was totally overshadowed by the Falklands War. It nearly led to England, Northern Ireland and Scotland withdrawing.

England was based in Bilbao for the opening group stages. The omens were never good. They'd chosen to stay at the beachside Los Tamarises Hotel. The *Daily Mirror* got there first. Veteran reporter John Jackson and his photographer sent back front-page pictures of a dead dog on the rubbish-strewn sand claiming that the players' only view in this workaday port city was of a refinery and 'dead dog beach'. My crew and I were swiftly sent in for a follow-up story. Not surprisingly we couldn't find a dead dog anywhere!

The tournament started well for England. They beat France 3–1 in their first match, with Bryan Robson scoring a dazzling goal after just twenty-seven seconds. High up in Bilbao's San Mamés Stadium, I watched with some optimism as it hit the back of the net. But it never got any better for these men with mullets.

England did beat the Czechs and the Kuwaitis.

But we ended up doing stories about how Ramadan had ruined the Kuwait team's preparations and why Basque extremists could be a threat to England.

In the second round in Madrid, England managed only goalless draws with West Germany and Spain and exited the World Cup with a whimper. And a third of our stories never made it to air on ITN, as the Falklands conflict dominated *News at Ten*.

But it was a great experience – my first World Cup – with a couple of bonuses. In Madrid, I got to interview former US Secretary of State, Henry Kissinger (apparently he liked football), and I saw the Rolling Stones perform at the Vicente Calderón Stadium behind a cloud of marijuana smoke. Spain's youth, liberated from the dictator Franco, were exploring their newfound freedoms with a passion!

There was rugby and golf, tennis and motor racing, boxing and bob sleighing to cover that year. And one event I hadn't expected.

ITN's sport editor Mervyn Hall, a splendidly larger-than-life character, loved an offbeat story. And he'd been tempted by an approach from a Norwegian explorer, who was planning a snowmobile expedition to the North Pole.

I was duly despatched to Oslo to check out this Polar plan and seal a deal to cover this Arctic adventure.

Ragnar Thorseth was everything you'd expect of a Norwegian explorer – gnarly, with a craggy face and wild beard, eyes like the Northern Lights and a long history of completely crazy trips by boats and sleds and snow scooters to every corner of the frozen world. He'd become the first man to row across the North Sea in a dinghy. He was going to be no pushover.

Ragnar was pushing a hard bargain. He wanted ITN to film his expedition to the Pole, but to give him all the footage to use as he wanted. And he was clearly talking to other channels. We wanted exclusive coverage and full control. It was becoming a battle of wills.

On the second night, his team proposed we all had dinner at a famous Oslo restaurant. We sat round one big table, consumed large quantities of reindeer steak and a lot of liquor. As the evening wore on, the aquavit, Norway's favourite spirit, came out. It soon became clear – and it was the last thing that was clear – that it was now just Ragnar and me who were drinking. The rest of his rugged gang of Vikings were the audience. Nobody had said anything, but this had become an informal contest – mano a mano. Or more like a test.

The Vikings filled our shot glasses time and again.

Each round, Ragnar and I slugged it down in one.

I almost lost count, but seemed to think they were about to pour glass number eighteen. I was nearly done. But I looked up to see spirit dribbling down Ragnar's ample beard. I saw an opening. I grabbed a bunch of flowers from a vase on the table and ate them. Then downed one last glass of aquavit. Ragnar Thorseth nodded, rose unsteadily to his feet and held out a hand. We shook. In the proud world of Viking adventurers, the Englishman had held his own.

ITN sealed the deal. We filmed Ragnar's spectacular snowmobile journey to the North Pole. And got a great picture story for *News at Ten*. Being sports correspondent, there was never a dull moment.

CHAPTER 8

INDIAN ALL-ROUNDER

'Anyone here got a visa for India?' The shout echoed across
the old ITN newsroom. 'Indira Gandhi's been assassinated.'

No mincing words when a big story breaks.

'Yes, I have,' I called out. As sports correspondent, I just
happened to be accredited for the upcoming England cricket
tour to the subcontinent.

'Get to Heathrow as soon as you can and we'll sort out
a flight,' said the foreign editor. And that's how I began my
unlikely role as ITN's Indian all-rounder.

ıııııııııııııııııııı

Hours later I was in a country and a city I'd never visited before
and knew precious little about. I had landed in New Delhi – the
suffocatingly hot and humid capital of a country that looked like it
was on the brink of civil war.

India's prime minister had been killed by her own bodyguards.
They were Sikhs, angered to the point of insurrection and murder at
what they saw as their boss's disregard for their holiest shrine, the
Golden Temple at Amritsar.

It had all started five months earlier, when Mrs Gandhi ordered the army to take control of the shrine complex and remove a militant Sikh religious leader. It resulted in a bloody battle with the loss of many lives.

In retaliation, on 31 October 1984, Satwant Singh and Beant Singh, two Sikh bodyguards, opened fire on Indira Gandhi in the garden of her official residence at Safdarjung Road. Beant, known as one of her favourite guards, was killed soon after by border police; Satwant was hanged five years later for his crime.

For the next four days, Delhi became a dangerous city as mobs took to the streets, hunting down Sikhs. Many were killed, thousands more driven from the city in a wave of violent revenge. Far from being a sports reporter, I became an ad hoc war correspondent, reporting on what seemed like anarchy as we witnessed Sikhs set upon and beaten by the crowds. We filmed their gurdwaras (temples) being attacked, shops and homes ransacked and set ablaze. There was little sign of the police intervening. Official figures suggested over 2,000 died in Delhi alone in what became known as the pogroms.

Indira Gandhi's funeral on the banks of the Yamuna River brought a moment of tranquillity after the days of violence. Several hundred thousand mourners gathered to watch the passing cortege, as leaders of 100 nations, among them Britain's Prime Minister Margaret Thatcher, paid their respects near the ten-foot-high funeral pyre, as India's assassinated leader was consigned to the flames and the gods. The huge security force nearby was a vivid reminder that the fires of sectarian violence were still burning too.

As the riots subsided I was reassigned to my original mission – the rather more mundane matter of an England cricket tour to India. But just flying to Mumbai, or Bombay as it was then still known, for the first Test proved quite a test in its own right. Video editor Fred Hickey and I turned up at Delhi airport confidently brandishing our tickets, only to find 500 other potential passengers doing the same. By the time what seemed like half the government, a handful of ex-maharajas and the airport manager's mates had picked off the best seats on a plane designed for 150, there weren't a lot left. We just squeezed in at the back. Clearly nothing was to prove prosaic on this passage through India.

Two days before the match, the England team and the accompanying media were invited to a reception at the residence of the British Deputy High Commissioner, Percy Norris. It was a pleasant, relaxed evening of fine hospitality – typical of the events organised for teams in those days when touring was a rather more leisurely sporting exercise. Mr Norris, a big cricket fan, told us how much he was looking forward to the Test.

But early the next morning I was woken by a call telling me that Percy Norris had been assassinated on his way to work. It was being reported that, as his chauffeur-driven car slowed in heavy traffic, a man stuck a gun into the window, fired two rounds and shot him dead. It was a bolt from the blue. There was nothing to suggest he'd been a target.

Mike Blakey, my BBC counterpart, and I found ourselves in a tricky spot. Neither of us had a camera crew. They were still en route. So we teamed up and went looking for a way to cover this breaking news story. We were crawling through the city in a taxi when we both saw a black object suddenly pointing into our back-seat window. We nearly jumped out of our skins. The method of Percy Norris's killing was still vivid in our minds. It turned out to be the handless stump of a beggar's arm, jabbed at us in search of a few coins. Mike and I were clearly more rattled by Mr Norris's death than we had thought.

Eventually, at the Wankhede cricket stadium, we tracked down a crew from state broadcaster Doordarshan, who were setting up ready to cover the Test match. After much haggling and the handing over of some persuasive paper money, they agreed to dismantle their outside broadcast unit and come with us to film our news story.

But our hearts sank when sixteen men and a load of equipment piled into a small bus and followed us out into the city. They were far from a typical news crew. A studio cameraman, who'd never shot a news story in his life, gamely lugged a huge OB camera around

Bombay's teeming streets so we could film our reports. Somehow Fred managed to cobble a story together and satellite it to London in time for our respective evening news bulletins. So this time I'd filed a report as a crime correspondent.

It was some years later before responsibility for Percy Norris's assassination was claimed by Abu Nidal, leader of a militant Palestinian splinter group.

It nearly put an end to England's tour. The players, who were clearly shaken by Norris's killing so soon after Indira Gandhi's death, were keen to abandon the series. But the team management, backed by the Foreign Office, persuaded them to continue. And after all the delays the first Test finally got under way.

The team probably wished they hadn't bothered when they lost heavily, by eight wickets. India had unearthed a new mystery leg-spinner by the name of Laxman Sivaramakrishnan, who took twelve wickets in his first Test and left England bamboozled by his googlies and the complexity of his name, which incorporated four Hindu gods. No wonder a team of mere English mortals came up short!

The local TV coverage we had to work with was interesting. Their ancient cameras were, like India itself, leaders in the non-alignment movement. Shot changes suggested the ball was moving from the sun-bleached surface of the Sahara to the emerald green fields of Ireland – all in the space of twenty-two yards. Luckily Fred was able to bring Indian technology into the late twentieth century with the help of his trusty Swiss Army knife.

At least I was back to covering sport – but not for long. Just as the cricket was coming to a climax, I got a call from ITN informing me of a horrific disaster at a chemical plant in the heart of India. The place was Bhopal. And my job was to get there fast: easier said than done using Indian transport. It took me a flight, two trains and a ten-hour taxi ride on some unspeakable roads to cover the 500 miles to the capital of Madhya Pradesh state.

I was met by some welcome old friends, Purshotam Talreja, the

UPITN agency cameraman from Delhi, and his nephew Sanjiv. Percy, as he was known, Sanjiv and I ventured into the city.

A leak from the Union Carbide pesticide plant had sent highly toxic gas and chemicals drifting across the city in the middle of the night. The fumes were as invisible as they were insidious. Worst hit were the densely populated shanty towns around the plant.

The sights and sounds that greeted us were pitiful. They were still carrying the dead from their homes by the hundred. Many had died in their sleep, others had woken to find themselves choking and unable to breathe, and some had even been trampled to death in the panic as residents rushed to flee the city and its unseen blight.

A cacophony emerged from the narrow lanes between the shacks, as people stumbled past us, their bodies convulsed with coughing. It was hard to find a single soul who wasn't contaminated. The gases had stayed low to the ground. Victims told us their eyes, their lungs and their throats were burning. They felt nauseous. Some led us to their homes to show us family members who had died in their beds. The emergency services were overwhelmed, unable to cope with the scale of the tragedy. Many of the dead, wrapped in simple white shrouds, were laid out along the side of the streets waiting under the baking sun for collection.

More than half a million people were exposed to the deadly gas cloud that fateful night. Over the years the death toll has climbed from 2,000 to 20,000. And still they're not certain of the actual number. Tens of thousands more suffered disabling defects from the poisonous gas clouds.

At the time, nobody could tell us whether the toxic gas was still in the air and still dangerous. We wrapped scarves round our faces to reduce the risks as we filmed, but we had little other protection. We took what precautions we could. We stayed at a small hotel on the far side of the city from Union Carbide; we ate only tinned food, drank bottled water and hoped for the best. Percy's motto for survival was: 'Give us this day our daily dhal.'

Each afternoon, after we'd filmed the latest story, we'd drive out to Bhopal airport in a clapped-out Hindustan Ambassador taxi. In the airport car park, Percy would bring out the largest, heaviest portable typewriter I'd ever seen and proceed to tap out his shot list or dope sheet, as it's known in the trade, in meticulous detail. It never ceased to amuse and amaze me how Percy would stick to his careful routine whatever the scale of the disaster around us.

Sanjiv and I would then record my voice track to go with Percy's footage. We'd package up the tapes, scripts and dope sheets and send them away on the afternoon flight to Delhi. Once there our editing legend, Fred Hickey, now known locally as Mr Hickory, would piece together our story, with the help of Percy's precise dope sheet, listing every shot, and satellite the finished product to London for *News at Ten*. He also became known as Guru Fred, achieving almost godlike status among our local colleagues for weaving magic out of pictures shot by cameramen, who'd never seen the edited, final version of their stories before. For thirty years they'd been filing pictures to London never knowing how they'd turned out. TV news by remote control.

'The pyres of mass cremations burned throughout the night,' was my opening script line for one of the most haunting images we filmed in Bhopal, as families brought their loved ones to be burned as part of the traditional Hindu funeral rites. I would never forget the sight of those thousands of tearful faces caught in the flickering light of the farewell flames.

But there were ugly scenes too, as flashy injury lawyers flocked to the city, seeing a golden opportunity to make millions out of the misery of victims. They offered to represent anyone who claimed to be afflicted, dangling hope in front of victims – the hope that mass action cases would squeeze a fortune from the US-owned Union Carbide Corporation. In turn, hundreds more people emerged with brand new coughs, seeking a fast buck or rapid rupee out of the misfortune of the genuine sufferers. In fact, legal cases were being pursued years after the tragedy, though precious little money ever reached the real victims.

Bhopal has long passed into history as the world's worst industrial disaster. And for one week I had turned into a disasters correspondent.

Back to sport again. I returned to Delhi just in time to report on the second Test. David Gower's side pulled off an unexpected victory at the Feroz Shah Kotla Ground to level the series.

But now sports correspondent turned into political correspondent as I set off to cover the general election that would determine Indira's successor. Her son Rajiv Gandhi was acting PM and led the ruling Indian National Congress campaign, the party now known as Congress I in Indira's honour.

Voting was held on three separate days over Christmas. So I thought it would be only fitting to film one of the highest polling stations in India, with plenty of snow on show.

Percy, Sanjiv, Mr Hickory and Lynn, who'd flown out from London so we could spend Christmas together, took a flight to Srinagar in Jammu and Kashmir state high in the Himalayas.

During the flight, I got chatting by chance to the Khuroo brothers. It turned out they were in the travel business and owned wooden holiday houseboats on the Dal Lake. They couldn't have been more welcoming.

When we landed they drove us to our hotel on the shoreline of the lake. And the next day, 25 December, they insisted on cooking Christmas dinner for us on board one of their houseboats. There wasn't a turkey or a pudding in sight. Instead, we were offered a stunning array of Kashmiri cuisine, featuring subtle and spicy curries. To drink there was Kashmiri chai – green tea with saffron, almonds, honey and spices. Warmed by a great cast iron stove, we ate sitting on cushions on the floor looking out over the beautiful waters of the Dal Lake.

Soon shikaras paddled up to our mooring. Small wooden boats, rather like the gondolas of Venice, they ferried people and merchandise around the lake. The shikaras that approached us carried baskets full of saffron and sapphires and local lapis lazuli for us to buy. It was too tempting to resist and the prices were good. Lynn bought a small sapphire ring and some lapis beads.

It was an unforgettable day and, without doubt, the most unusual Christmas we've ever had. The hospitality of these strangers was extraordinary. The Khuroos turned Kashmir into a lasting memory.

Early next morning we drove high into the snow-capped mountains above Srinagar. Eventually we reached a settlement that felt like it was on the roof of the world. All around us the villagers of Kud were trekking through the snow towards a low, single-storey building that turned out to be the communal hall. What made it so different was that the roof was a field of frosty grass that was being grazed by sheep and goats. Beneath the animals these hardy mountain people were busy casting their votes for a new Prime Minister.

It was bitterly cold, with an icy wind blowing snow flurries into our faces. Percy was constantly clearing flakes from his camera lens. The rest of us were just trying to keep feeling in our fingers. The temperature was well below freezing, and the place was hardly a scene of election fever.

But the locals seemed remarkably snug as they drifted to and from the polling station. We soon learned their secret – the kangri. This was an earthenware pot filled with hot charcoal hung on a leather strap around their necks. Kashmiri men traditionally carry a kangri beneath their cloaks or phirans. A personal winter warmer. They say you can always spot a Kashmiri man because he'll have burns on his chest from the time he fell asleep and forgot to remove his kangri.

It seemed that even in these distant mountains the electorate was remarkably well informed. They knew all about the turbulence following Indira's death. The majority said they would vote for Rajiv and the Congress Party in the hope of maintaining stability. Against the breathtaking backdrop of the Himalayas, it certainly made for a political story with a difference.

After hours of treacherous driving down snowy mountain roads we ended up in Jammu, the winter capital of Kashmir, where I'd arranged an interview with the former maharaja. Karan Singh, son of the last outright ruler of the state, was a Member of Parliament, once a leading light in the Congress I Party, now standing as an independent.

As befitting a man born into Rajput royalty, the one-time maharaja had tea served for us on the family china complete with silver spoons carrying the Singh crest. It was so civilised and genteel it felt like a moment from a bygone age.

Karan Singh talked of his concerns about simmering discontent over the central government's handling of the state and the growing militancy of Kashmiri separatists. He was right. We were lucky to see Kashmir then, before it was plunged into years of conflict.

Soon we were on our way back to Delhi and the climax of the election. As expected, Rajiv Gandhi won convincingly with his Congress I Party taking nearly 80 per cent of the seats in Lok Sabha, India's lower house, the largest majority since independence.

Within hours, I managed to get the first foreign TV news interview with India's new Prime Minister. 'Mr Clean', as he was nicknamed, was keen to tell me about his anti-corruption message, promising to rid the Congress Party of its legacy of fraud and arrogance. Always a reluctant politician, Rajiv was to last just one term as PM. He himself was assassinated in 1991, not by Sikhs like his mother, but by Tamil Tigers fighting for a homeland in Sri Lanka.

ITN foreign editor Maggie Eales sent a telex: 'Getting the Rajiv interview was a superb finish to a long run of great stories. The editor sends thanks for all your hard work. We thought you'd decided to stay and set up a Delhi bureau!'

But my Indian odyssey wasn't quite over. There was more cricket. Fred and I covered the Third Test in Calcutta, as it was then known. Sadly not from a luxurious press box in Kolkata's legendary Eden Gardens ground, but from the damp, rarely used attic of Indian TV in Delhi. We soon found we had a large lizard for company and plenty of mice as we recorded and edited the faraway cricket. I didn't tell Fred about the snake that I'd discovered lurking beneath his edit pack. And he only told me later about the huge, hairy spider in his cassette box.

We stayed on to report a historic England win in Chennai, which clinched the Test series 2–1. It was the only Test in which two England batsmen – Mike Gatting and Graeme Fowler – scored double hundreds in the same innings. Extraordinary: rather like most of my unexpected winter in India.

In another telex, news editor John Toker observed wryly: 'You are a true one-man band. Something of a loner. You seem to work much better when you don't have any help whatsoever from ITN and the foreign desk!'

Two and a half months after that call in the London newsroom, I finally flew home. I'd managed to combine being a sports correspondent with duties as a reporter of war, crime, disaster and politics. An England all-rounder in India. But it was just not cricket.

CHAPTER 9

ASIAN ODDITIES

When they said Asia bureau it sounded manageable.

Then I got there, looked at the map and realised the sheer size of my new patch. It stretched from the Khyber Pass in the west to Hokkaido in the east; from the Outer Mongolian capital Ulaanbaatar in the north to Dunedin on New Zealand's South Island. I was covering almost half the world – single-handed.

What had I let myself in for?

||||||||||||||||||||||

It was daunting enough without an early setback to my first for-eign posting. Back in London, the cameramen's union, the ACTT, demanded that a two-man crew was sent out to be based with me in Hong Kong. It was what I wanted too. But ITN's management rejected the idea, on the grounds of cost and precedent, and so the union blacked my bureau. Not a great start. And it was a fiercely fought dispute that was to drag on for over a year.

It also meant that I would be working with local crews hired from the news agency – Worldwide Television News – rather than my own dedicated team. Quality control was out of my hands and my patch was looking ever more daunting. With nearly fifty countries to cover, inhabited by more than 4 billion people, speaking over 2,000 languages, I was clearly going to need to some help.

As I'd learned from my earliest days in the business, a journalist's best friend was a local hire. I was never going to get my head round all these places and people, with their politics and patois, on my own. I needed fixers, finders, fast-thinkers, friend-makers and food acquirers – in other words, general factotums. And I needed one in every country where I was going to work.

Fortunately, I'd already nailed down a full-time deal with my main man, Tim Schwarz. We'd met up when he'd been our translator on the Queen's historic trip to China, and I soon realised he was just the man to help me run the bureau. Tim was a self-confessed leftie, who admired communism – in theory – but above all he had an extraordinary gift and a great appetite for languages. He'd studied Russian at Leeds University. Finding himself inexorably drawn to exploring the Eastern Bloc, he'd picked up German, Polish, some Czech and even a smattering of Hungarian. His Russian helped him converse with Borises in Bulgaria and the Balkans.

Then he'd turned his attention to Asia. Before long he'd mastered the tricky tonal subtleties of Mandarin Chinese. He'd fallen in love with a Cantonese singer, so he quickly learned her language in order to woo her and wed her. Somewhere along the line he'd spent a few months in Ulaanbaatar, cramming Mongolian while sharing a freezing flat with a Russian KGB agent who mainly ate yak. But that's a whole other story. Just to complete the picture, Tim, whose dad wrote scripts for *Coronation Street*, wore round, wire-rimmed glasses and sported a very studenty beard.

But, as I soon found out in China, he was the only Brit that I ever met who could get senior Communist Party officials to guffaw at the jokes he would tell in Mandarin, as they chowed down on platefuls of bear's paw and camel's hump. Banquets were a prerequisite to getting anything agreed in the land of Mao, especially if visiting journalists footed the bill. Tim had an uncanny knack of easing open impenetrable doors, parting opaque bamboo curtains and getting filming permits for the non-permissible. A couple of years on he was to keep us sane, safe and well informed during the Tiananmen uprising. More on that later.

In Bangkok, I discovered the ultimate smooth operator. Narunart Prapanya was a stringer for *Time* magazine and always found time to guide me round Thailand. Somehow he managed to get me and my cameraman into Khmer Rouge camps on the Cambodian border, on military drug-busting raids in the Golden Triangle, over the frontier into Burma to meet Karen rebel leaders, and could secure me an audience with just about any Thai bigwig or bandit that I wanted to meet. He had connections with everyone right up to the fringes of the royal family. And, almost as important, he knew a good place to eat in any corner of his country. He could also always acquire a bottle of Johnny Walker to help wash down Thailand's wonderful cuisine.

In Tokyo, WTN cameraman Tomoo Itoh, with his wild, sticky-up hair, was the all-purpose action man. He fixed things in a flash, filmed even quicker and drove to the satellite feed like a lunatic – mainly on the wrong side of the road. He appeared to be the only disorderly thing in the whole of Japan. But it worked.

South Korea became one of my favourite story haunts, partly because I found the most splendid travelling companion – Lee Eun-bong, EB Lee for short. Just EB to me. He was a driver I hired by chance at Seoul airport the first time I visited, but he soon became indispensable as I covered the pro-democracy demonstrations that were in full flow in the late '80s.

Whenever I flew in from Hong Kong, EB would meet me at the airport with unfailing punctuality. He had a fine head of hair, would always wear a three-piece suit and always asked about our mission. When I'd tell him we were heading straight into Seoul for the latest student demo at Yonsei University, he'd say in his heavily accented English: 'OK, we go to demolition. I get ready, boss.' EB would take off his jacket and waistcoat and fold them carefully in the boot of his car. Then he'd remove his splendid wig and place it in a special box. He'd pull on a leather bomber jacket, put on his shades, stroke his bald pate and declare:

'Right, JT, let's go get 'em!' And off we'd screech to Seoul and the latest democracy dust-up.

Before our first demonstration, EB took a detour on the way, stopping at a hardware store so that myself and WTN cameraman Claes Bratt could buy gas masks and helmets.

'How bad are these protests?' we enquired of EB.

'Pretty bad,' he said with a grin. 'You'll soon see.'

Then EB stopped at a telecoms shop. He wanted us to buy local walkie-talkies so we could all keep in touch. I soon discovered this was as much for him as for us. Among the fixers and drivers, a walkie-talkie handset was like an orb of office, a badge of honour. It meant you'd made it. You were a big guy working for a serious TV network.

To add to his stature, EB soon acquired an ITN cap and then got his wife, Yong Suk, to make a huge blue flag emblazoned with the ITN logo that he flew proudly from a special mast on the front wing of his car. EB was now a made man. We rode into broadcast battle at various demos in our Korean chariot, flying the ITN standard.

But we quickly discovered the protests were not to be taken lightly.

Thousands of students, leading a new movement against government oppression, conducted ferocious street fights with the police. In a typically South Korean way, they were very well ordered. They tended to start punctually at a given time and to end after four or five hours.

The students would charge the uniformed ranks, who'd respond with salvoes of tear gas canisters. The students countered the gas by smearing toothpaste under their eyes and covering their faces with cling film. They claimed it partly nullified the CS gas.

Placards with their demands and allegations played a big part in this theatre of protest. We noticed some banners were written in blood. Then we saw a university professor ripping off the end of his thumb with his teeth. We filmed as he began to write his message in his own blood, chewing his thumb time and again to ensure a flow of blood. Now we understood the passion that was driving these demonstrators.

The Great June Democracy Struggle of 1987 was to be a turning point. One student had his skull smashed by a gas grenade. When he died he became a martyr to a cause that was gathering momentum – the government was struggling to withstand the students' demands. In the end the government revised the constitution to allow direct elections, marking the beginnings of democracy.

It was the first of many occasions when I was to marvel at the lengths people will go to achieve a way of life we take for granted in the UK. Democracy was just something we grew up with, like electricity, running water, indoor toilets and now Wi-Fi – a basic human right. But for billions around the globe, democracy was just a distant dream. Many times in many countries I have witnessed the desperate struggles of those who demand no more than a reasonable say in how their countries are run. I've seen too many people die for democracy, while millions of us in the West can't even be bothered to go out and vote.

Reporting and filming in gas masks and helmets was never the most comfortable way to operate, but at least we could keep working, even in a hail of gas grenades. The problems came later when we went back to the hotel to edit. Basically, we had to strip off all our clothing and try to wash off the gas residue, otherwise we'd be left weeping, coughing, sneezing and struggling to see. The first time we managed to change into clean clothes without mishap and settled down to edit. But then I opened my notebook, which I'd had with me in the riots. Toxic gas trapped between the pages was released into the air and we all dissolved into a choking, wheezing mess. It was another half hour before we could start the edit.

There were lighter moments. One time I secured an interview with Kim Young-sam, a leading opposition politician and pro-democracy activist. He was a good-looking man and always smartly dressed. To break the ice, I complimented him on his suit, observing that it was made of fine Yorkshire worsted wool. He looked insulted and through the translator told me in no uncertain terms that his suit was made of the finest South Korean wool. I begged to differ. After years based in Yorkshire, I knew my stuff. For a moment, he seemed offended and I thought he might call off the interview, but I asked if I could explain. He nodded. I leaned down and rolled up his suit trouser. Inside was binding tape embossed with the words 'Fine Worsted' and the name of the Yorkshire cloth maker. Kim Young-sam looked taken aback. Then his face cracked into a big smile and he said in limited English: 'You, very smart man. You know many things.' And we went on to record a long and revealing interview. Six years later Kim became the 7th President of South Korea.

When you ran a whole continent, or two in my case, Asia and Australia, you could spend a lot of time dashing around at short notice. It was me or nobody.

Like the time I was on holiday with Lynn on the Philippine island of Cebu and Emperor Hirohito died in Japan. I left Lynn to it, not for the first or last time, and hopped on numerous flights to zigzag my way to Tokyo. I arrived in my holiday wardrobe – jeans and T-shirts. My first job was to buy a suit, not the easiest thing for a six-foot-tall, fourteen-stone Englishman in Japan. After several attempts I settled for a suit that fitted my chest, but which still had tragically short jacket arms and trouser legs. Cameraman Andy Rex, who flew in to join me on the story, thought it was hilarious and tried to get shots of my comedy suit into all our reports.

One of Andy's finest hours was in Hanoi. Andy, cameraman Tim Manning and I were among the first Western newsmen allowed into the Vietnamese capital since the end of the war a decade before. The story was a trial repatriation of Vietnamese boat people from

Hong Kong. They'd left Vietnam illegally and spent years in UN refugee camps. Now they were being welcomed home like celebrities – pawns in a complex game of international politics. The West was hoping the repatriation would staunch the never-ending tide of boat people. Vietnam was banking on its goodwill gesture helping to lift the economic blockade that was crippling the country's post-war recovery.

Filming the story was the easy bit. The Hanoi government, never known for being nice to nosy newsmen, was suddenly all charm and reason. 'You can ask any questions and go anywhere you like,' promised Hanoi's spokesman, Nguyen Khanh. 'Please write positive stories. Vietnam is putting on a fresh face.' But they didn't really trust us. We soon discovered that they sent their spooks to follow us everywhere to ensure we didn't dig up any negative stories.

The real problem was getting the story out of Vietnam. As Andy and I trundled into Hanoi Television, a compound of drab Soviet grey blockhouses, our hearts sank. We were shown to a pokey outhouse behind the bicycle sheds, grandly named 'Satellite Coordination Centre'.

As Andy unpacked his silver box of tricks, wide-eyed local engineers peered at the equipment like it was an Aladdin's cave of advanced technology. Andy gamely tried to patch his state-of-the-art 1989 gear into state-of-the-ark 1950s vintage circuitry, as chickens scratched and squawked beneath the legs of the giant transmission mast outside. Over cups of teeth-bending black tea and cigarettes of breathtaking harshness, transmission chief Mr Hong assured us that satellites had worked from here before.

Sure enough, later that evening, the equipment croaked and crackled into life. Andy's touch had turned ancient glass valves into modern magic lanterns. Our story was beamed halfway round the world, via Intel-Sputnik over Moscow, across Europe, via Goonhilly Downs earth station and into London, converted from PAL system to Russian SECAM and back to PAL.

'Seemed all right, mate. You've got a clear,' came a nonchalant voice of approval from the ITN control room in London, totally unaware of the miracle we felt had taken place. Minutes later our story from Hanoi was running on ITN's news at 5.40 p.m. We shook hands with our Vietnamese technicians, trying not to reveal our disbelief that it had somehow worked. They seemed as surprised as us.

We went out to celebrate. Tim, Andy and I were transported through the city on *cyclo-pousse*, cycle rickshaws. Hanoi's streets were almost silent at night. There was so little traffic. We coasted past once opulent villas and down tree-lined boulevards – crumbling reminders of French colonial days when Hanoi was nicknamed the 'Paris of the East'. A few soft lights glowed from little cafés. Electricity was in short supply. It felt like Vietnam had been left behind in a long-forgotten age, the legacy of war.

The restaurant was surprisingly good. Frogs' legs and steak French-style, washed down with Georgian red wine – culinary reminders of Vietnam's influences past and present. We almost needed another rickshaw to carry the wherewithal to pay. We settled the bill with wads of banknotes the size of building bricks – several of them. With inflation running at over 700 per cent, the dong was a near worthless currency, eroding by the week. I was reminded of that famous Trivial Pursuit question: where does a Vietnamese deposit his dong? Answer: in a bank.

On Friday night, most Westerners headed for the brighter lights of the Australian Embassy. The Billabong Bar – a typical oasis of ice-cold Fosters, Swan and Tooheys lager amid the palm trees – was packed with visitors, resident diplomats and aid agency staff. There was a bar like this in almost every capital in the less-developed world.

By incredible coincidence, I met a cameraman mate Ron Hurrell who I'd last worked with in Yorkshire fifteen years ago. He was with an Aussie government-backed project set up to teach local cameramen Western television techniques.

Later that year we were to cover another story about Vietnam's emergence from the war years – their final troop withdrawal from neighbouring Cambodia. They'd originally invaded Cambodia to drive out the murderous Khmer Rouge.

As they left after more than a decade, what Cambodians feared most was a return to the 'Killing Fields'. Outside the capital, Phnom Penh, we filmed inside the Tuol Sleng Genocide Museum that contains grisly reminders of Pol Pot's four-year reign of terror, when he tried to take the country back to 'Year Zero'. In an old high school where the Khmer Rouge tortured and exterminated thousands of their fellow countrymen, the skulls of the victims were lined up in rows, a haunting reminder of the atrocities of the recent past.

At the extraordinary temple of Angkor Wat, once the centrepiece of the Khmer empire, Cambodia's new young leader, Hun Sen, told me he would lead his people in one last fight to end the years of suffering. Nearby, children were training to defend their country. The local militia was mandatory for everyone over the age of sixteen, but many of them looked half that age, stunted by a childhood of malnutrition and slave labour in the 'Killing Fields'. When I asked how many had been orphaned by the Khmer Rouge, three-quarters of them raised their hands. They bravely pledged that Pol Pot would never return.

I wasn't so sure. The refugee camps along the Thai border, which were less than 100 miles away, were still full of Pol Pot's disciples. In the wasteland of war along this frontier, with its minefields and deserted villages, we got footage of heavy artillery exchanges between Hun Sen's forces and the Khmer Rouge.

As I left Cambodia, sitting with the departing troops on the back of a Vietnamese army truck, I wondered how Hun Sen and his new country would manage without them.

There seemed to be war everywhere in Asia. Sri Lanka was having a double whammy. We went to cover the Tamil war of liberation and got a bonus battle – guerrilla action from the Janatha Vimukthi Peramuna (JVP), a Sinhalese Marxist militant group. For two years they terrorised the centre of the country with violently enforced general strikes and assassinations. One favoured method they'd borrowed from South Africa's struggles was necklacing – putting burning tyres over a victim's upper body, executing them by fire.

My crew, Ian Robbie and Andy Rex, had seen the aftermath many times back home in South Africa. We filmed plenty of evidence of the JVP's crude and callous methods, most of it too gruesome to put on air. The entry in my notebook on Tuesday 8 August simply says: 'Burning body on main coast road near Kalutara. JVP death toll: July 1,070, 1–8 August 483.'

It was brutal.

The authorities didn't like us reporting on this latest Sri Lankan crisis and tried their damnedest to stop us. Driving down from the hill city of Kandy, we spotted a group of armed police at the side of a wooded road guarding a pile of bodies. Nobody was really sure just who was in the JVP. We suspected some renegade police and military were involved as vigilantes.

Ian and Andy said to me: 'Why don't you pop over and check it out. It looks like the correspondent's job.' Feeling slightly uneasy, I got out of our van and walked towards the police. They immediately raised and cocked their old .303 rifles and pointed them directly at me. They started shouting, mainly in Sinhalese. I got the gist of it: 'Clear off now or we'll shoot you.' I beat a tactical retreat. When I jumped back into the van at great speed Ian and Andy were chortling away, amused at my discomfort.

'We just thought that a correspondent is no great loss. At least we could still film the story.' Good old South African humour.

On the same trip, we had another heart-stopping moment on the Jaffna Peninsula.

We'd flown up to do a story on the Indian Peace Keeping Force, who'd been invited to help Sri Lanka's army deal with Tamil insurgents. They'd ended up becoming an army of occupation. We had paperwork allowing us to head to the frontline to see where Sikh troops were taking on the Tamil Tigers.

So Ian, Andy and I, with all our gear crammed into a tiny Morris Minor taxi dating back to the 1950s and headed out across the scrubland of the peninsula. We stopped by the roadside to film the funeral of a woman, a mother of four young children. Her husband told me 200 villagers had died in the past few days. He claimed they were innocent civilians caught up in the Indian shelling.

We'd nearly reached the frontline when we turned a corner and screeched to a halt at a makeshift checkpoint. Several imposing Sikh soldiers stepped onto the track in front of us, their automatic rifles trained on us. Then out came their sergeant, who nonchalantly pulled the pin from a hand grenade, shoved his hand through the window and held it just above our driver's crotch. The temperature was already in the mid-thirties. Our body heat went up another ten degrees. Talk about sweaty in that tiny car. Three sizeable newsmen and a rather portly driver all staring at a live grenade, hardly daring to breathe.

It seemed an eternity as the Indian peacekeepers checked our passports, our accreditation and our gear. We didn't look like Tamil sympathisers, but they weren't taking any chances. Then they told us to turn around and, as far as we could gather, ordered us in Punjabi to 'piss off'. We didn't need persuading.

We had a far more civilised reception in Pakistan when we went to cover Benazir Bhutto's first election campaign. The taxi driver who took us from Islamabad airport to the InterContinental Hotel introduced himself as Cecil, an unexpected name for a rangy, powerful Pashtun. He quickly decided I was the team leader and from then on called me 'Excellency'. On those grounds alone, I hired him for the whole trip.

Even Benazir seemed a little surprised when we arrived at her home in Larkana for an interview and heard me being addressed by my driver as 'Excellency'. But she didn't forget me or Cecil.

It was the first time I'd met her. She was a striking woman, dressed in her colourful shalwar kameez, a loose-fitting tunic and trouser suit.

It was her clothing compromise. The Western clothes she'd worn at Oxford and Harvard – jeans and designer dresses – were banned. And she didn't want to wear a burka. My cameraman on that trip, Colin Angel, commented on how the camera seemed to love her. She came across as charismatic and serene.

She seemed keen to keep us close. I got all the interviews I could have possibly wanted. Although her main audience was Pakistani voters, it appeared she drew comfort from knowing we'd get her story out to her old friends in the West.

As we followed her campaign through Pakistan, it was clear she was a cult figure to many, especially the nation's women. They thronged her jeep, jostled her burly bodyguards and threw rose petals. Benazir was driven by her dream of overthrowing those who'd thrown her father out of the Prime Minister's office nine years earlier and then hanged him.

She had plenty of opposition because of her heritage and her gender. But she seemed confident of winning as we filmed her at the polling station. She told me it was the first time she'd voted in a general election. Later we recorded the dramatic moment when she became Pakistan's youngest Prime Minister at thirty-six, its first woman leader and the first Prime Minister born since independence. In the end, just like her father, it was to cost Benazir her life.

Asia never failed to surprise.

CHAPTER 10

TIANANMEN

As a journalist, it's easy to think you're relevant, important, sometimes even crucial.

You can kid yourself into believing you really can make a difference. That you're helping to make the world a better place. That just by being there, reporting an event, you can influence how it turns out. I was soon to learn a very harsh and humbling lesson – that events can ride roughshod over your best intentions.

The year was 1989. The place was Tiananmen Square.

IIIIIIIIIIIIIIIIIIIII

We were filming an economic story in Tokyo when news broke of a student uprising in Beijing. We dropped everything and took the first plane to China.

It was Friday 21 April. Throughout that night we filmed and followed the young men and women as they marched from every university in the capital towards Tiananmen, the Gate of Heavenly Peace, a name that was to become redolent with irony.

By the early hours, at least 100,000 had gathered in the great square – the symbolic heart of Communist China. Beneath Mao

Zedong's unwavering gaze, the largest pro-democracy protest in a decade was taking place.

I can still see that image of a throng of students, below a full moon, clustered round the monument to the Heroes of the People. They had come to honour Hu Yaobang, the General Secretary of the Communist Party, who had died a few days earlier. The students saw Hu as a reforming hero, who'd led a movement favouring political liberalisation, and who'd stood up against more conservative factions in the Party leadership.

It was clear the students planned a defiant vigil to catch the attention of paramount leader, Deng Xiaoping, when he arrived at the Great Hall of the People later that day for a memorial to Hu.

The protesters dared to jeer Party leaders as they filed into the Great Hall and defiantly called for Deng's resignation for failing to listen to demands for greater freedom and democracy.

In the face of this direct and unprecedented challenge, the authorities backed down and allowed the student occupation to continue, avoiding confrontation. The students dug their heels in and so did we, little realising that we'd still be there nearly six weeks later.

From then on, the ITN team – me, cameraman Mick Deane, editor Andy Rex and producer/translator Tim Schwarz became part of the scenery.

Almost every day we walked with the students, filming them along the way, as they headed from their campuses to Tiananmen Square. Now they were attending rallies instead of classes. Their leaders were drumming up support to keep the momentum of the movement going.

They were just ordinary kids from the towns, cities and rice farms across China. We chatted to them about their hopes and dreams. They knew they were courting danger by taking on the Party but they said it was their time now, their generation. They wanted reform and a taste of democracy.

Mick used to call it 'The Long March' as we set off on the daily trek with the students, him shouldering a heavy camera. 'Well, at least a ten-kilometre march,' Andy Rex would chime in.

Mick soon became a highly visible and much-loved figure in the square: a tall, fair-haired, moustached man, wielding his camera, towering above the thousands of black-haired protesters. They seemed to instinctively trust Mick as a man who would tell their story to the world.

Mick had a strong sense of justice and felt it was our duty as newsmen to tell the students' story, which had been muted by the might of the Communist Party. 'We can't let the bad guys win,' he told me at the time. 'The people rely on us guys to be their voice.'

It was true. The demonstrations, not just in Beijing, but in many major cities, were barely reported in China. When they were, reports condemned the protesters as illegal mobs 'conspiring to poison the minds of the people'.

The students put up roadside posters to keep the populace informed, providing them with news suppressed by the official Chinese media. We saw members of the public giving students donations to keep the protests going.

It was clear the students, now joined by more workers, needed the presence of the international media to give their story a bigger platform and to take it to a wider audience. They told us we were their main hope. We felt the responsibility. So did some local newsmen. On 4 May, a symbolic date from the original Chinese revolution, the students organised a huge march in defiance of the government. And journalists from China's state news agency joined in chanting: 'Don't force us to lie. We want to tell the truth.'

Helping us get to the truth was my main journalist ally Jim Munson, the CTV News correspondent in Beijing. We'd struck up a firm friendship and a good deal a couple of years earlier: when we were in China we'd use Jim's bureau to work, and he would use our workspace when he was in Hong Kong. He and his cameraman Francois Bisson, whom we nicknamed Frankie the Bison, were great mates. We hunted for stories together and shared our material. Effectively, it meant we had double the news-gathering ability. Years later, Jim, a fearsome ice hockey player, went back to Canada and became director of communications to the then Prime Minister Jean Chrétien and later became a senator. A very different path to my own.

Together we met and interviewed the newly elected student movement leader Wu'er Kaixi, a charismatic 21-year-old Uyghur from Xinjiang province. He told me they weren't calling for a revolution, just the chance to have a hand in shaping China's future. He seemed entirely reasonable. But he was already a target for the authorities, dodging arrest by constantly moving to new hiding places.

Wu'er introduced a new tactic – a hunger strike. Hundreds of students pledged to fast until the country's leaders agreed to free and genuine talks.

Against this backdrop in Tiananmen, the Soviet leader Mikhail Gorbachev arrived for talks with Deng. The students saw Gorbachev as a hero for bringing in political reforms. They'd hoped to see him and for him to witness their protest. Yet they were to be cheated.

The chaos of China's biggest political upheaval in forty years of Communism meant Gorbachev wasn't greeted on the steps of the Great Hall in sight of the demos, but hurried inside for the ceremonials.

It was a moment of history – a handshake between Chinese and Soviet leaders healing a thirty-year rift – but it was the students in the square outside who were grabbing the world's attention. Incredibly, despite the huge security cordon, Mick and I managed to get up onto the roof of the Great Hall without being spotted. Mick got some amazing shots of the vast square below.

As I wrote in my report that day, these were the scenes Gorbachev would have witnessed IF he'd been allowed to enter through the front door: 'The ship of Communist Party power marooned amid an ocean of protest.'

In the days that followed, as we filmed among the students, it looked like Tiananmen was turning into a huge army field hospital. The effects of the hunger strike were beginning to take their toll. We could see students we knew growing weaker by the day. We talked to some. They were lethargic, but determined. Casualties suffering from dehydration and heatstroke were stretchered away for treatment. Nurses and doctors from Beijing hospitals volunteered their services. Free medical supplies were rushed to the square. It was becoming clear the cream of China's youth were prepared to die for democracy – and this was having an impact on the general public.

On 17 May, a massive new demonstration swamped the streets of central Beijing. This time it was tens of thousands of workers, streaming towards Tiananmen, in support of the hunger strikers. There were academics, civil servants, factory workers, miners, peasants up from the country, even soldiers – all demanding freedom and democracy. It felt like the mood had changed.

My report began: 'Something has snapped in China, unleashing a force for change that might be impossible to stop.' That's how it felt that day in May.

Certainly something was breaking. The government declared martial law and seemed ready to enforce it with armour. We had a tip-off that there were tanks on the outskirts of Beijing. We went on a hunting trip. Eventually we tracked them down in the distant suburbs. Discreetly we filmed a large convoy of tanks and armoured trucks. This was the first proof of a crackdown.

But as we were about to drive away with our precious pictures, we found ourselves surrounded by rifle-wielding soldiers. Tim, translating for us, said the troops wanted to know what we were doing. They wanted us to show them written permission, which, of course, we hadn't got. Then they demanded our footage.

Fortunately, we'd taken our usual precaution in risky environments of ejecting and hiding the main tape and replacing it in the camera with a blank tape. The all-important tape was hiding down the back of Andy's voluminous trousers. After some argument, we reluctantly gave the soldiers the blank tape and somehow Tim, in his masterful Mandarin, managed to talk us out of trouble.

We escaped and headed back into town. On the way we witnessed an extraordinary sight. A convoy of People's Liberation Army (PLA) trucks, water cannon and wagons loaded with barbed wire and tear gas had been halted by a human blockade. Students and citizens drove buses across the street and pleaded with the soldiers to go no further and not to harm the protesters. We had our story and had the proof. China's leaders had removed the gloves from their iron fists.

With martial law, came not only tension and tanks, but a telecoms shutdown. The authorities were determined to silence the foreign media. So satellites were blocked. Government envoys marched into CNN's control room and ordered them to stop transmissions. CBS News were broadcasting live until they were forcibly blacked out.

We had to think fast. For a few days, some TV networks kept broadcasting on undeclared satellite dishes. We made a deal so we could all feed material out of China. Then those dishes were found and taken out of commission. Now we had to send our reports as voice tracks over the phone. Video had to be smuggled out of the country by whatever means. Colleagues acted as mules, carrying hidden tapes in their luggage and flying to Hong Kong or Tokyo, where they could be edited and fed.

The British Embassy told all us Brits to stay at home and 'don't panic', which was helpful. Shades of Captain Mainwaring in *Dad's Army*.

We'd heard 250,000 troops had been sent to Beijing. Most were still being held at bay by human barricades around the city. We found some soldiers trapped in a schoolyard. Most were no older than the students. They were in full battledress and armed with assault rifles, the Chinese version of the AK47. They told us they'd been issued with live ammunition, but were uncertain of their mission.

We saw some young soldiers in tears and workers urging them to retreat. Others shook hands with protesters, their loyalties torn.

A war of words, not weapons, gripped Beijing as protesters and Party leaders tried to find a way out of the impasse. The PLA buzzed Tiananmen Square in helicopters. It was the nearest they could get. And there was an aerial bombardment of propaganda. After more than five weeks of protest the square itself resembled a foul-smelling squatter camp and we had to pick our way through a virtual rubbish tip to speak to the students.

Then torrential rain and a dust storm almost achieved what martial law had failed to do, all but blowing away the student camp. Soon refuse wagons arrived to sweep the square. In the warm spring sunshine, the camp of occupation began to look more like a country fair, with food and drinks vendors doing good business. The hunger strike was over. Things seemed more relaxed. The army finally made it to the square, coming in peace to raise the national flag.

It was hard to keep up with the mood swings in this emotional Chinese opera.

I ended my ITN report on 24 May with these words: 'Each day the pendulum of power swings at an ever more dizzying pace. All that's clear is that China's wily old revolutionaries are fighting for their political lives with cynical disregard for the voice of the people. Nobody dares guess at the final outcome.'

It was now a war of attrition. Veteran hardliners in the Party hoped to grind down spirits, demoralising and intimidating the demonstrators, with veiled threats of a military crackdown on counter-revolutionaries. That was an old Chinese euphemism for anyone failing to toe the Party line.

Under pressure and with protester numbers dwindling, the students rallied round a new symbol of freedom – a thirty-foot-high figure of a woman clutching a torch in both hands. They called her the Goddess of Democracy, a Chinese-style Statue of Liberty. It seemed to give them a fresh focal point and more courage. But

I noted at the time: 'The squatter camp on Tiananmen Square has taken on the tragic aura of a village of the damned.'

Soon after, my crew and I flew back to Hong Kong. It was decided we needed to see our families and enjoy a few days of rest and recuperation, after nearly six weeks in the square. We were meant to be replaced by a full relief team, but that didn't quite happen. The replacements weren't in place and ITN had only a skeleton crew on duty in Beijing when the PLA tanks rolled towards Tiananmen Square late on Saturday 3 June.

My team was having dinner with our families in the Hong Kong Foreign Correspondents' Club when we heard the news. We raced to our bureau and began filing reports, using whatever footage and reports were emerging from Beijing. By early on the fourth I was reporting: 'Beijing was turned into a bloody battleground as they fought over China's future. Lit by the flames of burning vehicles the students staged their final stand for democracy.'

The night-time pictures were eerie and graphic. But not precise. It was hard to pinpoint many signs of the killings being reported. There were no numbers at that time.

Within a few hours we were flying back into Beijing to pick up the story first-hand. We'd been away from the place for only a matter of days. But there had been one crucial day and we hadn't been there. Not being in Tiananmen on that night was one of the very few regrets I've had in my fifty-year career. A genuine snafu. But there was no time to ponder. We raced to put together the story of the slaughter in the square. The student uprising had quite literally been crushed. Witnesses told us they'd seen a line of 100 protesters linking arms as they were mown down by automatic gunfire.

In typical crude propaganda style, the state broadcaster merely said the PLA had cleared the square of 'thugs and outlaws'. No mention of students or workers.

One of my reports concluded: 'In one horrific weekend the Avenue of Everlasting Peace has been turned into China's street of eternal shame.' The broad avenues were hauntingly quiet. No cars, no taxis and, above all, no bikes. Gunfire still chattered through the streets as the army patrols tried to mop up any resistance.

There was one iconic image that immortalised the defiance and the suppression of the protest. A photographer we'd got to know and work with over the weeks, Jeff Widener of Associated Press, was on a sixth-floor balcony of the Beijing Hotel when he captured the pictures of an unknown man standing in front of a column of tanks.

Later we got hold of footage of the same incident in Chang'an Avenue, at the north-east corner of Tiananmen. As the lead tank tried to manoeuvre past him, the man in a white shirt danced into its path again, then scrambled on to the turret and shouted at the soldiers inside to turn back and stop killing people. It was a death-defying show of courage. Nobody knows what happened to the man.

After the massacre in the square, we were all finding it hard to film or take pictures. Troops were firing randomly at any of us out on the streets. We moved around the city with caution, filming from rooftops and hotel windows or even from moving cars. Western embassies were advising their citizens to leave China.

Interestingly, intelligence officers at the British Embassy were more than usually keen to hear what we'd seen on our travels through the city. We were obviously daring to venture out a lot further than they were. But it was risky. Like most foreign correspondents, we were threatened by hard-faced ministry men with arrest or expulsion from China. They always accused the media of distorting the facts. They tried to keep track of our movements and to limit what we could report.

State television broadcast the first footage of Tiananmen, four days after the crackdown, showing the square still strewn with rubble and burned-out vehicles. The photo op was restricted to Chinese media. We used the video, but we definitely didn't use their script, which insisted there had been no great conflict and that no one had been killed. It was the most outrageous and blatant contradiction of what the world had witnessed partly via its own TV screens.

In the days after the mayhem, it was clear that the democracy movement had been crushed and that the old guard in the Party were busy rewriting history.

They did their utmost to airbrush away all traces of the murderous assault. The uprising was portrayed as the work of a handful of counter-revolutionary villains, who'd attempted to overthrow the Communist Party. Students were slated as capitalist insurgents. Images of soldiers shooting wildly in the streets were replaced by official pictures of them saluting their Great Leader Deng, who stepped back into public view to prove he was the strong man who'd sorted out China's problems. The message: China's government had restored stability and the country applauded its methods.

The propaganda coup was breathtaking in its audacity. But behind this Communist charade we heard chilling stories of mass arrests and widespread retribution. Many of the student and workers' leaders were being hunted down, accused of treason. On the streets, there were Chinese whispers of hatred and despair; but people were too scared to speak out in front of our camera.

The spark of democracy had been snuffed out. And we had been powerless to stop it. For all the might of the international media, it seemed we'd done little to change the course of events. We were stunned and humbled at how the regime had acted so brazenly before our very eyes. We were naive enough to think those students were safe as long as we were there telling their story. The cameras of the world had proven to be no protection against a ruthless authoritarian government.

CHAPTER 11

COUP TWO

I remember it. Let's say, I have a hazy recollection.

It was my birthday.

I was forty. Lynn had organised a big party in our Hong Kong apartment. I'd been dashing around Asia so much, I hardly knew anyone in HK. So I spent the evening introducing myself and getting to know the entertaining social group Lynn had gathered in my absence.

||||||||||||||||||

'I was beginning to think her husband was make-believe,' I heard one young banker whisper to his shipping broker mate.

'No. I'm for real,' I butted in. 'It's just been a hell of a busy year for news.'

I worked out I'd been on the road three weeks in every month on average.

I promised to work less and stay in Hong Kong more.

I was just toasting that with a glass of some unspeakable Chinese liqueur called 'Three Penis Wine' when the phone went. It was London. 'There's been another coup in Fiji,' said the duty foreign editor. 'Can you pop down there, old boy?' It wasn't a question. Just a polite instruction. So I kissed Lynn goodbye, said cheerio to all my new pals and headed for Kai Tak.

When they said 'pop down', what they actually meant was a fifteen-hour journey via Sydney. Even then, I think I was still slightly inebriated by the time I reached Nadi International Airport in Fiji. I arrived to find this archipelago of paradise islands in a state of turmoil. Though, in such an easy-going place, it would be more accurate to say they were in a state of confused disquiet. Nothing moved too fast in Fiji. There were armed soldiers and checkpoints everywhere, but nobody was getting their sulus – Fiji's traditional kilts – in a twist. The cause of the coup had long been brewing – and there had already been another coup that year.

To shorten a South Sea Island story, Indians from the subcontinent brought in a century ago to harvest the sugar cane proved to be not only resourceful, but also rapid breeders. They'd ended up controlling the economy and the government. The indigenous island menfolk, who liked to play rugby or sit under palm trees imbibing kava, a mildly narcotic root drink, woke up one day and went: 'Holy crap, the Indians have taken over Fiji. We're not having that.'

But I soon found that colonial habits die hard, even during an insurrection. The moment we tried filming on the streets of Suva we were hauled off to the Information Ministry to register as foreign correspondents. The clerk laboriously wrote our details down in an old leather ledger and then issued work passes. Our lapel badges came with a fine Fiji crest and a space marked for the event. The clerk thought for a moment and then entered the words: 'COUP TWO'. It was the best press pass I ever wore!

Even then filming wasn't easy. We had an armed soldier riding shotgun in our taxi. Guards patrolled our hotel. As newsmen our every move was closely watched by military minders.

We soon met the leader of the rebellion. He was an impressive-looking army officer by the name of Colonel Sitiveni Rabuka, known to his mates as Steve. He'd declared himself head of a new interim government, determined to reassert ethnic Fijian supremacy and adamant about cutting links with Britain and the Queen.

We learned that when he and his breakaway gang of fellow officers stormed the Parliament they were wearing balaclavas. The stunned Speaker of the House demanded the leader remove his mask. When Colonel Steve revealed himself, the Speaker shouted in surprise: 'What the bloody hell are you doing here?' It turned out the Speaker was Steve's uncle. It all went down in Fiji's Hansard.

Every twist and turn of the revolt was relayed round the islands by coconut wireless, Fiji's version of the bush telegraph. They heard about the Queen's blunt condemnation of the coup and Britain cutting aid.

On a heavenly coral beach, me and my Aussie crew, Ray Jones and Paul Luxford, joined village elders as they drank kava. A strange brew. It numbed my lips and, in texture, reminded me of that old-fashioned kitchen scourer, Vim. The old men fretted over trade sanctions and the sudden loss of tourism. They knew it could be a while before they regained their reputation as the Friendly Islands.

What still passed for a government wasn't being too friendly with us media either. They'd shut down satellite transmissions. So our only option was to smuggle our taped stories out of Fiji through the main airport at Nadi. We'd lurk in the car park and approach outgoing passengers, slipping them a couple of hundred Aussie dollars to carry out our tapes, with the promise of more cash when they landed in Sydney.

When the authorities began to hunt down our tapes, we had to be more inventive. We unspooled our edited tapes from their usual BVU casings and hid them in cigarette packets, tampon boxes, sweet wrappers and even wound them into Fiji tourism VHS videos. It worked. Almost every story we smuggled out got on air.

What I really needed now was an exclusive interview with Colonel Steve. Being a keen rugby man, I'd heard that the island cup final between Nadi and Suva was being played in Nadi. I figured the

Colonel, a former Fiji international prop forward, was bound to attend. I was right. We reached the ground just as the final kicked off.

We'd driven over from the capital Suva – 110 miles away on the east coast – with our buddies from Nine News in Sydney, correspondent Mark Burrows and his crew. I'd got to know Mark from previous trips to Sydney. We'd discovered that the BBC team, led by Brian Barron, had got together with the other Aussie news networks and formed a casual consortium intent on carving us up professionally. So, as we crossed the island, unbeknown to our rivals, we called in a favour from some army officers we'd befriended. Once we passed through the main checkpoint, they agreed to blockade any further TV crews.

So we arrived at the rugby ground with no opposition, no pressure on our exclusive and the all-important airport close by. At first Rabuka seemed reluctant to talk to me. After the match I walked up to him and presented a military memento from another coup. This black cap with its US-style scrambled-eggs gold braid had been given to me by the dashing young leader of a coup I'd recently covered in the Philippines. His name was Colonel Gringo Honasan. I handed it to Steve Rabuka and said: 'It seems to be the year of the colonels. So, I thought you might like this for good luck.'

Colonel Steve was tickled pink. We soon got into conversation about coups I'd reported and great rugby matches I'd watched. Before long he'd agreed to an exclusive interview, telling me of his determination to win back control of Fiji for the indigenous majority. This massive, but very modest man seemed an unlikely military dictator – a title he told me he disliked intensely. He said that as a soldier with a British crown on his cap for the past twenty years he'd been hurt by the Queen's criticism, but he believed he was doing best by his country.

After leading two coups, Colonel Rabuka went on to become Commander of the Fiji Military Forces and later Prime Minister for seven years.

In contrast, *coups d'état* were a way of life in the Philippines. During 1986/87 alone there were six plots to overthrow President Corazon Aquino involving various members of the armed forces. I covered three of them. There were more coup attempts in 1989.

Filipinos had a flamboyant sense of theatre. So their coups involved hotels, TV stations, palaces, the Central Business District, as well as an array of military camps and airbases. They comprised frenetic shoot 'em ups, stagey stand-offs, endless arbitration and often a brave-faced back-down. These mutinies by the army ranged from the audacious to the absurd.

The first one I covered in Manila was led by disaffected soldiers keen to topple President Cory Aquino. They took over the Channel 7 TV station in Quezon City and attempted to grab a big air force base.

My ITN crew, Mike Inglis and Ray Cheeseman, and I got our worst-ever tear gassing outside Channel 7 as troops loyal to the government tried to smoke out the rebels. We'd been sprayed before, but the Philippines' CS gas seemed to be especially noxious, with an extra helping of pepper, that left us weeping, sneezing, coughing and vomiting.

We recovered in time to go for a bizarre evening run with the army chief, General Fidel Ramos, who was in charge of the siege. The chunky commander stripped to his vest and set off around the TV station at a steady trot, expecting us to run backwards in front of him to conduct our interview. Top marks to Inglis and Cheeseman for back-pedalling like Olympians.

When Ramos failed to talk the rebels out of the TV centre, his men stormed into the building and quashed the uprising.

Six months later, my passing acquaintance Colonel Gringo Honasan led his self-styled RAM rebels, Reform the Armed Forces Movement, into an uprising. They attacked the Malacañang, the President's palace, but were quickly repelled. However, they successfully seized an army camp, three TV stations and an airbase. Gringo was boldly demanding an end to 'overindulgences in politics which now pervade society'. Corruption in plain speak. Oh! And better conditions for soldiers.

We filmed government troops firing into the army base occupied by the mutineers. The two sides were blazing away at each other across a perimeter fence. Just yards from the line of ferocious fire, dozens of street vendors had pitched their carts and were busy selling cold drinks, ice creams, cigarettes and snacks to an ever-growing crowd. Coups were apparently a big spectator sport in Manila. But then they were almost as regular as local football matches.

These revolts could get nasty. Once we got trapped between the bad guys and a large group of nuns. With the rebels blasting away like lunatics, Mike, a good Irish lad left with no other option, crossed himself and then barged through the sisters to make his escape. He always felt bad about nutting the nuns.

Like most Filipino coups, it didn't take long to fizzle out. The attention span of the combatants seemed rather shorter than a gnat's. Unusually, this one cost a lot of lives. Fifty-three people were killed and over 200 were injured. But Gringo, seen as a hero by half the population, evaded capture and was later said to be living on a luxury yacht in Manila Harbour.

Coup plotters never seemed to get heavily punished. One lot were sentenced to twenty press-ups and most lived to fight another day or another insurrection. In Gringo's case he went on to become a senator and, with a lovely touch of irony, chairman of the Peace and Reconciliation Committee.

General Ramos, who'd once again quelled a coup, rose to number two in the Philippines. Five years later he was to become President. There was no place quite like the Philippines when it came to politics, plots and power games.

CHAPTER 12

FIRST GULF WAR

The banshee wail of sirens split the night air in the Saudi desert.

A Scud Alert.

Saddam was hitting back.

The Gulf War was officially under way.

iiiiiiiiiiiiiiiiiiii

As instructed by the military, the rest of the ITN contingent and I trotted down to the basement of our hotel in Dhahran and began pulling on our NBC suits. That's when the fun began. We'd been issued with this protective clothing – nuclear, biological and chemical suits to give them their proper name – a few days before. We'd all been put through drills on how to dress in under ninety seconds, and most of us had failed miserably. It was ludicrously unwieldy kit to get on in a hurry. There was a gas mask, breathing filter, a two-piece nylon suit impregnated with charcoal and rubbery overboots. The British Army called them 'Noddy Suits' because they had pointed hoods like the Enid Blyton children's character. Frankly, we looked as silly as Noddy and Big Ears, wrestling with all this gear as we tried to get dressed in a rush. We'd been warned that if we didn't wear it the weapons of mass destruction would kill us. That was the start of the great WMD saga that would go on for another twelve years through to the Iraq War.

High above us, Saddam's Scud missiles were whistling through the night sky supposedly armed with chemical warheads. Most of them were taken out by US Patriot surface-to-air defence systems or fell into the sea. But we were still kept in the cellars next to the kitchens for hours on end until we were given the all-clear. The only answer was a highly competitive Scrabble contest to keep us occupied. Alastair Stewart, known to his mates as Nobby in the Noddy suit, was a particularly tough opponent, often questioning my right to ring my wife back home to check on correct spellings. I strenuously defended the right to challenge his dodgy words. The battle of the newsmen raged on like a subterranean subplot to the real war being waged overhead.

After a few days of Scuds and Scrabble, sweating in our Noddy suits, we realised that no one was dying from nuclear or chemical fallout. So when the sirens went next we headed for the roof instead, so we could actually film the Scuds, rather than hide from them.

By now Operation Desert Storm was in its stride. This was the US-led coalition forces' response to Iraq's invasion and annexation of Kuwait. It was a huge $60 billion combat operation involving thirty-five countries, including the UK. For the media, it was a breakthrough moment in war reporting, with the introduction of live news broadcasts from the frontline and greater use of press pools, where reporters, photographers and TV crews were attached to military units. It gave us unprecedented access. So much so that it earned the nickname of the *Video Game War*.

On the day war broke out, 17 January 1991, I headed off with a camera crew straight up towards the Kuwait border to check out the action. We'd nearly reached the frontier town of Khafji when I heard yelling behind us. American voices: 'Hey, where the hell do you think you're going? Come back here or you'll get yourselves killed.' It seemed we'd gone over the frontline. The sergeant of this US infantry unit wasn't overly impressed with our cavalier charge to the border. He told us the Iraqis had been shelling Khafji for the past two hours. The local workers had evacuated. His men were going in to investigate.

In the spirit of US–UK relations, the sergeant allowed us to team up with his patrol from Kilo 33 platoon as they went in to check out the town. On the outskirts of Khafji, the sergeant told his men with a dramatic flourish: 'We're entering the badlands now.' You can always rely on the Yanks to give you a decent quote.

Khafji was a spooky place. It was known to be a hide-out for Iraqi terrorists. Now it looked more like a ghost town, with cars abandoned in the panicky evacuation. The sky around us was blackened by fire from a blazing oil refinery hit by Saddam's artillery. Overhead US helicopters kept a watchful eye on their comrades and us, as we got our first pictures of the real frontline.

Over the next month, I made similar journeys into the desert, along with ITN colleagues like Peter Sharp. However, we became a lot more careful after CBS correspondent Bob Simon, producer Peter Bluff and their crew strayed over the border and were captured by Iraqi soldiers.

In those early days of the campaign the war was being fought mainly in the air, with the coalition launching an extensive aerial bombardment of Iraqi targets. So I took up battle stations in the cutting room with ITN video editors Bill Frost, Peter Reid and Patrick O'Ryan-Roeder, where we spent our time turning around the amazing range of footage from the pool camera crews.

We were spoiled for choice. We'd never had such access to pictures from other news networks. There was great video of British and allied aircraft, with cockpit cams filming their bombing missions; also real-time footage of runway busting bombs, raids on Saddam's Scud missile sites and pinpoint strikes on Iraqi tanks. It was better than we'd ever seen before.

Out on the Persian Gulf, there were Tomahawk missiles being launched into the night sky from US battleships, secret stealth fighters scything through a desert sunset and Patriot missiles streaking up towards Scuds in our defence. My ears were ringing from the jet thunder of the unrelenting Desert Storm.

On the ground we had pictures of coalition troops preparing for the land war. Artillery firing practice, tanks turned into desert minesweepers, bomb disposal teams learning about the vast Iraqi minefields planted over the border, US Marines digging foxholes in the sand and the supply lines to arm, feed and water a force of nearly 1 million men and women. There was even a piece on the French Army's exotic food rations.

It was a bit like watching war porn as we sat in our darkened edit room, viewing hundreds of hours of explicit footage ranging from state of the art weaponry to Syria's splendid high-stepping female commandos. It was all too easy to forget that people were dying at the receiving end of all this firepower. And it would have been all too easy to be partial and jingoistic, cheering on the allies. I had to keep reminding myself to be objective, to write about two sides, not 'them' and 'us'. Calling the opposition 'the enemy' was not objective reporting.

I cut, scripted and voiced 110 packages in the first month of Operation Desert Storm, a record I don't think I have ever matched. My reports were not only being used on ITN, but also on CNN, the pioneers of live news. We had a deal with them to trade stories. They concentrated on live broadcasts and ITN provided them with packages.

After the war I bumped into a CNN tape editor, who told me with glee: 'Of course I know you, JT. I saw all your reports. In fact, I'm the guy that cut all the pauses out of your packages.' Sacrilege! It was well known in the trade that US networks liked their reports snappy, urgent and fast. They delivered words and pictures with the rapidity of machine-gun fire. Brits liked to pace their reports, with a few measured pauses for effect, 'Let the words breathe', as we always said. It remains a point of difference in TV news to this day.

The news production line was relentless. I had one enforced break when a toothache got so bad I couldn't think straight. I found a willing Egyptian dentist, who calmly carried out a full root canal procedure in the middle of a Scud attack. His hands were steadier than mine. I was back at the edit machine a few hours later. But mine weren't the only teething problems. The Allies had numerous logistical hassles trying to assemble such an unprecedented multinational operation. By now the liberation of Kuwait was growing close.

It had all begun seven months earlier when Saddam Hussein ordered the invasion of neighbouring Kuwait in a dispute over oil. I soon found myself posted to Amman, covering the plight of thousands of refugees fleeing into Jordan from Kuwait and Iraq. Cameraman Bernie Glancy and I regularly made a daily 400-mile round trip to film the desperate evacuees stuck in holding camps close to the Iraqi border. Scorched by day and chilled by night, these helpless people were stranded in the desert with little food or water. Jordan was struggling to cope with the crisis. The international community was surprised by the speed of events and the scale of the problem.

It took five weeks before we saw these squalid camps emptied and the refugees repatriated to their homelands. Few chose to stay in Kuwait under Saddam's military occupation, though we knew some expats, Brits among them, who had gone into hiding there. But for most Westerners in Kuwait and Iraq, there was no hiding place. They had been taken hostage by Saddam's regime.

Before long it was my turn to man the ITN Baghdad bureau. Like every other journalist flying or driving into Iraq there was that nagging anxiety that you might not get out again. I caught the plane from Amman to Baghdad with a one-way visa issued by the Iraqis. The return visa could be applied for only when you wanted to leave Baghdad. If you didn't get it, you'd become another of Saddam's human shields.

I soon met many of the British and Irish communities who now found themselves 'guests of the Iraqi government'. The word 'guest' had rarely sounded so sinister. It was strange and uncomfortable for us, interviewing our fellow countrymen and women, knowing that we would probably be allowed to leave, but they were trapped in Baghdad indefinitely. Saddam had made it clear that these men and women were held hostage to deter attacks against Iraq and to dissuade nations from joining the military coalition against him. Some were held at secret and strategic installations, but the Iraqis wouldn't let us near them. Quite simply they were human shields.

There were around 1,400 Brits trapped in Iraq at that time. They saw themselves as prisoners of war; they were free to live and work, but not free to leave. As journalists, we felt desperately sorry for these poor folk, whose only crime was to be in the wrong place at the wrong time. But we couldn't help them escape. The best we could do was tell their personal stories and hope that it would keep the pressure on Saddam.

The human shields did their best to remain positive. We filmed them at work and at home. Some were even camped out in the grounds of the British Embassy. The Embassy's Consular Section was still open, so I asked them to give me a passport, issued in Baghdad, as a keepsake. Some evenings we popped round for a beer and a chat to keep the hostages' spirits up. They put on brave faces, but they rarely masked their doubts and fears. It was a strange, uncertain existence.

The media's existence was almost as weird, billeted together at the eighteen-storey Al Rasheed Hotel. A huge advert at the airport billed it ominously as: 'The Al Rasheed – more than just a hotel'. And so it turned out. Word was that Saddam had had bunkers built beneath the hotel and bugs installed in every room so his spooks could spy on guests. Assuming it was all true, we made it our mission to drum up as much noise as we could to deafen the secret listeners. So, while we worked hard, we also partied hard in Baghdad. Iraq was a Muslim state, but very secular. Booze was cheap and plentiful.

The Rasheed was a gathering point for the media's big story beasts.

It was a great place to catch up with old pals from other networks. There was CBS producer Larry Doyle, who always had a fridge full of beer in his workroom. He was popular. CNN's Peter Arnett and Brent Sadler, a former colleague at ITN. BBC radio correspondent Bob Simpson, who'd been a great mate since local radio days twenty years before. He didn't like to be confused with his BBC TV counterpart John Simpson. As he saw John advancing imperiously down a corridor at the Al Rasheed one day, Bob commented: 'Oh look, here comes the she elephant.' There was an Aussie cameraman whose party trick was to drop backwards out of our fourteenth floor office, catch the ledge outside and then do pull-ups. All these while wearing a diving mask and snorkel. Baghdad could get to you like that. Journos on tour could be a raucous bunch.

CNN's executive producer Robert Wiener observed, in his entertaining book *Live from Baghdad*:

> In all my years on the road I have never seen anyone party harder than Jeremy Thompson and his crew from ITN. And it's testament to his physical stamina, if not his outlook on life in general, that Jeremy was always up and about early the next morning, when lesser mortals, including myself, felt like Big Ben was ringing in our ears. At 3 a.m., the ITN office made Animal House look like a tea party. A few hours later, the place could have passed a Marine inspection.

ITN Baghdad house rules were that everything had to be washed up and tidied before the last person went to bed. There was nothing worse than a messy office. We had parties to celebrate our arrival, our departure and just about any reason in between. Mainly the merrymaking was a relief from the tensions and fears of being isolated in a city in the global gun sights. On the office wall was a clock with Saddam's face at the centre and every ITN staffer pictured round the dial.

By my second tour in late 1990, Baghdad was getting more bizarre by the day. We were reporting on a constant stream of well-known faces heading to Saddam's palaces, proposing peace or pleading for hostage releases. They ranged from Labour MPs Tony Benn and George Galloway to French right-winger Jean-Marie Le Pen and Muhammad Ali. Eleven British women became stars on Iraqi TV when they asked Saddam to free their husbands. Two members of the Lakota tribe, going by the glorious names of Garfield Grassrope and Arvol Looking Horse, joined the pantomime of peace, inviting Saddam and US President George Bush to smoke their tribal peace pipe.

Then, in the middle of it all, Margaret Thatcher resigned as Prime Minister. ITN asked me for an instant reaction piece. It was interesting. Saddam tried to claim her downfall as a personal victory. Several of his ministers gloated, but then sounded uncertain about what it might mean for British policy on Iraq. A lot of British human shields went out and celebrated her demise. They believed her warlike rhetoric hadn't helped their chances of leaving. And while all this was happening, they were still finding time for a game or two of cricket in the grounds of the British Embassy. Nothing like a good cover drive to brush aside the cares of war. It made you proud to be a Brit. We are a strange bunch.

In keeping with the cricketing theme, we found an excellent driver to steer us round Baghdad, who turned out to be more loyal to ITN than Saddam. He went by the name of Hattem and soon acquired the moniker Len Hutton, after the great Yorkshire batsman.

Ten weeks later in Saudi Arabia, the ground war began. The coalition had by now achieved air supremacy, bombing Baghdad and beating up much of Iraqi's strategic infrastructure. That was Operation Desert Storm – now came Desert Sabre.

The armoured fist of the allied force punched into Kuwait and Iraq, breaching the defences. A show of overwhelming military might. The fighting lasted just four days. The huge Iraqi Army offered some resistance, before retreating or surrendering.

Close behind the liberating forces, we drove into Kuwait for the first time up a broken highway littered with abandoned Iraqi military hardware. It took us twelve hours from Dhahran, crawling behind allied troop transporters and artillery.

The light was going as we entered Kuwait City. Oil well fires were obscuring the landscape in a tenebrous haze. We made for the seafront. The plan was to meet our CBS buddies, who'd ingeniously lashed a flyaway satellite dish to a flatbed truck they'd hired in Saudi and driven to Kuwait. They arrived just before me and my crew. As did my ITN colleague Peter Sharp, who'd taken a sandier route up through the desert. The deal was that CBS would do the first live broadcast out of liberated Kuwait. Then it was ITN's turn. Sharpy wasn't fond of 'lives' and said I should do it. I told him it was his honour. He was the first ITN correspondent to arrive in Kuwait and he had a better story to tell. He'd seen more action. In the end, Sharpy reluctantly agreed to be first man up and made a bit of broadcasting history, then I sent my report. It had been a long few days in the desert. We were all exhausted but elated. It was only as we made our way to what was left of the Hilton hotel that we realised the streets were scattered with unexploded mines and bomblets. The place was a serious health hazard.

Early the next morning, I suggested to the ITN team that I push on north to see if I could get to the Iraq border. Cameraman Paul Carlton was with me. As we were leaving in our SUV, Robert Fisk, *The Independent*'s renowned Middle East correspondent, asked if he could come along for the ride. We had no idea what we might find. It was just a punt.

It didn't take long to hit the journalistic jackpot. Barely thirty miles out of the city on the main highway, Route 80, we came upon the most incredible sight: stretching up the hill ahead, almost as far as we could see, was a maze of mangled vehicles. There was everything from cars and buses to army trucks and tanks. A vast scrapyard where part of Saddam Hussein's much-vaunted army had been scythed down, as it tried to scuttle back home.

In its flight from Kuwait, this huge column of the occupying force had been trapped in a traffic jam of death. When the lead tanks had been halted by an air attack, they'd formed a chokepoint. Behind them a ragtag procession was backed up over three miles, caught in an aerial ambush. This was what American A10 pilots had tastelessly described as their 'turkey shoot'.

More like sitting ducks, we reckoned, as we filmed the carnage. It was a chilling place, this killing field in the desert.

There was the sound of a truck engine still running. We saw the spoils of war spilling from their vehicles – clothes, jewellery, children's toys, china and vacuum cleaners. A musical card that played 'Happy Christmas' when we opened it. A stolen Qur'an; the ultimate sacrilege. It was as if they'd tried to drive home with all the looted treasures of Kuwait.

A stench of death filled the air. Hundreds of Iraqi soldiers had been killed here. We saw the scorched shapes of men still sitting, sightlessly staring from the cabs of their burned-out trucks. It was macabre. There were weapons everywhere, like one vast forgotten arsenal. Evidence that most Iraqis had fled or died without even firing a round. Carlton picked up a Kalashnikov bent into a horseshoe.

Like scavengers checking their prey, allied helicopter gunships wheeled over this massive graveyard. A hillside where Saddam's boast of military power had finally perished. They called it Mutla Ridge.

As the three of us tried to bypass the logjam, we quickly realised we'd driven into a minefield. The desert strip beside the highway had been planted with explosives. We stopped, sweating. Then, Carlton jumped out of the vehicle, saying: 'Come on old chap. You drive, I'll guide you through.' With that he began walking carefully, but remarkably calmly through the minefield, plotting a path across the danger zone. Bob Fisk rolled his eyes in disbelief and muttered: 'Oh hell, I guess we might as well go for it.' And slowly, very slowly, I followed the ever-so-slightly crazy Carlton, still brandishing his curlicue Kalashnikov, until we were back on the highway beyond the carnage and the minefield.

We decided to push on to the Iraq border, passing fifty blazing oil wells – Saddam's revenge on Kuwait before the hasty exit. They sounded like rumbling thunder, as millions of dollars' worth of oil went up in flames. We met Egyptian refugees fleeing Iraq, who told us the Iraqis were massacring foreign Arabs. We even saw a three-legged dog, maybe less lucky than us in a minefield.

Iraqi soldiers were guarding their side of the border, looking hostile. Then I saw a camera crew without a camera. It was BBC correspondent Brian Barron and his loyal cameraman Eric Thirer.

They'd been my direct rivals and lively competitors when we were based in Asia. Thirer wandered over and explained that they'd got too close to the frontier and the Iraqi troops had held them at gunpoint and confiscated their camera. He was asking for a favour. Could he borrow our camera so they could film a stand-up?

It was a dilemma. I was certain from our days as rivals that Barron would never do me such a favour. But I respected Thirer. He was a great cameraman and a decent bloke. I said: 'Eric, I know Barron wouldn't lend me a camera, but I don't think the same way. So I'm doing this for you, if Paul agrees.'

Carlton reluctantly gave Thirer his camera for five minutes. Without it the BBC team would have nothing to show for their day's work, just an empty camera box. Do as you would be done by, was always the way I saw it.

We'd done a good turn and we also got back to Kuwait City with a great scoop – the massacre at Mutla Ridge and the Iraqi border. It was a scramble of an edit. I wanted to use every frame. It was that good. In the end I got a package running at 6'35" on News at Ten. They called it the Highway of Death. The ITN team who were with me gave it a round of applause – a rare accolade. It wasn't a bad way to sign off from the Gulf War.

CHAPTER 13

FLIGHT FRIGHTS

Heart pounding, ears popping, skin G-forced onto our cheekbones, we were trapped in a rickety transport plane that was trying to shake itself to bits as it approached earth at an alarming speed and angle.

'It's just a corkscrew landing, mate,' the gnarled old warrior sitting across the aisle told me, with a wink and knowing smile.

⁜⁜⁜⁜⁜⁜⁜⁜⁜⁜⁜

We were flying into Angola with Executive Outcomes, a motley crew of mercenaries hired by the government to help them win the civil war.

The problem was that the airstrip we were heading for was partly surrounded by Jonas Savimbi's UNITA rebel forces. They had anti-aircraft weaponry and liked nothing more than taking pot-shots at incoming aircraft. Hence the evasive action – a tight spiral of descent from 30,000 feet to tarmac, which felt like being in a skyscraper high lift plunging out of control. We landed, rattled, sweating, heads spinning, relieved just to have touched down.

The next few days were just as hair-raising as we filmed South

African-led war veterans putting Angolan recruits through some very vigorous training. Deep in the war-ravaged Angolan bush, they went through their full repertoire and sizeable arsenal, firing off everything they could lay their trigger fingers on. It was like a New Year fireworks show.

Set up by Eeben Barlow, a former Lt Colonel in the SA Defence Force, Executive Outcomes was manned by battle-hardened soldiers from Special Forces units, such as 32 Battalion and Koevoet, who'd built fearsome reputations as killers during the Frontline War in southern Africa. Ironically, they'd last been here with the SADF, fighting alongside UNITA against the very same Angolan government forces they were now training. Disillusioned with the new ANC-run South African regime, they were rather like US Vietnam veterans – misfits at home, but winning the trust of troops they were once trained to kill.

Round the campfire they told some grim stories of covert operations, kill missions and deniable assassinations. Black ops delivered with black humour. A week on the ground with these guys was as scary as the flight in and out of Angola.

Another time we were leaving Angola, we experienced the Luanda free-for-all. This was an unusual form of ticketing, which involved no boarding passes and no baggage handlers. We were herded onto the tarmac and told which plane was ours. The rest was up to us. First, we had to load our own bags.

Ian and I got ours on board OK. Then we started to help a Lebanese guy struggling to lift an inordinately heavy case. As we manhandled it up into the loading bay, it split open revealing great bricks of US dollar notes. We managed to strap it shut. As our eyes met, I said: 'Diamonds?' Our fellow passenger nodded sheepishly. 'Please don't say anything,' he pleaded. Then we had to scramble on board and bag a seat. Last one on was a sissy and a loser. There were way more passengers than seats.

We came across a similar situation in Nigeria. Lagos was always one of the worst places to work as a journalist – it was the 'Nigerian

Nightmare'. Endless hassle from officialdom, from police, from beggars, muggers and street vendors. Everyone seemed to want a piece of
you. Some would stop you filming or rip you off for permits. Others
would try to take the camera away, while one just tried to steal it. And
everyone wanted money. A foreign TV crew was a standing target.
The local maxim: don't use a tripod in case you need to leg it fast.
Then there were the traffic jams. It could take hours crawling a single
mile across the city and even then, brazen bandits would try thieving
through the open window as your car was trapped in traffic.

The best thing about Lagos was getting out of it. One time we
checked in at the airport, but there were no boarding passes, no
security checks and no semblance of order. We were ordered to walk
out to the plane and climb aboard via some very shaky, skeletal steps.
When the aircraft was full, the ground crew simply pulled away the
stairs. Dozens were left behind, trying to scramble inside. A couple of
unlucky ones just fell off the ladder as it was yanked away.

As you can imagine, foreign correspondents and their crews spend
an inordinate amount of time flying in all sorts of aircraft from jumbo
jets to airborne jalopies. And they waste even more time traipsing
through airports, checking large amounts of baggage in and out,
while trying not to scream at the inefficiencies. TV teams are connois-
seurs of crap travel, victims of squeezyjet and queasyjet, who spend a
working lifetime trying to blag their way into first class. So here are
a few more aerial anecdotes.

In India, in the 1980s, local airlines always seemed to be over-
booked. Bribery would sometimes get you a seat, but during the 1984
general election I found a near infallible way to get on board. I just
told whoever appeared to be in charge that I had an urgent British TV
interview with Prime Minister Rajiv Gandhi. They never questioned
it, often ushering me straight into business class.

On a flight from Phnom Penh to Siem Reap, in an antique Soviet
plane left over from the Indo-China War, my crew and I literally lost
sight of each other. The Antonov, which we renamed a Nose-drop-off,

suddenly filled with what seemed to be steam or condensed air. The aircon system had gone haywire and turned the cabin into a cool Turkish bath. Rauli Virtanen, an entertaining Finnish journalist who often travelled with us in Asia, jumped up and asked my cameraman Tim Manning to film a piece to camera. Rauli, who at that time had been to every country in the world bar three, explained that he was gathering material for a feature on strange saunas round the world – and this was one of his best so far. The cabin remained fogged until we landed.

We went from steam to smoke. As we left Skopje after the liberation of Kosovo on a charter flight of dubious pedigree, it was only moments after the plane had lifted off that the cockpit door flew open. It revealed a heavily moustached pilot, looking like Zapata from Zagreb, smoking a foul-smelling, black Balkan special. ITN's Mark Austin and I, sitting in row one, then spotted all the flight crew were puffing away on cigarettes as they took off. The cabin was quickly engulfed in smoke. Of course, passengers were prohibited from smoking. It was about the same moment Austin and I discovered our seats weren't properly bolted to the floor.

If it wasn't the humans, it was the animals. Flying into Kenya's Maasai Mara National Park on a wildlife story, our pilot did several low passes across the grass airstrip to scare off the buffalo before he could land. On the remote island of Boracay in the Philippines, it was monkeys that liked to clamber on board as the local shuttle plane prepared for take-off. It was all pretty informal. The airport building was a thatched hut. They weighed passengers and their luggage together on an old-fashioned set of scales. One time they were so overloaded, someone sat on my lap for the entire flight to Manila, while others squatted on the cabin floor, surrounded by their bags. Flights by Fred Karno.

'Watch out for the MiG fighters,' was a disconcerting warning I heard a few times during my travels across Africa. Flying into southern Sudan as the civil war raged below us was always a test of your nerves – mainly the nerves of the pilot. There were only a handful operating out of Nairobi's Wilson Airfield, who were foolhardy or hard-up enough to run charters into Sudan for journalists. We'd touch down to refuel at Lokichogio on Kenya's northern border. A strange, desolate staging post, Loki was a launch pad to Africa's wild west and even wilder north. From there we'd fly on into Sudan and bandit country.

The Cessna flyboys would aim to keep under the radar and hope they didn't get spotted by the Khartoum government's air force. They didn't fancy their chances against the Russian-made MiGs, even if they were Soviet surplus. We made a few trips in to report the war and the resultant famine. On one brief visit we filmed a local priest holding church services in a mud hut for his bedraggled flock. In the local tradition he had no front teeth, which turned his 'p's into 'f's. So when I asked him what he was doing, he told me: 'I am fraying for feace.'

The pilots would give us no more than an hour on the ground to film before they'd want to get the hell out. It felt like we'd held our breath for the entire white-knuckle ride until we regained the safety of Kenya. Ian Robbie and I had a similar experience flying into the jungles of Mozambique to interview the notorious Renamo leader, Afonso Dhlakama. More on that story in a later chapter when I'll tell you how we tree-hopped into a war zone in a prop plane well past its sell-by date, flown by Pilots for Christ. Quite literally, a wing and a prayer.

Somalia was hard to get into. Ian and I jumped on aid agency charters, food relief planes flown by Southern Air, a charter outfit with shady links to the CIA, and even the daily drug runs. Somali men like to chew qat or khat, a green narcotic stimulant that grows mainly in Kenya. So most days charters would fly in from Nairobi with enough qat to keep Mogadishu's men mildly stoned. You can imagine how we felt, lying on the sacks in the back of an old cargo plane. We called it flying high.

Southern Air did us a big favour one time when we were in the

Rwandan capital, Kigali. Ian and I had apparently filmed something the authorities didn't approve of and were trying to track us down for a 'chat', which we knew could be custodial. At the airport, we spotted a pilot we'd flown with before, who was about to fly out. He said we could have a ride if we could get to the plane without being spotted. Somehow, we managed to sneak past all the military guards and clamber aboard. No passport checks, no immigration stamps, no tickets, no boarding passes. Just a chance encounter with an old pilot mate and a lucky escape.

One of the hairiest flights was a charter to Johannesburg from Maputo, the capital of Mozambique. Ian and I spent the day filming refugees returning after the civil war and the miles of minefields they now had to contend with. Being around landmines always tends to raise your blood pressure, so it didn't help when we got back to Maputo airport to find our pilot pacing anxiously.

He'd heard reports of bad storms on the Highveld. Not ideal for our return trip. Ian and I were sharing the charter with the German ARD team, who had the bureau next to ours in Joburg. We clambered aboard and were soon airborne. We'd climbed to about 5,000 feet above Maputo when the canopy over my head suddenly blew open with a loud bang. Luckily I was firmly strapped in. But the notebook I'd been writing in was whipped out of my hands and vanished into the late afternoon sky. Our pilot told me to grab the canopy and hold it down while he executed a swift descent back onto the tarmac. This time he made sure my door and roof canopy were tightly secured before we set off again.

An hour or so later, as we flew up towards Joburg, we could see the storm ahead. Huge pewter-toned thunderheads filled our flight path and giant rods of lightning flashed and crackled earthwards. It was a real Highveld humdinger. We sat sweating and scared as our small prop plane was tossed about in the turbulent sky. After what seemed like an age, the pilot could see home base – Lanseria on Joburg's northern flank. The airfield was surrounded by lightning bolts, marching across our path like an irradiated army. They filled our horizon. But the tower told him to try landing when he saw a gap.

The little plane surged towards the runway, but the storm was too strong. We were buffeted and beaten back, the plane almost turning on its side.

I could see the pilot beside me, battling with the joystick, as jags of fire from the electric storm lit up his ashen face. He just held on, wrenching back the stick, tearing us from the suction of the storm. He fought for five minutes to keep his craft aloft and all of us alive.

Eventually, he was told to divert to Pretoria's Wonderboom airfield. As we were touching down, ARD's cameraman Nico said: 'Well! That was the third air disaster I've survived. I guess I must be lucky.' I made a note never to fly with him again.

We shook damp hands with our pilot and thanked him for getting us home safely. He admitted it was about the scariest experience he'd had in twenty years of flying. We all headed off to find a cold beer.

Talking of cold beers, by far the ugliest flight I've ever been on was the charter home after the First Gulf War. Newsroom bosses decided it would be a good, cost-effective idea to hire a large passenger jet to repatriate all the hacks from Dhahran in Saudi Arabia. Not a bad idea. Except they'd failed to take into account that many of us had been in the drink-dry deserts of Saudi and Kuwait for weeks, if not months.

So a plane load of reporters, photographers and camera crews from all the main TV stations, agencies and newspapers – many of them rivals – together with crate loads of booze was a potentially explosive mix, as we would soon find out.

It didn't take long for alcohol-starved hacks to turn into cheap drunks. The poor old cabin crew had to deal with media mayhem on a mega scale in a confined space. There were people being sick, others crashing out in the toilets, fights breaking out, some surreptitious sexual activity in the rear seats and all manner of bad behaviour.

In fact, we were so unruly and indecorous the pilots told us they weren't willing to fly us all the way home. So they landed in Rome and insisted we had a night to sober up before they'd complete the flight to Gatwick.

For many newsmen and women, the riotous reporter antics didn't stop there. Some tried to add to Rome's ruins, while others attempted to ruin themselves. Most poured back onto the flight from hell the next morning, looking suitably dreadful, but quite a few simply disappeared, making their way back to London and their various newsrooms days later.

The scene at Gatwick was a bit like A&E, as a couple of hundred hangovers hove into view. Besuited editors were there to welcome home their heroic troops from the war zone, but they ended up looking on with a mixture of despair and disgust, no doubt wondering what sort of media monsters they were managing.

My longest flight began in Manila. I'd been in the Philippines covering the latest political upheaval, which had led to another *coup d'état*. It had been a lively couple of weeks, so me and my ITN crew, Mike Inglis, Ray Cheeseman and Patrick O'Ryan-Roeder, were looking for a nice relaxing flight home. Our flight was anything but. We'd barely taken off when our British Airways captain came onto the intercom to announce the first problem – a mechanical fault had shown up on his instruments. The captain apologised and said he was having to divert to Kuala Lumpur to get the plane checked out. It was to be the first of many apologies.

We hung about on the runway at Kuala Lumpur for several hours in stinking heat with no air-conditioning as mechanics tried to figure out the fault. In the end, the pilot said sorry again and told us we'd be staying overnight. So twelve hours after we'd set off from Manila – a two-hour flight away – we found ourselves having an unexpected stopover in Kuala Lumpur. At least BA paid for the hotel.

Thirteen hours later we were back at the airport expecting a new plane. But BA insisted they'd sorted out the mechanical glitch and ushered us on board the same flight again. There were more problems and more delays. When we eventually were told to prepare for take-off, I could see many fellow passengers starting to look more than nervous, especially in economy. It was packed with petrified Filipina maids and amahs heading back to the families who employed them in the UK. Mike Inglis and I decided on some improvised social welfare. On our heads we plonked pillow covers that looked like a cardinal's scarlet biretta. We grabbed a couple of bright red BA blankets, taped them to our arms, stood in the aisles and persuaded the whole of economy class to flap their arms like us to help get the plane airborne. It seemed to work. The jumbo jet lurched into the air and 100 Filipina girls giggled and clapped in relief. Being good Catholic girls, they may have thought we'd been sent by the Vatican, or maybe they just knew Brits were crazy.

By now we'd spent a couple of days on this flight and were starting to make ourselves at home with a bit of impromptu decorating. The Philippines is renowned for its hand-crafted wooden birds, anything from decoy ducks for American hunters to beautifully carved parrots. We'd all bought a few to take home. The crew's gaffer tape came in handy again as we made bird mobiles to hang from the overhead lockers. We'd also made such deep inroads into the BA drinks supply that they ran out of champagne. Otherwise, the flight seemed to be smooth enough, until the latest captain came through with yet another effusive apology. The old mechanical fault had reappeared and we were going to have to put down again. This time it was Abu Dhabi. And another torrid wait on a roasting runway.

It took so long to fix the problem that we had another change of cabin crew. This time the ITN team stood at the top of the steps and saluted them on board, welcoming them to Flight 032. It really was starting to feel like our plane more than theirs. The BA crew had obviously been warned we were in a playful mood, verging on the psychotic, after being cooped up on a jumbo jet for over three days. They treated us with that weary, long-suffering care parents reserve for amusing, but difficult children. By now we'd taken up squatter's rights in First Class. It wasn't long before Inglis and I, in full stewardess outfits, were serving drinks to the handful of other passengers still on this hapless flight. A kind Egyptian woman helped perfect our make-up. The fearful majority of passengers had chosen to leave the plane at various stops along the way, literally too frightened or superstitious to stay aboard.

By the time we made another unscheduled stop, this time in Cairo, most of the remaining stalwarts of this blighted BA plane leapt at the chance to leave. But, somehow, the aircraft limped into Heathrow in one piece. It had been just over fifty-six hours since we set off from Manila.

Ironically, it was the day that state airline British Airways was privatised. Not a great start to the new enterprise. And not a great end to our trip. As we stumbled through immigration and luggage reclaim half asleep, a BA apologist thrust an envelope in our hands with £100 in cash inside – hush money we assumed.

A haunted flight, hangovers and jet lag had left us looking pretty messy. As we emerged into the arrivals hall, I could see Lynn waving with joy and relief. Then I saw her jaw drop as she took in the sight before her. Four bleary, bedraggled and heavily bearded newsmen trudging towards her, looking and smelling more like characters out of *Castaway*. Four days in the same clothes. The welcome home embrace was tentative to say the least. 'Well, there's one good thing to come out of it,' said Mike. 'Four days overtime!'

CHAPTER 14

YUGOSLAV WAR

Sometimes as a reporter you see a story through from start to finish. Other times you get only snapshots, frustrating fragments of the big picture. The Yugoslav War was like that for me. I witnessed the beginning and the climax.

In between I had run news bureaux in Africa and the USA for over seven years and all that time the fighting was still going on. I started covering the conflict with ITN and finished it with Sky and, without a doubt, it was one of the scariest places I've ever reported from.

||||||||||||||||||||

The day I arrived, Slovenia and Croatia had declared independence, the first signs that the old Yugoslavia was unravelling. Tito, the strongman who'd held together this Balkan state made up of six socialist republics, had long gone. The Berlin Wall had fallen, the Eastern Bloc had come unstuck and now Yugoslavia had reached breaking point.

The small alpine state of Slovenia immediately raised a new national flag in defiance of the federal government in Belgrade. We reached the border with Croatia just in time to film Slovenian armed police putting up a makeshift sign declaring this was now an international frontier.

They then began patrolling proudly beside a hastily erected, colourful beach umbrella, presumably all they could find in the rush to proclaim their independence. Each morning, when we passed through the border, they would park a caravan outside and use it as their office. Every evening when we returned we saw the caravan had been blown to bits by Serbian artillery. By the next morning there was a new caravan. Stubborn folk these Slovenians.

Three days later what we witnessed just down the road was far less amusing.

By now Yugoslav Army tanks and armoured columns were rumbling into Slovenia to suppress the uprising. On the main highway from Croatia to the Slovenian capital Ljubljana, cameraman Mike Inglis and I had come across a convoy of lorries forming a barricade to halt the heavy armour. As we were filming, we heard the roar of warplanes. We ran off the road and dived for cover among some trees. Several of the lorry drivers followed.

Moments later MiGs from the Yugoslav Army screamed over our heads, strafing and bombing the lorries. They'd clearly been ordered to blast away the blockade. The noise was terrifying as the planes made several low and lethal passes over the highway before disappearing beyond the wooded hills.

Still filming, Mike and I moved cautiously back to the A2, now strewn with broken and burning vehicles. We found several of the civilian drivers writhing in agony on the ground. We counted seven dead. Nearby a farmhouse and livestock had been destroyed. The farmer lay dead beside his smouldering barn. His daughter looked on in tears. The first casualties of a conflict that was to claim more than 100,000 lives over the next decade. The Yugoslav War had begun.

By the time we drove into Ljubljana it felt like the city was on the brink of civil war. The people of Slovenia were literally up in arms. Shocked and angered at the Yugoslav Army's attempts to intimidate them, they were preparing for armed resistance. I talked to Matjaž and Dushan as they patrolled the streets of their capital. Only the week before they had been an office manager and a truck driver; now they were part of the country's 30,000 strong volunteer force, fighting for their independence. 'We've had enough of Serbia's threats and bullying,' Dushan told me. 'It's time to be our own country.'

The tourist brochure I picked up in Hotel Lev boasted: 'Discover the Sunny Side of the Alps.' For the moment, the sun had been replaced by the grey clouds of conflict.

It was David and Goliath stuff. The lightly armed Slovenian defenders taking on the military Yugoslav giant. But their country was ideal for guerrilla warfare. We watched as the Slovenians harassed and halted, taunted and frustrated the army's advance. They put up roadblocks, barricaded the troops in their barracks, cut off supplies, planted booby traps and minefields. And it worked. They thwarted the military might of the Serbian President Slobodan Milošević.

Mike and I joined one Slovenian militia group made up mainly of farmers in plaid shirts armed with hunting rifles and grenades on a wooded ridge. A ragtag outfit, who'd managed to trap an armoured column of Yugoslav tanks and artillery in the narrow valley below on Highway One for six days. When the column tried to withdraw, the militia attacked and stopped them moving. It was a short but bloody battle. One of the wounded, a 21-year-old conscript from Serbia, was weeping in pain and grief. Next to him was his best friend, who had been shot dead.

During a pause in the fighting, the Slovenians allowed us to walk down the hill to talk to these young Yugoslav soldiers. We could see that they looked hungry and frightened. They told us that they'd been trapped for nearly a week without any supplies and were waiting for help to arrive. They asked us for food and drink. We didn't have much to offer.

Then a local Slovenian farmer appeared with milk and water for them. The Yugoslav recruits were pathetically grateful. I asked the farmer, through our interpreter: 'Why do you care? Surely these men are your enemy?' To which the farmer poignantly replied: 'Yes, but they are still human beings.' It was something we were to hear many times in this strange war, which would pitch brothers against brothers, neighbours against neighbours.

Pasha Pantich, the sergeant in charge of these lads and their mobile anti-aircraft guns, told me the soldiers all wanted the violence to stop. They blamed the politicians for the conflict and killing. His unit just wanted to get home alive and in peace. And this was only week one of a war that was to last a decade.

The following day there was an even more extraordinary scene, as a group of weeping mothers arrived all the way from Belgrade, 350 miles east, to plead for their young, conscript sons to be allowed to go home. This war was already tearing families apart.

Before we left Slovenia, I thought we should take a look at the Austrian border to the north. I wish I hadn't bothered. We knew it would be tense as the Austrians were seriously worried the fighting would spill over into their country. But when we drove across the frontier high in the Alps near Jesenice something else spilled over. The Austrian border guard took an instant dislike to me. He jabbed his AK47 through the back window into my face, in fact literally up my left nostril. Goodness knows what I'd done wrong, but he treated me more like a terrorist than a TV reporter. Mike jumped out of the driver's seat and did a lot of animated mime, to show the guard we were harmless and armless, and that we'd turn straight round. Finally the growling guard backed off. Slightly bruised and rather offended, I retrieved my British passport and we hightailed it back over the border to the 'safety' of war-torn Slovenia.

The consolation was that we found a delightful alpine village, perfect for a feature piece on Slovenian independence. It had pretty chalets, families gathering in the summer hay and proud people demanding freedom from Yugoslavia's crumbling economy and ethnically divisive politicians. It seemed miles from the war we'd witnessed, until I saw military uniforms drying on a washing line and the local carpenter with a Kalashnikov.

In the village inn in idyllic Srednja Vas we heard more about the locals' age-old hostility to the dominant Serbian majority, which was at the root of many of the region's problems. As we listened, the innkeeper served us a plate of delicious local cured ham. He grated raw horseradish root over it. It was the first time I'd tried it that way. Delicious. It was one of those unexpected lunches you never forget. A day later a ceasefire saw Slovenia begin life as an independent republic, but sadly it was just the beginning of the Balkan wars.

When I returned to Yugoslavia three weeks later I was soon plunged into the heart of bandit country. By now Croats and Serbs were at each other's throats. Neither side had declared war but ceasefires were fragile. The distrusted Yugoslav Army was the only entity keeping the warring ethnic factions apart.

In the Triangle of Terror on the Croatian–Serbian border between Osijek and Vukovar, the army grudgingly agreed to take us on patrol. ITN cameraman Eugene Campbell and I squeezed into an old personnel carrier with eight nervous young conscripts and their officer. In the stifling heat, this armoured sweatbox, reeking of smelly soldiers, stale tobacco and engine fumes, trundled noisily through some of the most hotly contested territory on earth.

Eugene filmed, the lads clutched their rifles and I scribbled in my notebook to still the nerves. For four hours, we monitored border villages that had seen some of the most vicious fighting. The squaddies told us one of their comrades had been shot dead on this same route the night before. When they reached Sarvač, where it had happened, the patrol turned back. They said it was too dangerous. The road was mined. For them, this Croatian-held village was a no-go area.

The fault lines were emerging. The Croats saw the army as a threat, if not the enemy, while armed Serbians, manning a barricade up the road, seemed relieved to see the Yugoslav Army patrol. Out of the slit windows of the APC we saw fifty federal tanks dug in, apparently forming a buffer zone to keep the factions apart. We passed in and out of Serbian- and Croatian-held territory. It was a battered landscape of blasted homes, deserted villages and bristling militias. This was the Krajina, the disputed border lands.

When we returned to the army base in the Croatian town of Osijek, I'd rarely been as pleased to leave a vehicle. It had felt like a tin coffin in a shooting gallery. I checked the local paper on this latest ceasefire day. The headlines were not about peace, but tips on how to blow up a tank.

At a nearby graveyard, they were burying twenty-year-old Mario Vuknič, a Croatian guardsman killed in a shoot-out at Dalj, a village we'd passed earlier where twenty-two people had died in a gun battle. The mood was one of mourning, but the whispers were about revenge. Yet curiously, as a Serbian funeral procession passed by, the Croats stood aside respectfully. It was a poignant reminder that this awful conflict was being played out among neighbours. United in grief, divided by the gun.

Three weeks later I was back, as ceasefires crumbled into all-out conflict. The strategic Croatian border town of Vukovar had become a major flashpoint, beleaguered by Serb militias after days of vicious fighting.

It wasn't far from here that my colleague David Chater was badly injured when he took over reporting duties from me a couple of weeks later. David was sheltering in a church tower near Vukovar with local militia fighters when he was shot in the back by a sniper. Surgeons saved his life, but David lost a kidney. However, this didn't stop him from returning to a highly successful career with ITN, Sky and then Al Jazeera.

Many of the stories emerging of slaughter and savagery at that time were too gruesome to report in detail. In war, it was always difficult for a correspondent to know where to draw the line. Maintaining some decency amid the brutality of battle can be difficult, but I always figured the viewer didn't really want to know every grisly fact.

The self-styled Captain Hawk, one of many wannabe gun-toting Rambos I was to encounter in this combat zone, offered to act as our escort. With his Croatian militiamen riding shotgun, we sneaked into Vukovar through the back door, along rutted tracks and maize fields high enough to screen our approach.

As we entered the town through a series of checkpoints, the guns were silent for once. Five days of fighting had shattered Vukovar, now almost deserted by local civilians. We saw a car hit by a mortar; inside were three charred bodies. From the gaping window of a shelled house, a man shouted to us that the Serbs would never get him out. We filmed teenage boys armed to the teeth preparing to defend their homeland.

Captain Hawk stroked his moustache, fondled his gun and told us his men were now defending Europe's last frontier against communism. But he admitted they were trying to do it with rifles and homemade grenades.

Within days I'd heard a similar story – but from Serbs. How this came about was chance or perhaps just plain clumsiness. We were driving through the contested area of Krajina some forty miles south of Croatia's capital, Zagreb, when, unbeknown to us, we'd crossed an imaginary green line. One moment we were in Croat territory, the next we were confronted by hostile Serb militiamen manning a barricade of tractors and hay bales. They had to be farmers. I got out of our car, raised my hands and walked over. I told them we were British journalists and we'd like to hear their side of the story.

They relaxed a little, whispered among themselves and then invited us to follow them. We were taken into their village of Blinja and soon found ourselves in a small farmyard being plied with homemade slivovitz, a local brandy made from damsons. It was tasty, but tended to burn like battery acid as it took a fast route to your stomach. It seemed to make these men of arms an awful lot jollier, which, as an unarmed journalist, I was pleased to see. I'd observed that much of this Yugoslav War was fuelled by slivovitz – bottles were handed round before battles. Booze probably enhanced the bravery and brutality of the combatants.

Anyway, the Serbs of Blinja told us how they'd been surrounded and cut off by Croatian police for almost two months. They showed us their village shop with bare shelves and said they'd been left with no public transport, no phones, no fuel and their food supplies were running out. After forty-five years of peaceful coexistence, their Croat neighbours had turned into their enemies. Yet these Serbs had no desire for Milošević's 'Greater Serbia'. All they wanted was ethnic harmony in Yugoslavia and a slurp of slivovitz.

Interestingly, the farmers of Blinja had respected the large 'Press' sign we had stuck on both flanks of our car. But increasingly that wasn't the case. It was clear to us that the media had become 'piggy-in-the-middle'. With trust the first casualty of this cognate war, all sides had lost faith in the fourth estate. In fact, they'd chosen to see us as anything from spies to propagandists for their opponents. We even saw militias trying to pass themselves off as press to sneak up on their enemies, while others went to war in ambulances to disguise their deadly intent. It all went to undermine the status of independent non-combatants, from journalists to medics. Instead of feeling like I was accepted as a neutral observer, objectively reporting the unfolding drama, I'd never felt more like a target. For me, Yugoslavia marked a sea change in the way journalists were treated in war zones. From then on I sensed that combat reporting was turning into an ever more risky and dangerous business – broadcasters now had bulls-eyes on their backs.

On a last sortie, I crossed the Sava River from Croatia into Bosnia to film a war memorial that explained some of the historic hatreds that were once again wracking Yugoslavia. In a peaceful woodland clearing were the mass graves of 360,000 people massacred by the Ustaše, Croatia's Nazi collaborators during the Second World War. Most of the victims were Serbs.

In a nearby village, those old ethnic fears had been revived. I talked to Serbs, now sheltering in Bosnia, after fleeing from their village just across the river in Croatia. They were refugees barely a mile from home. They told me they'd lost everything when their neighbours turned against them. It was becoming a familiar tale. So far the crisis had only tainted the fringes of Bosnia, but it was a potentially explosive mix – home to Serbs, Croats and a Muslim majority. Ethnic passions were already inflamed by talk of nationalism. Some fearfully whispered the phrase 'ethnic cleansing'.

It was early September 1991. I signed off my final report: 'Croatia has all but closed its borders. Just one bridge remains open across the Sava River to Bosnia – and the only export now is trouble.' It was eight years till I was to return to the Balkans and the conflict was still raging.

CHAPTER 15

THE MANDELA YEARS

It was an inauspicious start to my relationship with Nelson Mandela.

As he walked free from Victor Verster Prison in South Africa's Western Cape on Sunday 11 February 1990, I was 1,800 miles north in Lusaka trying to coax his comrades into action.

||||||||||||||||||||

The African National Congress had run its 'government in exile' from the Zambian capital for almost thirty years, ever since their movement had been banned in South Africa. They'd kept the Struggle going from here and mounted countless military actions through MK, their armed wing.

But as we flew in to get their reaction to Mandela's release, it felt like the ANC leadership had been caught by surprise.

At the Pamodzi Hotel, watering hole of the party elite, some old hands seemed more interested in which foreign correspondent would buy them a round. At an ANC gathering in a local hall, officials broke into song as news filtered through of Mandela's walk to freedom. But it was hardly spontaneous. As cameraman Tim Leach and I filmed interviews it was clear they still couldn't believe it had really happened. They'd been told Mandela was free after twenty-seven years, but none of them had seen it for real on television.

Zambia's colourful President Kenneth Kaunda was far more upbeat. He had plenty to say, as always. He invited the international media round to his exotic State House, with its own golf course and wild animals roaming the grounds. There, in his gardens, he knelt down and prayed, giving thanks for Mandela's release. 'This is just incredible. I can't believe it,' he told us. 'This act by de Klerk has prevented a revolution in South Africa.'

As we watched grainy TV footage of Mandela's release, you could sense the expectation, the excitement and the uncertainty. These exiles in Lusaka, many of whom had served time on Robben Island, were among the few who knew Mandela. To the rest of the world he was a mystery man. An enigma. Most knew his face only from an old image as a freedom fighter. Nobody could guess what impact he might have on South Africa after twenty-seven years behind bars.

The next day, the ANC got its act together, and with considerable help from the travelling media, they organised a party. At last there were genuine signs of euphoria. Something for us to film, thank goodness. Pallo Jordan gave me an answer in keeping with the Head of Propaganda: 'We're obviously very elated for Comrade Mandela.' But he still couldn't resist the familiar resistance rhetoric. 'Of course, we'll intensify the armed struggle, while we work out our strategy.'

They were cautious about the SA government's motives and wary of returning home. But they were bewildered by the speed of events. Looking back, it was hard to believe these men and women would be running South Africa in little more than four years' time. The next time I saw these warriors of the long Struggle they were back in SA, wearing smart suits and fancy titles, like minister, director or chief executive.

Tim's sound recordist on that trip, Daniel Krebs, a Swiss-born ex-chef, got a call from home to say his wife had given birth to a baby boy. Daniel asked me what I thought he should call his son. In the mood of the moment, I said: 'How about Nelson Mandela Krebs?' He liked the sound of it.

It was a while before I was to meet Mandela. Two months after his release he came to London to be honoured with a victory concert at Wembley. I managed to throw a question at him amid the media scrum. He confirmed he wouldn't be seeing the Prime Minister. 'We have serious differences with Mrs Thatcher,' he answered sternly.

It wasn't until I took up my post as ITN Africa correspondent in late 1991 that I had a chance to talk to Mandela face to face. I arrived in Johannesburg just as the CODESA talks, aimed at negotiating an end to apartheid, got under way. The National Party government of F. W. de Klerk, Mandela's ANC and all the main parties were involved. In a break between sessions, I grabbed a chance to introduce myself to Mandela as a new member of the foreign press corps. Courteously, he welcomed me to South Africa, saying with a smile: 'We hope you'll have much positive news to report.'

To my amazement, from that day on, he never forgot my name. Every time I saw him he would say with unfailing politeness: 'Hello Jeremy. How good to see you. How is your family?' And I wasn't the only one. He seemed to remember the names of most correspondents. We found it hard to comprehend how a man of seventy-three, who'd spent twenty-seven years in jail, and now had the weight of the world on his shoulders, could find time to learn our names. It was all part of his extraordinary charm.

After all those years in enforced hibernation, he emerged into the sunlight and exceeded even his own myth. I found he was charismatic and amusing, but tough and canny, handling the political exchanges like a veteran. He'd had twenty-seven years to prepare and he wasn't wasting time.

F. W. de Klerk told me some years later that he'd decided to release Mandela because he was a man with whom he could do business and he knew his country had to change. But it was hardly all sweetness and light between them. De Klerk soon discovered that Mandela was a fighter, not just for freedom, but for democracy and equality.

The talks took place against a backdrop of murder and mass action. But one incident changed the mood and the tone.

Early on a Thursday morning in June 1992, we received reports of a massacre in a small township forty miles south of Johannesburg called Boipatong. We raced out there to discover a horrific scene. As we walked into the little shanty settlement there were bodies littered everywhere. It looked as if they'd been mown down at random. Some shot, some hacked to death. There had been no specific targets; everyone in sight had been slaughtered. Forty-five deaths in all. It was stomach churning.

Relatives were still searching for blankets to cover their loved ones. Through their sobs I began to gather their stories. Elizabeth Rameledi told me she watched petrified as her husband and her mother-in-law had been stabbed to death. Not even their family dog had been spared.

Nearby lay the body of 29-year-old Maria Mlangeni. Neighbours said she'd been expecting her first child next month. In a tiny bundle lay the remains of nine-month-old Aaron Mathope. He'd been stabbed in the head and his mother had died alongside him. The baby's grieving father told me how they'd been attacked in the night by Zulu-speaking Inkatha gangs. Some residents claimed the killers had been accompanied by white policemen.

Now in daylight we filmed police removing the bodies. They refused to comment on their alleged involvement. Yet again the term 'third force' began to do the rounds. It had long been thought that elements within the government's security network paid agent provocateurs and gangs to carry out hits that would terrorise the public and undermine the ANC. Residents of Boipatong were certain they'd been attacked by Inkatha supporters from the nearby Zulu workers' hostel.

Mandela swiftly accused de Klerk's government of complicity in the attack, through a state-sponsored 'third force' aimed at destabilising

At Sevenoaks Prep School, 1957 – with a fly on my cheek!

Budding young reporter at BBC Leeds in 1974.

Dodging tear gas in Seoul with cameraman Claes Bratt, 1987.

Striving for the perfect script, Manila, 1988.

ABOVE LEFT Sweating at Angkor Wat, Cambodia, 1989 – the Khmer Rouge weren't far away.

ABOVE RIGHT Riding with Vietnamese troops as they finally withdraw from Cambodia in 1989 – the real end of the Vietnam War.

LEFT Royal tour to Cameroon, 1990.

With Ian Robbie in Mogadishu in 1992.

Not the luxury hotel we were hoping for! With Ian Robbie in south Sudan, 1993.

Commentating as British troops enter Iraq at Safwan border town, 22 March 2003.

LEFT The Blairs on election night, 1997 – taken by Alastair Campbell just before he dropped my camera!

BELOW Me and volcanoes – this time it's Mount Etna, 2002.

ABOVE My last chat with Nelson Mandela at his Johannesburg office in 2007.

RIGHT An Emmy for Sky's special report on *Pakistan: Terror's Frontline* in 2009.

LEFT Interviewing golden girl Jessica Ennis at the London Olympics in 2012.

LEFT Two fine Springbok captains Jean de Villiers and Francois Pienaar at Mandela's memorial service, Johannesburg, 2013.

BELOW LEFT A great man – Mick Deane.

BELOW RIGHT New tech man – presenting via mobile phone from the Paris terror attacks, November 2015.

RTS for News Programme of the Year 2016.

Our great escape – on safari in South Africa.

Team Thompson at Londolozi, 2016: Lisa, me, twins Josh and Ewan, Adam, Lynn, James, Bella, Fiona and Sophia.

My last Sky road trip crew – Andy Portch, Chris Curtis and Kenny Stewart during the 2016 US election.

ABOVE A word with Trump, New Hampshire, 2016.

LEFT One final show – Washington DC, November 2016.

the country. We were seeing another side to Mandela. This was the steel core beneath the charm. It was the first time since the talks began that he challenged de Klerk head on. He threatened to call off the negotiations and inflict a campaign of mass unrest on the country.

It was a turning point. I knew then that I was seeing a shift of power from de Klerk, the last leader of the old white nationalist regime, to the black majority of the ANC. Mandela had become a force to be reckoned with.

Two days after the carnage I was back on the dusty streets of Boipatong as de Klerk swept into the settlement to offer his condolences. The scene that followed was unprecedented in South Africa. As the President's heavily armed convoy stopped for him to talk to the residents, his car was mobbed by furious crowds chanting: 'Go away, murderer.'

His worried security guards struggled to form a barrier to shield him. I could see de Klerk through the back window. He looked genuinely shaken. A white South African President had never before been openly booed and jeered at.

Trapped inside his car, he'd come face to face with the raw emotions of his black countrymen, now incensed at his government's failure to stop the violence. De Klerk was forced to abort his visit after less than ten minutes, chased away by the grieving shack dwellers of Boipatong. It was humiliating.

However, few South Africans would have seen that story on their televisions.

Looking back, it seems extraordinary that the apartheid government was still trying to control what went on air at home and abroad. Foreign broadcasters were obliged to satellite out from SABC studios in the main cities. Censors watched every story we fed, ready to eject and reject anything they didn't like. It was a game of cat and mouse trying to slip sensitive stories past the censors.

Cameraman Ian Robbie told me how, in the darkest days of the Struggle in the 1980s, most South Africans were unaware of the violence and conflict. The troubles were barely mentioned on the heavily censored state-run TV. When Ian tried to explain what he'd filmed and witnessed in the townships to friends, neighbours and even family, they often refused to believe him.

Back to 1992 and the bloodshed was far from over. Three months after Boipatong I was to witness at first-hand another massacre, different in dynamic, but equally deadly.

We'd flown down to the black homeland of Ciskei to cover an ANC march demanding that all homelands should be absorbed back into South Africa. It was controversial. The ANC wanted to start mobilising supporters in Ciskei. They accused its military leader, Brigadier Oupa Gqozo, of being a puppet of the white government. They wanted him out. He warned that any protest would be met with force. The scene was set.

A defiant crowd of at least 50,000 ANC supporters, led by their Secretary General Cyril Ramaphosa, began to march from King William's Town, up a long hill, towards the Ciskei capital, Bisho. Ian Robbie, soundman Gugu Radebe and I were waiting, along with more media, on the grassy bank of the Bisho football stadium. As the marchers approached the homeland border, we could see Brig. Gqozo's brown-uniformed troops of the Ciskei Defence Force, moving down a slope towards the frontier fence. They were armed with rifles. We all assumed it was just a warning, a show of intent.

As the first wave of ANC protesters broke the defence force lines, we heard the crackle of automatic weapons. For a moment we thought they were just firing in the air. But then marchers all around us began falling to the ground. I could see blood spreading on their clothing. Some were moaning, others screaming in pain. Suddenly it was mayhem. Now we knew they were shooting to kill. Hundreds starting running, crouching low to the ground, zigzagging, trying to flee the gunfire. Some fell before they could escape.

Ian, Gugu and I were totally exposed filming at the top of the stadium. We dived to the ground and rolled down the grass bank,

Ian still filming. Gugu was clinging onto his microphone kit, while I was left with the extended tripod, which turned into a fibre and rubber octopus. Its legs and spreaders became entangled with my limbs as I cartwheeled down the hill. We were terrified. Somehow we found some cover behind a van. We ended up half buried under a pile of people, some alive, some wounded, some dead. Amazingly, Ian kept his camera rolling throughout – and in focus. His footage was remarkable and revealing.

The Ciskei troops had opened up with no warning. It was a relentless fusillade. They fired over 425 rounds. I timed the first burst at one and a half minutes: ninety seconds of sheer horror. Men, women and children fled in panic. It sounded like the gunfire had come from three different directions. I was totally disoriented.

When the gunfire stopped, the three of us decided to make a run for it, looking for more substantial shelter and a safer place to film from. As we set off, a second volley rattled out across the open field. More people were felled. The firing lasted at least a minute. Live rounds cracked just above our heads and now they were launching grenades too. We kept running, weaving, making for a solid-looking building. We got to safety, gasping for air, lungs tight from fear and acrid smoke. Later the troops would claim they'd been fired at first. We could find no evidence to support their claim.

On this one-sided killing field, the targets clawed their way to safety, dragging their wounded comrades. Some were no more than teenagers. In all, twenty-eight demonstrators died that day. Just ten weeks after Boipatong, another massacre had plunged South Africa into even deeper crisis.

Predictably, de Klerk put the blame on the ANC's mass action campaign. The ANC accused him of propping up an unpopular black homeland.

In those days we had no live link to feed the video back to London. While we were still filming, ABC bureau chief Mark Foley realised the magnitude of the story and wisely booked a charter to fly us all back to Johannesburg without delay. A frantic edit and these extraordinary pictures just made it onto the *ITN Early Evening News*. The footage was to win Ian Robbie the accolade of Royal Television Society News Cameraman of the Year. Rightly so. His work that day, like every day I worked with him, was brilliant, brave and utterly professional.

When I finally got home late that night, I found Lynn still in a state of shock. She'd been planting flowers out in our garden in Joburg when she received a call from the Foreign Desk: 'Hi Lynn, just to let you know Jeremy and the guys are OK.'

Not having a clue what had gone on in Bisho, Lynn said: 'I know. Thanks.'

Then it quickly dawned on her that this was no normal call. 'What do you mean?' she asked.

'Oh, there's been a shooting in Bisho, a massacre, a lot of people killed. But we've heard from Jeremy and his team and they're safe.'

Lynn told me she'd gone cold and shaky at the thought of it.

It wasn't the first or the last time she received one of those unnerving phone calls. Once again I realised just how much I asked of Lynn when I was away on stories. Waiting at home, always anxious in case the phone rang with bad news, she's been incredibly strong for me, coping courageously with the risks and uncertainty of a reporter's life.

Early the next morning we flew back to Bisho as Nelson Mandela arrived to pay homage to his fallen comrades. Standing beside yellow wreaths, he told us he held de Klerk's government responsible for the deaths. Then to my surprise he turned to me and said: 'Jeremy, you were here yesterday. Please tell me what you saw.' So I talked him through those minutes of terror, as objectively as I could. He listened and nodded.

Later that day I discovered the Ciskei Massacre had a link to another dramatic episode from the Struggle. Treating the casualties at Grey Hospital in King William's Town was nursing sister Ntsiki

Biko – widow of one of South Africa's greatest black icons, Steve Biko. The woman, who had experienced the tragedy of the freedom fight so personally, told me she was shocked by the massacre, but feared it might not be the last.

On the fifteenth anniversary of Steve Biko's death at the hands of the South African police, Mrs Biko took me to his grave in a quiet cemetery at Ginsberg. With great sadness, she reminded me how the leader of the Black Consciousness Movement had died of brain injuries in prison after three weeks of brutal interrogation. He was thirty. And deaths in custody had not stopped. More than 100 had died that way in the past year alone.

Ntsiki Biko bore her loss with great dignity. She told me her main hope was that her husband, whose life was sacrificed in the name of democracy, had not died in vain.

Later, in East London, I spoke to Donald Woods, the newspaper editor whose book on his friend Biko inspired the film *Cry Freedom*. He told me he believed Steve's death had focused the world's attention on the injustice of apartheid. A martyr, who had paid the ultimate price for his beliefs.

The heartache, the suffering and the sacrifice of the Struggle. Even Nelson Mandela was vulnerable to the emotions of love and loss, as I was soon to discover.

CHAPTER 16

CRY FREEDOM

She had held his hand as he walked free.

It was a great South African love story.

A fairy-tale that had begun when a young ANC activist named Nelson Mandela had married his beautiful royal bride, Winnie Madikizela, in 1958.

They made a handsome couple.

The king and queen of the Struggle.

||||||||||||||||||||

When Mandela was locked up by the apartheid regime six years into their marriage, it was Winnie who carried on the fight. Her many supporters dubbed her the 'Mother of the Nation'. She was charismatic, undoubtedly, but she was becoming an increasingly controversial figure.

The government harassed Winnie and detained her for her activism before eventually banishing her. Some reporters remember her fondly from their visits to see her during exile at Brandfort in the Orange Free State in the '80s.

But the image was to become tarnished by her support of neck-lacing – burning people alive using petrol-filled tyres. Then there were allegations that she was implicated in murders; details of her adultery emerged; her views became more radical; her leadership a threat to the party.

The pressure on Mandela from his ANC comrades was enormous. Winnie had gone from loyal wife to major liability, beset by scandals about her personal life. Yet he clearly still loved her.

For several days in April '92 we'd seen an increasingly tired and troubled-looking Mandela as he side-stepped our questions about his marriage. We gathered from those close to him that he was still besotted with Winnie. But in the two years since his release from prison the love that had held them together for so long had begun to cool. It seemed that Winnie almost resented his worldwide fame, which had stolen the spotlight away from her. Her ego couldn't cope with his towering presence.

Then on 13 April, we were summoned to Shell House, ANC's HQ, for a news conference. When Mandela walked slowly into the conference room he cut a tragic figure. There were no prizes for guessing the topic. His sad face said it all. In his now familiar, slow and careful way, he announced that his 34-year marriage was over. The words seemed almost too heavy to project. There was pain in his eyes as he still proclaimed his devotion to Winnie. It was the first time I had really seen Mandela's soul exposed. He looked heart-broken, close to tears.

He said they had parted with no recriminations. 'I embrace her with all the love and affection I have felt for her all these years in prison and outside.'

As the press conference came to an end he stood and looked at us. Then said: 'I hope you will appreciate the pain I've gone through.'

For a moment you could feel the sympathy of the media for the Old Man.

It was tough witnessing a man of seventy-three talk about how a long love affair had ended and having to bare his soul before the watching world. Then there was the usual stampede as news crews and reporters rushed off to tell the world the news.

Mandela had always insisted he was a party man first and fore-
most. He may have been seen as the leader, the shining star, the
driving force, the essence of the African National Congress. But
Madiba told me he saw himself as merely part of the team, just the
one chosen to be a figurehead. So, in the name of the ANC, he'd been
persuaded to dump Winnie for the sake of his party and his people.
Quite simply, Mandela had taken one for the team.

Back in his office, he told his national executive: 'Boys, you must
make sure Winnie toes the ANC line. She must never leave the party.'
He was hurt by her betrayal. But, in the end, a hard head won over
a broken heart. His marriage was the latest victim of South Africa's
freedom struggle. Yet there was plenty more grief and heartache
to come.

A year later came the moment that could have destroyed it all.
Four gunshots that triggered a wave of emotion and hatred so strong
that we all feared South Africa would disintegrate into a racial, civil
war. A moment that was maybe Mandela's biggest test.

It was Easter Saturday, the tenth of April, a sunny autumn day.
In the racially mixed suburb of Dawn Park, Chris Hani was standing in his driveway holding a copy of that day's *Star* newspaper
when he was gunned down. Hani was no ordinary victim. To young
blacks, Chris Hani was a hero. As a former head of Umkhonto we
Sizwe (MK), the ANC's military wing, he'd spearheaded the armed
fight against apartheid. Now leader of the South African Communist
Party, he had become a powerful advocate of peaceful change, a
man seen as a future President. In popularity, he was second only to
Mandela. Chris Hani had always told us he was willing to lay down
his life to free his country and he'd already survived two assassination attempts. But not this time. The tragedy was witnessed by his
traumatised fifteen-year-old daughter, Kwezi.

By the time we got to the scene some twenty miles south-east of
Johannesburg, senior figures from the ANC were already gathering
at Hani's front gate. Winnie was weeping openly. Tokyo Sexwale,

a member of the National Executive, choking with emotion, told me he feared there could be dire consequences. Party legends Walter Sisulu and ANC chairman O. R. Tambo arrived to pay their respects. They all looked shocked at Hani's violent death and were fearful of the fallout.

Police soon told us they'd arrested a forty-year-old white man near the scene.

Hani had always been hated by white extremists. In his MK days he'd been one of South Africa's most wanted men. The implications of his death were enormous. If it turned out to be a government conspiracy, we knew the racial and political tensions simmering just below the surface could erupt with volcanic force. Blacks could turn on whites. Extremists would gain traction. The hopes for democracy would be dashed. It was a recipe for Armageddon.

The next day, Easter Sunday, South Africans prayed for peace and feared the worst. Outside Hani's home, where he'd been comforting the family, Mandela told me he was seriously concerned at the threat of turmoil.

Only hours later we were filming burning barricades in townships, the first sparks of the violent reaction we'd anticipated. The protests gathered momentum. Marches were held. Vehicles were stoned and petrol bombed. A white TV cameraman's car was hit by a bullet. It was a time when I was grateful I'd accepted Gugu's advice to put the skull and crossbones bumper sticker of the Orlando Pirates soccer team on my car. He always said it would give you cred and safe passage in the townships. I tested the Pirates' protective powers to the limit.

The government deployed extra troops to maintain order. I deployed all our reporting resources to cover the crisis. It wasn't going to be much of an Easter holiday.

By now police had arrested and charged Janusz Waluś with Hani's murder. Waluś was a Polish immigrant, known to be fiercely far right and anti-communist. Later Clive Derby-Lewis, a Conservative

MP was charged with giving Waluś the gun. This apparent white extremist conspiracy was fuel to the racial tinderbox. The blue touch paper was almost alight.

The nation held its collective breath. Roelf Meyer, the government's chief negotiator, told me later that South Africa had been at a 'tipping point for forty-eight hours'.

Now it was all down to Mandela. He pushed the government for an election date. He wanted something concrete to calm his people.

Three days after the assassination, the ANC leader appeared on SABC, state television, with an appeal for restraint in the memory of Chris Hani. He was the very image of authority, wearing large, gold-rimmed glasses. 'Our grief and anger is tearing us apart,' he told the watching nation. 'A white man, full of prejudice and hate, came to our country and committed a deed so foul that our whole nation now teeters on the brink of disaster.'

Then the brilliance of Mandela as he explained how information from a white neighbour of Hani's had helped track down his killer. 'A white woman, of Afrikaner origin, risked her life so that we may know, and bring to justice, this assassin.' After the cold-blooded murder of Hani, he said it was 'time for all South Africans to stand together against those who, from any quarter, wish to destroy what Chris Hani gave his life for – the freedom for us all'.

With this masterstroke, Mandela defused the racial time bomb ticking in his country. In this short TV address he had projected his authority and confirmed his leadership. It was the moment I felt Mandela had assumed the presidency from de Klerk. Even though it was another year until he officially took the title, he looked to me like the man in charge.

Years later F. W. de Klerk told me he knew only Mandela could ensure the assassination didn't spark great violence and conflict. 'I couldn't do it, persuade the people. Only Mandela could do it and he rose to the occasion.'

It wasn't long before he got de Klerk's government to agree an election date. As a political operator, he had turned a time of peril, with South Africa on the precipice of disaster, into an opportunity for progress. Somehow Mandela had held the nation together. Now people began to believe he could lead it too.

But Mandela was losing those he trusted at a crucial time. Hani's death was a terrible blow, not just to his party, but to Mandela personally. He undoubtedly saw Hani as a shining star in the democracy movement, a man of character and conviction, his heir-apparent.

Then, just a fortnight after Hani's murder, Mandela lost one of his oldest friends and allies, Oliver Tambo. They'd known each other for over fifty years. O. R., as he was known, was one of the corner-stones of the ANC. He'd kept the banned movement together for thirty years in exile, building up its military wing.

Mandela and Tambo had set up South Africa's first black law practice in 1952. Many years later, Tambo became President of the ANC before handing over the job to Mandela. He died from a stroke at the age of seventy-five. For Mandela, who was just one year younger than his friend, it was a reminder of his own mortality and the urgent need to complete his walk to freedom while he was still able.

Hani, then Tambo, both gone in two weeks. They were body blows to Madiba. When I interviewed him shortly after the news, his grief was palpable. As I watched him sitting just a couple of feet away, he looked weary, immeasurably sad. A man of seventy-four feeling his age.

I asked him: 'How saddened are you that comrades like Chris Hani and Oliver Tambo couldn't see your vision fulfilled?'

He paused, gathering his thoughts, fighting his emotions. For a moment I thought he might cry. It was eight seconds before he answered. He measured every word: 'That is a tragedy. Their pass-ing is a disastrous blow to the democratic forces of this country.' I had never seen him look this troubled. The weight of history and expectation were oppressive.

Yet this extraordinary man never failed to surprise. Despite all the political setbacks, the endless violence, the split from Winnie, the personal tragedies, he was dragging his people towards democracy through sheer strength of character. Yet there were many more battles still to come.

CHAPTER 17

VALENTINE'S DAY

I'd picked it because it was the poorest country on earth.

Or, in the words of the UN's Human Development Report, the least developed, with the lowest quality of life.

Pretty damning, really, when your home nation, judged on life expectancy, education and personal income, comes out bottom of the world.

Welcome to Sierra Leone in 1992.

||||||||||||||||||||

I'd been asked to film some features to coincide with the Rio Earth Summit, a grandiose UN gathering in Brazil aimed at making the world a better place – aren't they always. It turned into the largest environmental conference ever held, attracting over 30,000 people including more than 100 heads of state. And ironically costing about as much as sad, little Sierra Leone's annual economic output.

Ten thousand journalists alone attended this extraordinary eco-fest. So I thought it was only reasonable that one journalist should focus on the country that might benefit most from the 'caring' world's efforts to ensure a healthier planet. A country where I learned that 20 per cent of the population survived on less than one US dollar a day, where hunger was rife, access to water restricted, electricity virtually non-existent, education limited and where healthcare was so unaffordable or unattainable that life expectancy was barely thirty-nine years.

But just getting to Sierra Leone proved hard enough. There were no direct flights from my base in Johannesburg. It either meant criss-crossing the continent using operators of questionable airworthiness or flying via Europe. We went for the safer option – big planes run by airlines we'd actually heard of. But, in the extra time it took Ian Robbie and I to get there, the unexpected happened. They had a *coup d'état*.

On 29 April a group of young military officers marched into the capital, Freetown, and took control of the government. And, by pure chance, we were the only foreign journalists there to report on the overthrow. Sometimes, as a hack, you just get lucky.

From the airport, we took a taxi into the city, not sure what to expect. But it didn't take long for our garrulous cabbie to fill us in on the background to the coup. Ian and I were fairly nervous, being quite new to African coups. Our driver insisted there wasn't much to worry about. There was no fighting. Everything was 'cool, man'.

We were shocked by how poor the place looked as we drove slowly into the centre. And slow was the only option. The roads were so bad, you couldn't speed. They were an endless checkerboard of deep potholes loosely held together by hardcore. The tarmacadam had long gone. And the rains had come, turning thoroughfares into mud affairs.

Freetown looked more like a shabby shanty town than a capital city. But at least the streets were quiet. There was an uneasy calm about the place. It seemed the coup had been bloodless. And possibly accidental.

Here's how we heard the story of the uprising. A year back, Sierra Leone had been plunged into a civil war against a rebel army called the Revolutionary United Front (RUF). Led by the notorious Foday

Sankoh and backed by neighbouring Liberia, the RUF aimed to overthrow what they saw as the corrupt government run by the Freetown elite.

Sierra Leonean soldiers fighting on the frontline against the RUF were so poorly armed, clothed and fed that they became disheartened. Many claimed they hadn't been paid for months. In the end, a group of six young officers, led by Captain Valentine Strasser, set off for Freetown to demand a better deal for their troops. When word of their approach reached the capital, it proved enough to scare the government out of office; the President took flight, quite literally. Joseph Saidu Momoh, who'd run the country for seven years, jumped on a helicopter and fled for neighbouring Guinea, where he lived out his days in exile. The rest vanished into the night.

So Strasser and his fellow officers found the offices of state deserted. And, with the help of a few canny old backroom fixers, they were persuaded to install themselves in power. So, at the age of twenty-five, Valentine Esegragbo Melvine Strasser became the world's youngest Head of State.

Strasser told me a few days later that he'd had no plan for a coup. He'd merely come to town to demand a better deal for his men: clothes, food, pay and a few bullets. He wasn't asking much. In the end, he got a lot more than he bargained for – the reins of power.

It was so Africa. You couldn't make it up. An accidental coup; a ragtag army; a Head of State fleeing in panic; a captain who finds himself President at twenty-five, running a nation on its knees; and me, the only chronicler for miles. I felt a bit like Evelyn Waugh's Boot of the *Daily Beast* stumbling into a Graham Greene novel of West African intrigue.

Clearly my priority was an interview with the new President. But, still struggling to come to terms with his sudden and unexpected elevation, Strasser was proving elusive. His advisers told us he'd be ready to face the camera in a couple of days. They suggested we took a tour of the country.

First stop – the frontline, where it all started. It was a long slog to the eastern border with Liberia. There, in a torrential, tropical downpour we found Strasser's troops. They were a sorry, sopping bunch, dressed in plastic ponchos, T-shirts and flip-flops. Hardly an elite defence force. They carried weapons, but were quick to tell us they'd run out of ammunition weeks before. And they couldn't remember when they'd last been paid. The news of Strasser's startling success lifted their spirits. All they needed now, they told us, were the supplies he and his fellow officers had gone to demand.

On the way back to Freetown, Ian and I stopped to film one of the country's most lucrative and infamous resources – blood diamonds.

The conditions were atrocious. We watched the so-called miners panning for precious stones in huge mud wallows, bloated by the rains. It was back-breaking and dangerous work. The silt-streaked workers – men, women and young boys – told us they witnessed comrades dying in this treacherous bog almost every week. And yet they earned only a pittance.

The ones who really profited were in the nearby town: the dealers, many of them Lebanese, who bought stones from the miners and sold them on. And this was just the starting point of a blood diamond trade that fuelled the war that was consuming Sierra Leone and which would continue to do so for another decade.

Back in Freetown, I wanted to understand more about the country's parlous and impoverished state. The general hospital provided answers in abundance. As Ian aimed his camera down the largest ward, it was apparent many of the windows had no glass. The bed linen was far from freshly laundered, there were no lights and precious little equipment on display. The patients looked pitifully vulnerable. To complete this stark and haunting image, there was a vulture perching on a rail just outside the ward, peering in at the sick and dying.

Downstairs I found a surgeon carrying out a procedure, not in a well-equipped surgical theatre, but crammed against a window in a side room so he could use natural light to operate. A plasma bag was hanging from the window frame. He told me, with a resigned shrug: 'We're lucky if we get power for more than an hour a day. So we just have to keep on working by whatever light is available.' I asked him about the impact on healthcare. 'Well, we lose more patients than we'd like. We have to do the best we can.'

Near the harbour we found thousands living in a squalid shanty town where toxic waste trickled between the shacks in bile-coloured rivulets. The levels of sickness were alarming. It was obvious what was left of the health system couldn't cope. Not far away were the steps that symbolised the return to Africa of the first freed slaves from the Americas. Freetown had been named in their honour 200 years prior. What we witnessed here hardly looked like two centuries of progress.

We'd heard there were numerous political prisoners being held in the city, not so much victims of the current coup, but more likely left-over casualties who'd fallen foul of the previous patrimonial regime.

I sent a message to Strasser saying that we'd like to meet the prisoners. Somewhat grudgingly his people granted us access to the Central Police Station, a crumbling white pile dating back to British colonial days. Inside, a grumpy sergeant, with a crumpled uniform and face, led us through to a large room at the back. I still couldn't see any cells. Then, to our amazement, the officer reached down and prised open a sizeable trapdoor. As it creaked upwards, Ian zoomed in to the hole beneath, filming a dozen dazed and blinking faces staring up at us. The air that belched up from this pit was putrid. The prisoners were trapped below the floorboards in their own waste. I asked about their crimes. None of the police officers seemed to know or care. Just something to do with the usual political bedlam, they suggested.

A couple of days in Sierra Leone was ample time to see why it had fallen to the bottom of the global pile. Plenty of problems for the new President and plenty of questions.

Finally, after several days of badgering, we were granted an audience. Ian and I were ushered into the President's office. Sitting behind a vast desk was a big, gawky young man, wearing military fatigues and Ray-Bans. It turned out Ray-Bans were de rigueur. When we met Strasser's Cabinet we were struck by the fact that every one of the members wore the mandatory sunglasses. But then, like him, they were all aged about twenty-five.

I tried to engage the Big Man in casual conversation as Ian set up the camera, lights and mic. It wasn't easy. Strasser was not a gifted talker. Things got even harder when we rolled the camera. I asked a few starter questions about how he felt suddenly finding himself President and what were his priorities. He mumbled a few monosyllabic answers. It wasn't going to work. His comments were essential for our report. Ian buttoned off the camera. I got Strasser to stand up and stroll round the room with me in an attempt to put him at ease. He cut an impressive, muscular figure, like a loose-limbed heavyweight boxer. But he was no Mandela. The contrast in leadership ability couldn't have been more stark. Strasser was a shy, diffident lad, ill-prepared for running a nation of 4 million people.

I felt some sympathy and asked him what he really wanted for his people. He said, quite simply, an end to the years of corruption. He wanted to clear out the greedy, grabbing elite, who'd bled Sierra Leone of its wealth and left most of his countrymen in penury.

I told Strasser this was a good, strong message. Then I helped him draught and learn a short script and coached him how to deliver it. Eventually, Ian rolled the camera again and the rookie President told us:

'I want to clean up my country. I want to rid Sierra Leone of corruption and incompetence. I want to give my people a chance, to help lift them out of poverty.'

We got there in the end. A few coherent sentences was all I needed. It was a brief, but powerful statement of intent. But we still had no footage of this 'man of action' in action.

'Mr President, I need some pictures of you with your people,' I explained.

'I don't know how I can help, Mr Thompson,' he replied. 'I'm rather new to all this, as you have no doubt gathered.'

'Well, I like this image of you cleaning up your country, Mr President,' I went on. 'I think it sends out a strong message of intent.'

'Go on,' he said, looking puzzled.

'Well, if you don't mind me saying, your capital is in quite a mess. Perhaps you and your Cabinet would consider cleaning the streets?' I suggested.

'What, literally?' the President asked, with eyebrows raised.

'Yes, literally.' I said. 'I think that would do the trick.' Sometimes you just have to try your luck.

And so it was that early the next morning, the President of Sierra Leone and his merry band of young military officers, all dressed in their best fatigues, turned out on parade on the grimy streets of Freetown, wielding not weapons, but brooms and shovels.

Before a bemused crowd of local citizens, who'd been duly rounded up to witness this moment of history, Ian filmed Strasser and his youthful Cabinet sweeping clean the boulevards of their dilapidated capital city.

It was an unforgettable sight. You couldn't have made it up. Lining the streets, incredulous residents, the women in wonderfully bright-coloured dresses, applauding with increasing enthusiasm as their brand new, fledgling Cabinet brushed away the muck and rubbish. Talk about symbolism. Even the young soldiers, who'd initially looked reluctant and somewhat sceptical about their latest marching orders, entered into the spirit, sweeping and shovelling with new-found vigour, still wearing their Ray-Bans of course.

When we'd got enough footage, Ian and I left them to it. But a few hours later we received a message from the President's office inviting us to join him at his official residence. That evening Ian and I drove out to what was known as the Presidential Palace, a grand mansion on Juba Hill, with spectacular views over the city of Freetown. As the sun went down, from this elevation the capital almost looked charming. A quilt of colourful, chaotic buildings behind an Atlantic shoreline, a crescent of white sand and palm trees.

The story of this mansion seemed to sum up Sierra Leone itself. It was the brainchild of Siaka Stevens, who led the country for nineteen years as Prime Minister, before becoming President. Stevens, whose regime was infamous for its repression, corruption and mismanagement – extreme even by African standards – got his government to build him this palace. Later in his presidency he enabled legislation so that the building could be gifted to him.

And before he left office he sold the palace back to his impoverished nation – earning himself a sizeable profit. Another great African allegory.

As I chatted to Sierra Leone's latest leader, Captain Valentine Strasser, on a terrace high above the city, it was clear he wanted to shake off his nation's reputation for graft, extortion and nepotism. And he felt he needed some help.

Unexpectedly he said: 'Mr Thompson, I have been most impressed by your advice to me and your understanding of my country's problems.'

I told the President I was flattered by his words. But I was just doing my job.

But he wasn't finished. 'I would like to ask you to consider becoming my Information Minister or at least my media adviser.'

I did my best not to choke on my beer. Was he really serious? How do I deal with this diplomatically? After all, I was in a country where past Presidents had thought nothing of imprisoning or eradicating anyone who said no to them.

'Mr President, I am very honoured that you have thought me worthy of helping your government,' I replied. 'It is a weighty proposal. I'm sure you'll understand if I ask you for time to think about your offer.'

With that, I nudged Ian and nodded discreetly towards the door. We thanked the President for his generosity, made our excuses and left.

'Quick, let's get to the airport and get out of this place,' I said to Ian. 'I'm not sure how this'll end up if we stay any longer!'

Within hours we were in the air, never to return to Sierra Leone.

As a footnote, it is worth reporting that Strasser lasted four years as President before he too was deposed in a coup led by his own soldiers. He and his 'boys', as his junta was known, were initially seen as saviours – but Strasser was no saint. His government executed twenty-nine alleged plotters without trial and he refused to hand over power to a democratically elected government.

Maybe I was right to be wary.

The next I heard of him he'd enrolled at Warwick University, but never completed his degree. A few years later I read a paragraph in a London evening paper, reporting that the former President of Sierra Leone had been mugged in Stoke Newington, east London.

Last I heard, he was back home in Sierra Leone, a washed-up alcoholic, living with his mother in Grafton, east of Freetown, surviving on a very small state pension.

CHAPTER 18

BLACK MAMBA
AND THE BAD MAN

He was the world's most wanted man, known as the Pol Pot of southern Africa. Like the Khmer Rouge, he ran a guerrilla army legendary for its brutality, for its mass killings, mutilations, abductions and the exploitation of child soldiers. And, as long as I'd been in Africa, I'd wanted to meet the mysterious Afonso Dhlakama, leader of Mozambique's notorious resistance movement, Renamo.

||||||||||||||||||||

For me, Dhlakama and his fighters were the very essence of Dark Forces on the Dark Continent.

An army of seemingly murderous and malicious vagabonds, who'd emerged from the bush of Mozambique to wage a fifteen-year-long battle for control of their country.

Renamo's reputation was as awful as it was awesome. They were known best for their thuggery, their uncanny ability to appear from nowhere, maim and terrorise opponents, then vanish back into the jungle without trace. It was guerrilla warfare at its most vicious and most effective. Renamo had managed to sustain this almost endless battle of attrition and destabilisation, surviving on limited resources, holed up in the forests ever since Portugal had grudgingly granted Mozambique independence in 1975.

It was a fascinating story, with a touch of danger and mystery. I was determined to get to Dhlakama, to find out more about him and his movement. Could he really be that bad? Were his tactics as savage and inhumane as his enemies alleged? Or were all those hair-raising reports magnified in the murk of war?

The main motivation for our trip was the rumour swirling through the bush that he might, at long last, be willing to consider a peace deal. But tracking him down turned out to be quite another matter.

A tip-off started me on a telephonic trip through an intricate web of contacts, most of them anonymous, some just answering to cryptic first names. I should have realised all along that the key lay just a short distance from the ITN bureau in Johannesburg.

After all, Renamo – the Mozambican National Resistance – had been set up by the white Rhodesian special forces in 1976 as an anti-Communist rebel group to stop the newly independent Mozambique supporting black guerrillas threatening to overthrow Ian Smith's Rhodesian government. South Africa's armed forces then took up sponsorship of Renamo as part of the country's Front Line States policy, creating friendly buffer zones between themselves and their radical African enemies. Renamo was encouraged as an insurgent force to disrupt Mozambique's Marxist-leaning Frelimo government and prevent them supporting the ANC's anti-apartheid movement in South Africa.

So, unsurprisingly, there were quite a number of well-placed, if somewhat shy, white South Africans who could point me in the right direction for a trip to the dark heart of Mozambique and a rendezvous with Renamo.

Cameraman Ian Robbie and I were advised to head for Malawi. There we were told to make for Blantyre, check into a small motel and wait for a call from a man named 'Charlie'. It was all rather like a bad Boys Own adventure – long on trust and short on information.

Curiosity won over caution and Ian and I set off for Malawi. We artfully donned non-journalist disguises – shorts and loud, flowery Hawaiian shirts – and did our best to blend in as regular tourists. I'm not sure we were that convincing.

Ian had swapped his usual Sony Betacam for a holidaymaker's handycam, so we looked a lot less like a news crew. We were now officially 'undercover'.

Two days went by without a call from 'Charlie'. If you're looking to kill time, Blantyre is not the place to do it. In fact, time had passed by Blantyre long ago, a small, bland dusty town of faded colonial charm and not a lot of distractions. We quaffed a few cold beers, chewed a few stringy chicken legs and tried to go largely unnoticed. Though it's strange, when you're on a bit of a secret mission you just feel that you stick out like a polar bear on a sun bed. Two large, anxious white blokes in a one-horse African town with nothing much to do but wait. It's probably all in the mind. But it felt like everyone in Blantyre was looking at us suspiciously. We might just as well have been wearing trilbies with 'Press' stuck in the hatband.

Eventually the phone call came. Thank God. 'Hello, it's Charlie. Get yourselves down to Blantyre airport. Round the back of the hangars on the far left you'll see an old blue Piper Aztec. I'll meet you there.' The way he said 'Parper Eztik' suggested we were likely to meet a white, male Rhodesian/ Zimbabwean. And so it turned out.

Ian and I, still doing our best to look like trouble-free tourists, had the taxi drop us outside the airport, then walked the last few hundred yards to make sure we weren't being tailed. Who knows if anyone was watching us. But we'd experienced enough of Africa to suggest there was always somebody who wanted to know what nosy journalists were up to, particularly when they had 'guilty' stamped in their passports. It was one of those trips where paranoia sets in early and never eases its stranglehold on your throat or that knot deep in your guts.

We sidled our way to the quietest corner of the airfield and peered round the last rusty hangar. What we saw made our hearts sink even lower than the new annual base point we'd achieved in the past couple of days. Apprehension turned to sheer anxiety.

Out on the cracked, weed-lined tarmac was the shabbiest small aircraft we'd ever seen. Single-engined as we'd feared. (Try not to fly anywhere dodgy with one engine was an African credo we broke with disappointing regularity.) Sure enough, loading the plane was a gnarled man of around forty-five in the inevitable khaki shirt and shorts that said 'old Rhodie'. And peering out from the back window of the craft, a peeling sticker that radiated the words: 'Pilots for Christ.'

We never found out if Charlie was his real name. We suspected it wasn't and just called him Biggles. We introduced ourselves to 'Christ's Pilot' and soon learned he was very committed, if you know what I mean. He'd fought with Rhodesian Special Forces in the latter days of the War of Independence and helped to set up Renamo as a tool of the white Rhodesian government. Since then he'd found God and now combined a little light missionary work in Mozambique with aerial chauffeuring duties for Dhlakama – just to keep his hand in with his old pals in Renamo. God really does move in mysterious ways!

We certainly felt intrigued at being flown in the very plane that ferried Dhlakama to his many clandestine meetings with the men who fuelled and funded his brutal war. But it was hard to imagine how the guerrilla leader had survived numerous trips in this shabby shuttle. Especially when we saw Charlie loading the nose cone locker with a potentially incendiary mix of full fuel cans, old bicycle wheels and a car battery – the recipe for an airborne explosion that would take him much closer to his God, an awful lot quicker than perhaps even he had planned.

Ian swiftly intervened, with some common sense science that persuaded our gung-ho pilot to unload his flying tinderbox.

Eventually, we limped off the ground, lurched away from Malawi and launched ourselves into the mysterious world of war-torn Mozambique.

It was soon clear that Biggles was intent on tree-hopping. He was flying at no more than 400 feet, hugging the canopy of the forest. When we inquired why, he, all too casually, explained that we could get shot down at any moment either from ground fire or by government MiG fighters. Neither Ian or I could actually recall Frelimo – Renamo's sworn enemy – having much of an air force. But that hardly helped us relax. The thought of a Soviet-made fighter closing in on this juddering piece of junk was difficult to banish from the mind. As the tired little plane croaked and chugged its way deep into the war zone, Biggles turned to me and said: 'Eh! JT can you see that hole between your feet?' I looked down past my knees and sure enough there was a large round vent, through which I could feel the breeze and see tree-tops rushing by not far below. 'That's where they shot us last time we did this run,' Biggles chortled with relish.

Ian and I were bad flyers at the best of times. He tended to feel sick, and me, just plain nervous. If you don't get the physics of why lumps of metal should stay airborne there's not much you can do to soothe the nagging doubt. Now, suspended over one of the nastiest killing grounds in the world, damp and sweaty palms had spread into a total body experience.

On the return flight – and I'm amazed to recount that we did make one – Biggles's wife, who appeared as if by magic for the ride home, told us another tale that gave us a similar warm, cosy, closer-to-one's-God glow. In that unmistakable white female Southern African pitch that could cut facets on De Beers's best diamonds, Mrs Biggles explained with missionary zeal: 'We picked up this plane from a scrapyard and sort of put it back together using an old manual. We didn't know anything about planes and we had no money.'

And she added with a beatific smile:

'So God helped us make it work and taught us to fly. Really, it's a miracle that it's in the air at all.' Amen!

Just what we were thinking.

After an hour or so of jaw-clenching tension, we dropped even lower towards the forest canopy and Biggles began an unnerving wing-dipping manoeuvre like a dying bird.

'Just looking for the landing strip,' he called back brightly. 'I know it's near here somewhere. It's always a bit difficult to find,' he added reassuringly.

We swooped and jived for several minutes until we saw what was little more than a tear in the tree-line. As Biggles plunged the plane towards it, a brown letterbox of earth opened up amid the greenery. And he posted us down into it. It was amazing how well hidden it was. It didn't look big enough to land a child's balsa wood glider. But suddenly we twitched, straightened, flattened and crunched to earth, bouncing wildly for a hundred yards before slamming on all the anchors, just short of an imposingly solid line of trees. My favourite part of flying had always been the touchdown.

As our pilot cut the engine, the Piper's asthmatic wheezing was replaced by a new, more aggressive sound that filled the bush. A buzz-saw roar that could have been the war-cry of over-sized mosquitoes, if we hadn't caught the glint of sun on metal.

We stumbled unsteadily off the dirt landing strip, through the first stand of trees and into a small clearing. There, revving their muddy steeds, were the cream of Renamo's leadership astride 250 cc scrambler bikes. It was some sight.

One of them stepped down and walked towards us. He was a slightly rolypoly figure, about forty years old, in smart bush camouflage fatigues, wearing Buddy Holly-style black-rimmed glasses.

'Welcome to free Mozambique. I am pleased you have arrived safely,' he said in passable English, with a heavy African–Portuguese accent. 'I am Afonso Dhlakama.'

So here he was. One of the most hated and feared men in Africa. Portrayed by his enemies as a butcher and a barbarian. Leader of an outfit that had become known in the 1980s as the Khmer Rouge of Africa. One human rights report accused Renamo of using excessive force against the civilian population including 'burying alive, beating to death, forced asphyxiation, drowning and random shootings'.

At first glance he didn't look like a monster. Outwardly he was welcoming and courteous. But a man who'd led such a feared band of outlaws for thirteen years was clearly no fool and no saint. You don't get accused of war crimes and crimes against humanity by chance.

The next thing I knew I was clinging onto this notorious rebel for dear life, arms clutching around his ample midriff, as the President of Renamo gunned his bike and we careered off into the dense bush. It was a hair-raising ride, a slalom course through hardwood trees deep into his secret lair at Gorongosa. Behind me Ian was clamped onto a senior general, but somehow still managing to video this extraordinary scene.

We finally emerged into an opening dotted with thatched huts of various shapes and sizes. This was the primitive headquarters from where Dhlakama had masterminded much of Renamo's fifteen-year guerrilla war against the Marxist Frelimo government. The camp went by the whimsical name of Casa Banana. With only the most basic of equipment and intermittent funding from friendly governments and sympathetic right-wing businessmen and churches in the USA, it was amazing to think what an impact Renamo had made. What an infamous reputation they had built. What mayhem and misery they had conspired to bring to Mozambique. All done in the name of freedom. Although it was by no means a one-sided war. Frelimo had played their part.

By this time the war had claimed nearly a million lives, created over 3 million refugees and brought the former Portuguese colony to its knees – economically, physically and emotionally.

When we sat down for our formal interview, Dhlakama didn't want to talk about fighting. He dismissed my questions about the allegations of atrocities and the rule by terror as: 'No more than Frelimo propaganda.'

This man of war wanted to talk about nothing else but peace. It was clear that a ceasefire accord with Frelimo was only weeks away. Dhlakama and his generals knew they now faced perhaps the toughest of all their campaigns – reshaping Renamo's notorious reputation and preparing for democratic elections. Turning a guerrilla army, ostracised by the outside world, into a respected political party was no easy task.

Dhlakama insisted that, whatever we might have heard abroad about Renamo, it was a popular movement, support by almost half of Mozambique's 15 million population. To try to prove the point, he took us on a journey through a string of villages in the region. Whatever the truth in the dirty war of disinformation that clouds any civil conflict, reporters have to go by what they see and hear, read between the lines, ferret out the reality, sense sincerity, grow an instinct for injustice.

As I looked into the eyes of the malnourished, rag-dressed men, women and children we encountered along the way, I saw no fear or loathing, just exhaustion. Far from running in terror, these people clamoured around Dhlakama, welcoming him as a hero, showing genuine adulation. It was hardly the image of a man who, his opponents claimed, ruled only through intimidation.

Yet these were traumatised people in a broken land, shattered by a vicious civil war that had destabilised society and destroyed the infrastructure. We saw roads and railways that had been blown up, schools smashed to the ground, local government buildings trashed. Hardly a shop or a home left standing was undamaged. The war had left in its wake a trail of destruction.

And, as if that wasn't bad enough, they now had to contend with another of Africa's favourite tortures – drought. A natural catastrophe to compound the ravages of human conflict. As we travelled on with Dhlakama through this parched and wasted landscape, we found villagers scraping the last drops of water from dried-out river beds.

In Khande village we came across missionaries – a rare sight in rural Mozambique – handing out food. For the residents it was their first meal in three days. But they were meagre rations – a few bowls in a land where 3 million people were on the brink of starvation.

Oh Africa! So beautiful and so barbarous. As a paid observer, such scenes always raise that debate about one's role in life. Do you stop to help or can you do more good by alerting the world to the troubles you have witnessed? I've generally gone for the latter. But I'll never be sure.

Of course, politics can breed poverty and this was no exception. There was food aid in the region. But the relief routes into these villages were kept closed by Renamo for fear they would be infiltrated by Frelimo soldiers. Tough luck, folks! You're going to keep starving in the name of security.

But, for all that, they still seemed to dote on Dhlakama. Probably he represented their only hope. By the time I met him, he knew his people were dying of war fatigue. The only struggle left in them was the fight against famine. His best chance of helping them was forsaking violence and proving to a sceptical world that Renamo could be a force for good instead of evil. Afonso was no angel, but he was a realist as well as a rebel.

Within a month, Dhlakama and Frelimo President, Joaquim Chissano, had signed a Peace Accord in Rome. Two years later they contested Mozambique's first democratic election. Frelimo won by a short head and Dhlakama became the opposition leader.

It was a useful lesson. Never write your story in advance. Woe betide the journalist who sets out on an assignment with one eye already shut, impaired by the mote of preconception. But there was one last, dramatic image of that trip that was even more vivid than the rest.

At breakneck speed, we were racing back to headquarters on Renamo's preferred form of transport, the trail bikes. Ian and I were clamped onto our respective generals, clad in their rough serge combat uniforms. The smell suggested neither men nor garments had seen soap in a generation. It was more like cuddling a Stinking Bishop cheese than a fetid general.

We weaved and bucked along narrow bush paths, ducking under vines and branches. Suddenly we lunged down into a donga – a dry stream bed. Ian's bike was just in front. From their rear tyre something spat upwards. In that instant it looked like a black hosepipe rearing six feet into the air. As my bike shot by, I could have sworn I saw the hosepipe open its gaping mouth, spread its narrow hood and crack down towards me like a whip. It brushed my back. I felt a deadly draught. Then we were gone, up the steep bank and away. My general turned back from the handlebars and shouted into the wind: 'Black mamba.' I could have crapped myself, if I hadn't been hanging on so tight in every sense.

The black mamba, *Dendroaspis polylepis* to give it its full name, is arguably Africa's fastest and most venomous snake. It can grow up to thirteen feet long and move at fifteen miles an hour. Two drops of its venom can kill a human in little more than thirty minutes without proper medical treatment. I'd read up on snakebites. First comes the paralysis, then the shock, the nausea, the headaches, the sweating, the fever and the lapses of consciousness. I didn't need reminding that this remote bush hideout was about as far from medical treatment as you could possibly get. Bush veterans say all you can do is sit under a tree and wait to die.

Then I remembered. The mamba had missed! It didn't stop me sweating and shivering for quite a while though.

'That was mighty close,' said Ian as we were dropped off at our thatched hut. 'My guy was shaking as he held the handlebars – and he lives here.'

He quickly dug out the iron rations. A bottle of single malt whisky and a packet of biltong. We never went anywhere in Africa without our life-saving provisions.

'You look like you need a drop,' he said, laughing.

I replied in time-honoured team fashion: 'Silly not to!'

'Happy birthday, Jeremy,' Ian said as he lifted the whisky flask in a toast.

Bloody hell! I'd completely forgotten. It was 23 September, my birthday.

I'd survived another year. But only just!

CHAPTER 19

SOMALIA: WHY I BLAME MYSELF FOR BLACK HAWK DOWN

Imagine Mad Max and the Thunderdome for real, run by psychopaths on narcotics in a vast, bleak sandpit filled with the leftover hardware of the Cold War. A box full of grown-up fireworks guarded by kids with their pockets stuffed with matches and seemingly no conscience.

Welcome to Somalia circa 1991–92.

ıııııııııııııııı

As our aid flight banked over Mogadishu, below lay a city in partial ruins. The civil war that had erupted after the downfall of President Siad Barre had laid waste to large swathes. At first sight it was a patchwork of white and pastel buildings pockmarked almost beyond recognition. Cameraman Ian Robbie and I looked at each other with some apprehension. 'God, what have we let ourselves in for here?' I muttered above the whine of the plane's twin engines.

As we stepped out onto the crumbling tarmac of Mogadishu airport, we were met by some heavily armed lads, who barely looked out of their teens.

'Hello, my name is Mohammed. This is your security.'

We looked round at a battered Toyota jeep. Several young men brandishing AK47s hung out of the doors. It seemed that Save the Children (STC) Fund, who'd agreed to host us in Mogadishu, meant us to get to their headquarters safely.

Off we set, at breakneck speed, through shell-shocked streets, with horns blaring, much shouting and cursing and even more gun waving. We soon realised that just about every vehicle we passed was a variation on the same deadly theme.

These were war machines. SUVs turned into light military gun carriers. Flatbed trucks and four-wheel drives with machine guns mounted on the back. We saw some bristling with anti-aircraft guns and anti-tank weapons. There was even a lorry with a Stalin Organ – a multiple rocket launcher – strapped on its deck. They were battlewagons like we'd never seen before. This was the light cavalry of the Somali warlords. Ian filmed this alarming array of improvised fighting vehicles as we careered through the dusty, damaged streets.

At the Red Cross's fortified HQ, the staff explained that NGOs had been stopped from bringing in private security from outside Somalia. It was so dangerous, they'd had to change their code of conduct allowing them to hire local clan gunmen to protect their personnel. They'd got round some local red tape by paying for them with money termed 'technical assistant grants'. So, in time, these Mad Max gunships became known as 'technicals'.

Senior STC staff loaned us Mohammed and his band of brigands as protection during our three-day stay and warned us not to venture out without them. Sound advice.

As we got to know him better, Mohammed agreed to show us his store of weapons – a garage full of RPGs and machine guns. It seems they were all too easy to pick up.

For years, Somalia had been a proxy battleground for the Cold War superpowers. As that war thawed, this desert nation became a dumping ground for military hardware. You could find anything from a pistol to an old Soviet T55 tank, dug in to a weapons cache or simply left lying around. We'd never seen so many instruments of death.

Now this carelessly discarded arsenal had been commandeered by the warlords who'd filled the power vacuum after Siad Barre's demise.

Our 'security team' took us to the green line. Every war-torn city has one. This divide between north and south Mogadishu was marked only by a ghost town – the haunting bombed-out shells of once fine colonial mansions. This was the epicentre of the fight for control of the city between the clans of Mohamed Farah Aidid and Ali Mahdi Mohammed. They'd literally carved the place in two.

We watched and filmed the exchanges of fire across the green line. Enough to keep the two sides at munitions distance apart.

There was an air of anarchy amid the sound of artillery fire. 'Somali Music', the locals called it, with barely a hint of irony. It was hair-raising stuff. But our security man Mohammed seemed to know how to keep us out of the firing line, while still enabling us to get good footage.

Amid the chaos of conflict, the aid agencies, the few that hadn't been scared away from the country, did what they could for an increasingly desperate population caught up in this madness. By early 1992, over half of Somalia's 10 million population were in severe danger of starvation or disease from malnutrition.

At a makeshift medical centre on the outskirts of the city, we filmed a weeping father carrying his four-year-old son Ahmed in a plastic shroud. He told us the little boy had been ripped to shreds by shrapnel. We heard from medics that dozens of children were being killed or maimed every day in this slaughterhouse of a city.

At least 20,000 Somalis had been killed or wounded in the previous six weeks.

A British nurse, Joy Riordan, one of only a handful of foreign aid workers who'd braved the war, told me conditions were desperate. There were twice as many patients as beds in what was left of Mogadishu's hospitals. In pitiful, unsterile wards, staff did their best to patch up mutilated warriors and their victims.

And all around were signs of a man-made famine growing worse by the day. Food was power to the clan warlords and incoming relief supplies were the levers of their power. Firearms were more plentiful than foodstuffs, so at Mogadishu docks the warlords requisitioned food aid meant for the masses and made sure it fed only those who would support them in return.

The result: more than 300,000 people died from malnutrition in the early months of 1992.

Just outside Mogadishu we filmed a camp of a quarter of a million residents driven out by the fighting, now on the brink of starvation.

From Baidoa to Bardera it was the same story: clumps of emaciated, dying people at every turn. It was impossible to forget the faces of all those hungry children.

Into this failed state, this nightmare of violence, this place of anarchy, flew James Jonah, a west African, who was the United Nation's Under Secretary General. His mission: to broker a ceasefire. For two days we followed him around the city, filming his ever more desperate pleas for cooperation. At least he managed to get a meeting with General Aidid, the warlord running the south side of Mogadishu. But even with a private army to protect him, he couldn't get safe passage over the green line to meet his main rival, 'President' Ali Mahdi. A failed attempt in a failed state.

There wasn't a lot of faith in the UN after it pulled its mission out of Somalia a year before because they deemed it 'too dangerous'. Defeated and bemused, the UN envoy headed for his plane.

Ian and I, knowing we had more than enough material for a cracking report, also made plans to escape. But worryingly, at Mogadishu airport we found all aircraft had been grounded by an intense battle in the area. We were in trouble. There seemed no other way out.

Then we remembered, James Jonah had mentioned he was flying out by private jet. Our security man, Mohammed, reckoned the UN plane must be parked at an old airfield called Baledogle, forty-five miles to the west of the city, away from the fighting.

An hour later – after a ride of bone-jarring ferocity in our 'technical' – we raced onto the runway just in time to see the UN's sleek executive jet revving up ready for take-off. I jumped out, sprinted onto the airstrip and started waving my arms in front of the Learjet. I could make out the pilots glaring at me in astonishment. Slowly, the engines subsided. Then a side door opened and steps unfolded.

The UN Under Secretary General greeted Ian and I with a very stern look, but softened a little as we described the battle we'd left behind and how, without his help, we'd be trapped in Mogadishu indefinitely. We needed to get the story out. He took pity on us.

Five minutes later we were sinking into the soft leather seats of this purring UN jet, snapping open cans of wonderfully chilled beer and glancing back at the hell hole from which we'd just escaped. Left behind in Mogadishu, a fuming BBC crew, still looking for a way out of Somalia. Sometimes you get lucky.

In Nairobi, we cut and fed our story to ITN in London. It went down well. On *News at Ten*, it was the first real glimpse of how bad things were in Somalia. And we beat the BBC on air by a day. Later we headed to the legendary terrace bar at Nairobi's Norfolk Hotel and raised a cold Tusker ale to toast a decent story and a fortuitous escape. 'Thank god for that,' said Ian. 'That's our toilet trip of the year out of the way and it's only 3 January!'

Boy, did he speak too soon. Somalia wasn't going to let us go that easily.

In the following months, Ian and I were to return six times. We called it the 'year of living rough'. Weeks of mosquito nets, insect repellent, bed rolls, water filters and iron rations. Tenuous ceasefires had made little difference. The fighting continued. The famine grew ever worse.

Flying in on an aid flight one time, we became only too aware of how desperate and dangerous a business it was trying to feed the starving millions. Our plane was immediately ringed by security trucks as the sacks of rice were unloaded and rushed off to Red Cross feeding stations under armed guard. We heard all too many stories of international relief being plundered by marauding gangs of gunmen, with no regard for their fellow Somalis. This was a man-made famine.

We found that hundreds more squalid camps had sprung up round Mogadishu. Some people sheltered in the shells of bombed-out buildings, others squatted in old schools – education had ceased to function. More hungry, wasted figures huddled in the sand dunes by the Indian Ocean.

At one small camp we filmed, we were told twenty people had already died that day. Malnutrition and disease were rampant. A young woman called Faduma was barely clinging to life herself. Just outside her tattered tent, she showed me where eight of her ten children had been buried in the past week. She no longer had the strength to weep.

In the town of Baidoa, 200 people were dying every day. There were more body bags than food sacks. The body wagon made twice daily rounds as people were urged to bring out their dead. It was like some awful medieval tableau. When we followed the wagon to a cemetery in the desert we found the gravediggers couldn't keep up with the death toll.

It was one of those many moments as a journalist when you, once again, question your role as an eyewitness. How can you really help? The first instinct is to reach out. To buy food, to find medicine, to take them to a better place. But the scale of the catastrophe is so often overwhelming.

I'd long ago decided that the best way I can help is by bringing the plight of such people to a wider world. To alert governments and agencies through television news and hope it will spur them or shame them into action in such a way that will ease the suffering. Sadly, I've often been disappointed.

By now Ian and I had hired an interesting new security detail.

When we arrived at the airfield, there was no transport waiting for us. Just a line of dusty, battered 'technicals' manned by an ugly bunch of gun-toting 'taxi' drivers.

I picked the nastiest-looking leader, mainly on gut instinct. He didn't have much English. Just a rasp or two. He told me his name was Abdi. He had four brutes with him. I reckoned that in a shoot-out with the rest, they'd win.

So I hired him. We agreed on US$150 a day for the whole crew. He seemed happy enough. Well, he sort of grimaced gleefully at me through the stumps of blackened teeth. We shook hands and off we drove. Though we suspected his loyalty would last only as long as we had dollars.

Abdi certainly seemed like the kingpin in this part of town. He was a scary-looking character. He wouldn't have been out of place as one of Blackbeard's pirates. It took just one stare for most people to get out of his way.

Down at the docks, he soon proved his use. Unloading the aid ships often turned into a wild dog fight, with four rival clans demanding a share of the food before anything could move. It was accompanied by incessant arguments and plenty of gunfire. Food was leverage and currency.

On one occasion a clan gunman took exception to Ian filming the whole fractious process. He raised his Kalashnikov, pointed at Ian's chest from a couple of yards away and appeared to pull the trigger. It jammed. In a flash, Abdi rushed in, grabbed the man, pushed him away and wrenched the gun out of his hands. It was a frightening moment. But one that formed an unlikely bond between a British TV news crew and an unreconstructed old villain. Abdi had proven he was our security man.

Ian and I were intrigued by a hole in the windscreen of Abdi's tatty Toyota. So we asked how it got there. Abdi told us in sketchy, but graphic English. 'Man have car. I have gun. I go bang. Now my car.' As simple and savage as that.

The hole was exactly at head height on the driver's side. It all made sense.

Abdi was clearly not a man to be messed with. Before running shot-gun for us, he'd been a gun for hire, fighting for a warlord.

'What exactly did you do?' I asked.

'I kill,' said Abdi. He wasn't a man to waste words.

Naturally we dubbed him 'Abdi the Killer'.

On one trip, he drove us through bandit country around Baidoa to the small town of Wajit. It took us five hours to go just sixty miles on a rocky track through semi-desert scrub. Halfway there, Abdi stopped for food. That was just after he'd leaned out of the cab and shot a dog that was running alongside. No explanation. Just Abdi's Highway Code.

The food place was rudimentary. A wooden shack, the Somali equivalent of a truck stop. Fast food feral style. Out came lunch. Tin plates piled high with fatty goat. Abdi and his crew devoured the meat like they hadn't eaten for days. Vultures are more dainty on a carcass. Abdi graciously offered to share. We declined and stuck to our biltong and dried fruit rations.

When we finally reached the isolated town of Wajit, a tragic scene awaited us. Within minutes we were greeted by hundreds of residents who appeared from nowhere. They looked at us with pleading eyes.

The local elder explained that, months before, relief workers had promised them food supplies. The townspeople had cleared and marked a makeshift airstrip in the bush. And then waited. And waited. And waited. But still no food had come. And every day a few more starved to death.

They had simply been forgotten. For weeks they'd lit fires along the runway to guide in the food planes. Now they had given up the fires and almost given up hope.

When they saw us, they thought we had finally brought them food. I've rarely felt as bad in my entire career than in that moment when we dashed their hopes. I promised we'd carry their appeal for help to the outside world. I'm not sure they even understood the concept.

As he chewed on camel skin, just about the only sustenance left, Yusuf Asman, the head man, said plaintively: 'Nobody seems to care about us. What can I tell my people? Why is the world ignoring us?'

But help was to come to Somalia eventually.

At that time, we shared our ITN bureau in Johannesburg with ABC News. Their correspondent, Don Kladstrup, used to come in to our edit room and watch our Somalia reports with growing enthusiasm and, as he admitted, a little bit of envy.

'I just can't get New York interested in the place,' Don told me. 'It's off their radar. And I know it's a great story.'

But things were to change for Don, for the US and for Somalia.

Kladstrup finally persuaded ABC to let him and his cameraman, Tim Manning, go to Somalia. They joined us on one trip, so we could show them the ropes. It was to have some impact.

The images were so powerful and the story so strong that ABC soon got feedback that the US President George Bush Senior had watched Kladstrup's report in the White House and demanded action.

Before the end of the year, the UN had approved a peacekeeping force, led by the United States, to ensure the delivery of humanitarian aid.

And so it was that Ian Robbie and I found ourselves standing on the beach beside Mogadishu airport late into the ink-black night of 9 December 1992, filming some very startled US Marines emerging from landing craft.

President Bush's Operation Restore Hope was meant to be a top-secret insertion of peacekeeping troops. Much to their surprise it turned out to be a media circus.

Most journalists in Mogadishu seemed to have known about the timing of the operation for hours.

Ian and I had holed up near the airport in the house of a local chief we'd got to know. As was the local social custom, he and his friends chewed qat, as they chatted about the US 'invasion'. Then they kindly tipped us off when they heard the warships were off the shoreline. Out we raced with camera rolling and lights ablaze to capture the moment.

It was pandemonium. The US Marines, who'd clearly been over-prepped for the mission, ran up the beach Rambo-ready, all pumped up and aching for action. Only to be greeted by a horde of hacks, armed only with microphones, cameras and notebooks. The Marines didn't see the funny side.

It was the night when an 'unopposed amphibious assault' turned into a media ambush. A bunch of US Navy Seals looked ready to kill us for exposing their 'secret insertion'. One Marine went head over heels down the slippery ramp of his landing craft and had to be stretchered away. Several others lost their way. Another squad officiously rounded up some dozy old porters, who'd been asleep in a hangar, cuffed them and marched them off to detention like they were international terrorists.

A platoon of Pakistani peacekeepers, who'd been in town for a few months, looked on with the amusement of old hands, puffing away on their Woodbine cigarettes. Their officer, with a look of disgust on his face at the Yankee behaviour, whipped out his penknife, cut the cable ties and freed the unwitting prisoners. That sparked a US–Pakistan stand-off that lasted several hours until tempers abated.

Nearby Marines fired on twenty newsmen, ordering them to lie face down in the dirt, until they realised their error. The US mercy mission was in danger of being more humiliation than humanitarian. It wasn't an auspicious start for UNITAF – the Unified Task Force.

A total of 37,000 personnel were shipped in, two thirds of them from the US.

In the end, the operation began to come together. However, there were some curious photo op moments as US troops in full combat gear handed out sweets to very streetwise Somali kids, who were soon trading with them.

The media had a good many run-ins with the Press Ops set up in the dilapidated US Embassy. The Major in charge of communications didn't seem to have a lot of answers. Never a good thing when faced with a pack of rapacious war reporters.

'I'll take that question,' was his standard response to just about anything we asked. We gathered this meant he would make a note of our question, get an answer from the relevant generals and pass it on to us, when it suited them. But we soon realised he never came back with an answer. So after a few days of this pantomime, I asked him a question about the latest military operations.

The Major replied: 'I'll take that question.'

To which I said, somewhat facetiously: 'No, you won't. I don't want you to take that question out of this room. Answer it now or give it back to me and stop messing us about.'

That met with strong murmurs of approval from fellow hacks and a look of blind panic from the American officer, who didn't seem to know what to do or say. Unsurprisingly, media briefings became few and far between.

If their bureaucracy sometimes bumbled, their intelligence often creaked.

A few days after the landing, I'd arranged to meet top warlord Mohamed Farah Aidid. We filmed an interview on an open rooftop just a few hundred yards from the US HQ and discussed a possible peace deal with his rival, Ali Mahdi.

It turned out that at this very moment the US Marines were looking for Aidid because they believed his men had fired on a US helicopter.

An hour or so after our interview, US forces bombed that very same stronghold as part of their security crackdown. The place where we'd done the interview was no more. But Aidid had long gone. And fortunately so had we. It seemed our intel was a step ahead of the Yanks.

The following year another special forces operation against Aidid spiralled into the First Battle of Mogadishu, as it was known. During the exchanges two US helicopters were shot down. The ferocious firefight to recover the aircrews was retold in the movie *Black Hawk Down*. It was to be a turning point. Within a matter of months, the new President, Bill Clinton, ordered the mission to be scaled down.

It makes you wonder about unintended consequences. How our focus on the Somali conflict triggered a US news network into action and how that persuaded an American President to send in troops. Were we, indirectly, responsible for the chain of events that led to Black Hawk Down?

As for Abdi the Killer, it seemed his conversion from gunman to good guy continued. He ended up as head of security at the aid agency Care in the town of Baidoa. And we heard some years later that he'd been killed defending their compound from looting bandits.

CHAPTER 20

A BRIGHT SKY

I was hired by Sky in a pub. I shouldn't have been surprised, as it was the way they did business.

Informal, unconventional, no messing around. The approach had come out of the blue.

|||||||||||||||||||

I was running ITN's Africa bureau at the time but I had flown back to the UK in the summer of 1993 to attend a hostile environment course. However, names can be deceptive. This wasn't what it sounded. It was nothing to do with saving the planet, combatting global warming or treating mozzie bites and nettle rashes. It was all about surviving in conflict zones.

Now most of us attending this course, from ITN, the BBC and various other news agencies, had been doing that for decades. But, all of a sudden, our bosses were consumed by a newly acquired need to care for us. The sceptics among us felt it probably had much more to do with keeping insurance premiums down when we were sent on assignments in harm's way.

And there were plenty of wars about in the 1990s.

So off we went for three days of battlefield training at an elegant country house in Hampshire. The course was run by a bunch of former military men, who'd spotted a gap in the market, providing safety training to anyone working in high-risk areas.

The ex-squaddies had done their best to turn the manicured woodlands of Hampshire into a Malaysian jungle. There were booby trap bombs in rhododendron bushes, make-believe minefields beneath the oak trees, ponds masquerading as poisoned rivers and lots of other jolly surprises for us in their replica war zone.

We learned first aid on an inflatable dummy. We treated sucking wounds with a plastic bag and three pieces of tape. We were told how quickly someone could 'bleed out', how to deal with phosphorus burns, what to do in the event of a nuclear attack and many more handy hints.

Then there were the practical exercises. To the sound of gunfire and mortars, we raced round the gardens in small teams patching up large ex-soldiers, who told us to imagine they'd had limbs blown off or who were lying in minefields or who had large lumps of broken glass or metal spikes stuck in them. With fake blood squirting everywhere, we learned triage, treated those 'patients' we could, applied tourniquets, gathered severed hands and fingers, and then carried the 'victims' away from danger on stretchers concocted from blankets and fence posts.

My cameraman Ian Robbie was a brilliant shell-shock case, hamming it up in masterful style, as we tried to stop him walking into 'enemy lines'. This bit was all about recognising PTSD – post-traumatic stress disorder – which our instructors seemed to think we'd probably been suffering from for years, considering all the conflicts we'd reported on. Comforting!

As if that wasn't enough grovelling around in the dirt, they rounded it off by ambushing us and taking us hostage. This involved dragging us out of our Land Rover, tying us up, sticking a hessian sack over our heads and attempting to disorientate us. One hack punched an instructor, a couple of others escaped into the woods, while the rest of us were left face down on the ground and given the old terror treatment. Anyway, we all survived, took it in good part, had a laugh over a few beers later and completed the course feeling a wee bit wiser.

In the midst of all this fake gore, field dressings and first aid tips, I received a mysterious and cryptic phone call. A woman, calling herself Mrs Forrester, rang to say an on old friend from Sydney and Hong Kong wanted to get in touch. She gave me a number.

When I rang it later, away from inquisitive ears, it was answered by Ian Frykberg, the head of Sky News. Frykers, as he was affectionately known, was a giant of an Australian, whom I'd first met at the Nine Network in Sydney, where he was, at various times, head of current affairs and head of sport.

We had got to know each other better when he had come to Hong Kong to set up a Nine Network news bureau, which was similar to my own operation. Lynn and I were able to fill in Frykers on the need-to-know about Hong Kong and the region. And Lynn ended up finding an office and an apartment for the new Nine correspondent. As Frykers always used to tell me admiringly: 'Mate, your wife's a bloody good bloke.' He was hugely grateful for our help and now seemed intent on returning the favour. He said he'd got a proposition for me and suggested meeting up in London before I headed back to South Africa.

A couple of days later I met him at his local, the Gloucester Arms on Sloane Street, just round the corner from his home in Lowndes Square. It became clear in the months to come that Ian did a lot of business in the Gloucester.

The landlord always had a bucket of Frykers's favourite bottled beer on ice behind the bar, ready for the Big Man. Like many an Aussie, he liked his bottles on ice and drunk straight from the neck. That evening he was on Molson, the Canadian lager. As I mentioned, Frykers was larger-than-life. He was built like a square granite block, weighed twenty stone and had once been a formidable prop forward in Sydney club rugby.

'Look mate,' he said after a bit of a catch-up chat. 'Here's the deal. Rupert wants to take on Ted Turner of CNN at his own game. He's talking to CBS about a global 24-hour news channel jointly run by CBS News and Sky News.'

'About time too. Sounds like a great idea,' I told him. 'But where do I come in?'

Frykers explained that Rupert Murdoch had instructed him to beef up the Sky News reporting line-up ready for the big news channel challenge and he wanted me as his first recruit. I was seriously flattered. I liked what I'd seen of Sky. At ITN, I'd worked with CNN a lot during the Gulf War and the Balkan conflict. I was in no doubt that 24-hour news was the way to go. It felt like it had to be the future. Waiting all day to put out your story on *News at Ten* already seemed like an old-fashioned concept. Appointment to view, as it was known, was already being tested by the news channels' round-the-clock availability.

We agreed that I'd go home and discuss it with Lynn and let him know my answer without delay. My gut, not for the first time in my career, told me this was a great break. A gamble, maybe, as Sky News was still in its infancy. It had been going for only four years. It had had a few successes but I knew it still wasn't taken very seriously by the veterans at ITN and the BBC.

'I like the idea of being in on the ground floor of a new project,' I told Lynn. 'Of hopefully having an impact, perhaps helping to shape how people see Sky News and putting my experience to good use.' Lynn agreed that I should say 'yes' and give it a go. I'd been at ITN eleven years. It was time for a change of direction.

Frykers and I got together again at the Gloucester over a few more cold ones. Though in my case it was a few pints of bitter. I told him I was keen to join. We talked money. It was a lot more than I was getting at ITN. That was nice, but I never had and never would move just for the cash. If the job wasn't the right one, I figured the money would never make up for it.

'So what do you want to do? Where do you want to be?' Ian asked. 'It's your pick, mate.'

I'd never been made an offer like that before. But I had no doubt in my mind. 'I'd like to stay in South Africa, if that's OK with you. The story is amazing. We could soon be reporting the end of apartheid and the country's first truly democratic election. I want to see the job through.'

So we agreed I'd become Sky's Africa correspondent and then discussed staffing the new bureau. He said he'd leave it to me to sign up the right people, find a bureau, rent cars and sort out equipment. 'Just tell me what it's all going to cost.'

Frykers wanted to know if there were others who might be interested.

Soon after I got a few colleagues and mates from ITN round a dinner table and told them what was on offer. Sworn to secrecy, we felt like conspirators as we chewed over the pros and cons of going to Sky News. Reporters Peter Sharp and David Chater were keen from the start. So was my old sports unit teammate, Mike Nolan. They were to sign up within weeks. Others were more nervous at the idea of leaving a great news organisation like ITN – they felt Sky was too much of a gamble.

Mark Austin, who'd moved from the Beeb to take on my old job as ITN sports correspondent and then succeeded me in running the Asia bureau, was tempted to move to Sky. But in the end he decided not to risk it. His career at ITN was on the up. Not for the first time in my career, there were other colleagues who thought I was stark, staring mad for switching channels, especially such a new venture as Sky.

Several ITN mates were sceptical about Rupert Murdoch himself. Having seen how his newspapers operated, they were worried about editorial interference. How much would we be compromised as journalists if we moved to Sky? I told them I trusted Frykers's word on this and if I ever felt my independence was being undermined, I'd be the first one out of the Sky door.

To help Frykers with recruitment I suggested a couple of senior reporters' names at the BBC, who might fit the Sky bill. A few weeks later, Frykers told me it had been a waste of time talking to them. 'Those BBC guys just don't get it. They don't have the right work ethic, mate. All they want to know about is pensions and what holidays they'd get. I want journos who are hungry for stories.'

Back in Johannesburg, I told my bureau team what was going on and asked who'd like to join me in moving to Sky. It seemed they trusted me. 'If you reckon it's good,' said Ian Robbie. 'Then we're with you.'

Ian was on board, as was Rolf Behrens, the Channel 4 cameraman in our joint bureau. Our loyal Zulu sound recordist, Gugu Radebe, was less sure. He'd been with ITN for years and was reluctant to leave them. Pearlie Joubert, the producer I'd recruited a year before, said: 'Yes please. It sounds fantastic.' And I persuaded another producer Glenda Spiro to join me from the BBC's bureau. I was left to negotiate their deals and their salaries, which they agreed were entirely satisfactory.

When it was all sorted out, Frykers said he'd fly down to do the deal. Just meet him off the plane and book a good place for lunch were his orders. Now this was style the Sky way.

He took a twelve-hour overnight flight from Heathrow. I picked him up at Joburg airport and drove him to a restaurant not far from the bureau in Auckland Park. Sky's brand new Africa team was sitting round the table, all of them meeting the boss for the first time. We had a splendid lunch with some top-class South African wines. Over coffee, Frykers opened his briefcase and skated contracts across the table to one and all. They read and signed their contracts, looking pretty pleased with themselves. We had one last drink, put Frykers in a taxi to the airport and he flew home to London. All in one day. Just like that. How to sign up a new bureau and impress people. Now that was class.

It said everything about why I liked Sky. It was straightforward, no nonsense, say it as it is management. They made decisions and carried them out. And everyone knew where they stood.

I guess it was Administration by Antipodeans. From the start it had been run by them. Rupert Murdoch had invented Sky. The news channel was his pet project. He was proud of it and always backed it, even if it didn't make money.

The first head of Sky News was John O'Loan, an unflappable Aussie I'd first met in Sydney a decade before. The head of sport was another Aussie acquaintance, the dynamic David Hill, one of several recruits from Channel Nine. They were affectionately known as 'the Marsupials'. It was a far cry from the politically correct, cautious corporate beast that Sky became in the twenty-first century.

The main Marsupial in the old days was Sam Chisholm, a Napoleonic New Zealand nugget, who'd steered Channel Nine's success with ruthless efficiency. By the time I joined Sky, Murdoch had brought in Sam to run Sky or BSkyB as it was in those days. Though his first task was to rescue it before he could run it. And needless to say, Sam had hired his old chum, Ian Frykberg, to take over news from John O'Loan.

So I joined a news outfit run the Aussie way. It wasn't tabloid, but they liked the news to be bright and breezy. There was none of the old stuffiness that could creep into terrestrial news bulletins. It was presented in a more relaxed and accessible style from colourful studios, with big, bold graphics on screen. The management style was cavalier compared to anywhere I'd worked before.

For someone with a healthy dislike of authoritarian management, from headmasters to head honchos, this was right up my street. It was management light. There was Frykers in charge and his deputy. Programme output was left to the executive producers, who were in charge of each three- or four-hour segment of the day's news shows. These EPs were virtually autonomous, with very little interference from management. Rupert never did tell us what to report! Tightly run home and foreign desks assigned stories to news-gathering teams, home and abroad. And there was a sense that everyone was empowered. Ideas from reporters and producers were listened to. We all felt part of the same project. But one project that didn't last was the Sky–CBS worldwide news channel.

When push came to shove, Murdoch took one look at the bottom line and canned the whole idea. Taking on Ted Turner was one thing. Losing money over it was quite another matter for Mr Murdoch.

It resulted in losing Ian Frykberg as our boss. He felt badly let down by the collapse of the deal and believed promises had been reneged on. On top of that, Murdoch moved Kelvin MacKenzie, who had been editor of *The Sun* for thirteen years, out of Fleet Street and inserted him into BSkyB. Not surprisingly, MacKenzie soon starting to tinker with the Sky News business. And that was the final affront for Frykers. He left to set up a hugely successful agency negotiating sports rights.

A few months before he left there was a very Sky moment, when Frykers called me back to London, and invited me round to the Gloucester Arms. Ostensibly, it was to chat about the upcoming election in South Africa, but he said he also wanted to buy me a drink to say well done for winning an Emmy. Ian Robbie and I had recently picked up this prestigious award for our ITN coverage of the Ciskei Massacre.

Then, unannounced, Sam Chisholm blew into the pub like a small tornado, shook my hand vigorously and said: 'Bloody brilliant, mate. You boys winning that gong for your coverage. Bloody brilliant. That's why we bought you. Top-class reporting, mate.'

I said my thanks, explained that it was for ITN before I moved to Sky and said I hoped we'd soon win awards for Sky.

'Yeah, you will, son. You boys are the best.' Sam continued. 'I guess you'll be wanting some more money, right? How much do you want?'

It wasn't the sort of question a boss, let alone a really big boss, like the CEO, had ever put to me before. It took me a moment to grasp what he was on about. Seeing me hesitate, Sam said: 'Come on, son, name a figure. You deserve more money. I know you took a gamble coming over to us.'

So I plucked up courage and plucked a figure out of the air. It was nearly double what I was earning, which I already thought was generous. I assumed it would be the start of negotiating downwards. Not at all. Sam shook my hand and said: 'Great, mate. Like your style. That's a deal then. OK, Frykers, sort out the man's new salary as soon as you can.'

With that, Chisholm, like an aggressive and overworked Santa on Christmas Eve, vanished from the pub, leaving behind a bemused hack with a bounteous gift. What a place to work!

The editorial production line at Channel Nine Sydney continued to keep Sky in bosses. Sam brought in Ian Cook to replace Ian Frykberg. I'd known Cookie from my first reporting tours to Australia when he was head of Nine News and he was always generous in helping out a travelling hack far from home. He became known as the 'Smiling Assassin' for his ability to hire and fire staff with the same fixed, thin-lipped grin on his face. He was a good news operator and built Nine News into the market leader.

Cookie promoted Mike Nolan to be his no. 2 and they were in charge for the next couple of years. Sky News went from strength to strength, gaining more viewers and a steadily growing reputation for rolling news.

I was covering the Atlanta Olympics in July 1996 when I got a call from Nolan suggesting all was not well at the top. He thought Cookie was shafting him and wanted rid of him. He also thought it might be Sam Chisholm who was up to mischief and wanted to give both of them the heave-ho. Nolan was right about some or all of it. It wasn't long before Chisholm gave Cookie and Nolan their marching orders.

After a few weeks without real leadership at Sky News, I rang Frykers to find out what was going on. It had been two years since he'd left, but he was still close to Chisholm and knew what he was thinking. He told me Sam was looking for a new head of Sky News.

'Well, I know a guy who might be right,' I told him. 'He's an old mate of mine called Nick Pollard. He was one of the best executive producers of *News at Ten* that I ever worked with. He's now heading up Channel One, the cable news venture.'

'OK,' said Frykers. 'I'll mention him to Sam. See what he says.'

A few days later, Sam rang me: 'Now, this Pollard bloke of yours, I've never heard of him. Is he any good? How do you rate him?'

'Very highly,' I told Sam. I thought it might be a good time to finally have a Brit in charge at Sky News. Nick had nearly thirty years' experience as a journalist. Like me, he'd worked his way up from a local paper, in his case the *Birkenhead News*, through local radio and on to network television news at the BBC and ITN.

'Right,' said Sam. 'Bring him round to my apartment and I'll have a look at him.' Sam sounded a bit like a man thinking about buying a dog. But it was just his unique, slightly terse and insensitive style.

So, auspiciously, on Friday 13 September, I met up with Nick Pollard at Marble Arch tube station and walked round the corner to Sam's elegant mansion flat. On the way, Nick asked me: 'Why don't you want this job? You'd be good as head of Sky News.'

'Honestly, Nick, I wouldn't,' I replied. 'I'd be bloody awful. I'd probably fire half the staff for not being good enough! Seriously, you've got the patience and management skills to deal with two or three hundred people. I've never wanted to manage. I just like telling news stories.'

It was probably the strangest job interview we'd ever attended. Nick was the candidate. I went along because I'd proposed him and vouched for him. If Nick failed, it was probably going to be my fault. Sam launched off a few quick-fire questions, asking Nick why he wanted the job and why he thought he was qualified.

Sam drifted away from the interview and just talked for about an hour on any subject that had caught his interest that week – television, the economy, politics, sport. In fact, anything but the matter of Sky's next head of news. Sam always did like talking and his favourite topic was himself.

Eventually he seemed to remember we were in the room. By then he'd obviously decided the job was Nick's.

'So the first thing you've got to do is go into your office and tell Ian Cook he's fired and that you're now head of news. Right?' Sam at his most pugnacious.

'Is that right? Or are you expecting me to fire him for you?'

Nick, clearly taken aback, replied: 'Well, it might be better if you were to fire him.'

'So now you're telling me how to do my job. Is that right?' Sam blustered on: 'Look, mate, nobody tells me what to do. You understand?'

You were never sure if Sam was deadly serious or just revelling in a poker-faced wind-up to test his victim. Poor Nick looked a bit nonplussed. But then Sam said: 'Good. That's settled then. When can you start and how much do you want?'

Before Nick could reply, Sam gave him a salary figure and we all shook hands. The deal was done. Sky had a new head of news. And he was the first Englishman.

CHAPTER 21

AFRICAN SKY

It was a hell of a start to Sky's new Africa bureau. One minute we were having a quiet Sunday lunch, putting steaks on the fire. The next thing, we were under fire.

I won't forget the date. It was 9 January 1994.

My very first assignment for Sky News.

‖‖‖‖‖‖‖‖‖‖‖‖‖‖‖

I'd invited my new bureau team and their families round for a summer Sunday, lazing by the pool in Johannesburg, cooking steaks on the *braai* (the typical South African barbecue). But I just had this nagging feeling we should check out an apparently small event in a township some fifteen miles south of the city.

South Africa's first democratic election was just four months away and the country was still riven with tension and violence, as rival factions waged turf wars ahead of the vote. The ANC wanted to show the media how they'd brought peace to Katlehong, a ramshackle black community on the frontline between ANC supporters and a workers' hostel that served as the local Zulu Inkatha stronghold.

ANC leading lights, Cyril Ramaphosa and Joe Slovo, were planning a brief walkabout and speeches at a local stadium to prove how peace had come to this troubled township. No sooner had they stepped out of their car onto the hot, dusty streets than shooting broke out. We filmed as the two ANC chiefs were hustled away to safety by their bodyguards. Many of us journalists were left diving for cover in the devastated and deserted homes on the frontline in this urban war zone. The rattle of automatic gunfire echoed round the broken walls of this frightening no man's land. Local ANC guys claimed the shooting was coming from Mazibuko hostel on the slope above us. ANC self-defence unit comrades rushed past us with AK47s at hip level, spraying bullets wildly at their Inkatha enemies.

For a few minutes, I was one of several hacks trapped in the empty shells of houses. Someone shouted for us to make a run for it. We dashed, low and weaving, away from the metallic mayhem. Rounds were fizzing and pinging all around us. Suddenly, AFP photographer Abdul Shariff cried out in agony as he fell to the ground just a few feet in front of me. He'd been shot in the back. More rounds whined over our heads. A radio reporter right behind me screamed. She'd been clipped in the arm. The rest of us hit the deck and crawled for cover under a hail of gunfire. Others dragged wounded colleagues to safety. But it was too late for Abdul. He died before they could get him to hospital. Another victim of South Africa's mindless, unstoppable and often indiscriminate violence.

My cameraman Ian Robbie had filmed the whole, awful incident, with amazingly steady focus. I know I was shaking. We were all in shock. Somehow, we got ourselves back into work mode. Such events have to be reported. Still spattered in blood, Ian and I quickly recorded a piece to camera. I can still remember the words: 'For journalists like us, we only occasionally glimpse scenes like this, but for the people who live in this battlefield of Katlehong this is an everyday occurrence.' It was another harsh reminder of the daily existence of so many black South Africans in those last days of apartheid. This township was on a virtual war footing, but at no time was there any sign of the police.

Back then, live links were pretty rare. So, I phoned my first eyewitness reports from the scene and then drove to the bureau in Johannesburg to edit and satellite the dramatic images back to London. It led the news that evening.

The next day Sky's head of news Ian Frykberg rang to say well done, in his own droll Aussie way. 'Mate, I hired you to win awards, not end up dead,' said Frykers. 'Go easy, mate. And, by the way, not a bad story.'

The violence in South Africa was unrelenting in the following months leading up to the election. It felt like almost every political faction was conspiring to derail the country's first democratic vote. Mandela even accused the government of exploiting this carnage to frighten blacks from voting.

But throughout this mayhem, Nelson Mandela somehow managed to radiate an inner calm that gave people hope. On 11 February 1994, the fourth anniversary of his release, we joined him as he returned to Robben Island where he'd spent eighteen of his twenty-seven years in jail. This bleak, rocky outcrop, known as the Island of Seals, is barely five miles from Cape Town across Table Bay. Yet it must have felt like being chained up in the middle of the Atlantic for Mandela and his fellow political prisoners. No one ever escaped. The beauty of Table Mountain and the Mother City were within clear sight, yet unreachable.

Now the whole of South Africa was tantalisingly within Mandela's reach as he made this emotional trip back to prison. I watched him carefully aboard the ferry boat. For a while he seemed lost in his own thoughts, staring at the island as it drew closer, breathing in the familiar salty air, maybe trying to comprehend the enormity of his journey from prisoner to would-be President.

As he stepped onto this stony outcrop in the ocean, he was greeted by a sound that had haunted him for eighteen years – the wailing of the siren. But this time he was back as a free man.

Inside the jail he strode down the once familiar concrete corridor and into his old cell. I asked Prisoner 46664 what his emotions were as the memories came back to him. 'I'd forgotten how small it was,' he told me as he spread his arms out to touch the walls of a stark room that was just six feet square.

The barred window faced out onto a yard where the prisoners exercised. He looked wistful as I showed him old, sepia photos of his days of manual labour. The jail was built from stone and lime hewn from the island's quarries. Madiba recalled how they sweated here seven hours a day. His eyes were permanently damaged by the glare and alkalinity of the limestone.

I asked him and his comrades whether they ever sang. With a laugh, Madiba and his old ANC allies gave us a rousing rendition of 'Shosholoza', a folk song that embodied the spirit of the Struggle. It was a poignant reminder of South Africa's past. But Mandela's trip down memory lane had a serious purpose, providing powerful images to boost the ANC's election campaign. Madiba had been sent to this island by the architects of apartheid so that he would be forgotten by the world. The experience turned him into a legend who could never be truly caged.

The big question we were asking was whether twenty-seven years in jail had prepared him for the presidency and the pitfalls that lay ahead in those early months of 1994. The dying days of apartheid were turning into a self-destructive drama.

South Africa was close to anarchy, in danger of tearing itself apart. The Zulus were on the warpath. Chief Mangosuthu Buthelezi's Inkatha Freedom Party was threatening to boycott the election. A state of emergency was declared in KwaZulu-Natal. Some moderate whites were emigrating, others were on shopping sprees, stockpiling supplies in case of the worst. Hardline Afrikaners were digging trenches and hoarding weapons ready to defend a white republic. Several black homelands were in revolt. Amid all the violence, volatility and uncertainty, it seemed impossible to hold an election.

On the fourth anniversary of his unbanning of the ANC, President F. W. de Klerk gave me an exclusive interview on Sky. He was remarkably confident about the future considering the chaos across the country. I remember he told me how resourceful and resilient South Africans were. That was why they'd find a way of making the election work. Though he couldn't resist a dig at the ANC, telling me they weren't fit to govern.

Once the camera stopped rolling, F. W. was in amicable mood and surprisingly open about his thinking. It was a rare off-the-record insight. He told me it was the events of 1989 – Gorbachev and the fall of the Berlin Wall – that had persuaded him change was inevitable in South Africa. He realised he could no longer hold back the tide of history. He just hoped he could still have some role in the future of his country.

As we parted, F. W. shook my hand firmly and said: 'Now, you're a keen golfer aren't you? Let me know when you're ready for a round.' Then he added with a wry smile: 'I might soon have a bit more time on my hands.' As always he wished me: '*Alles van die beste.*' This translates as: 'Everything of the best.'

But his optimism seemed misplaced, as I stood in downtown Johannesburg not long after, reporting on rampaging mobs and fierce gun battles. The Zulus of Inkatha had taken their fight to the heart of the nation's largest city. There were few more scary sights than a Zulu impi, a battle group, dressed in tribal gear, wielding assegais and clubs called knobkerries, shields and guns, as they stomped and chanted their way into combat. We'd filmed them many times over the years. But I still found them way more intimidating than any modern army. It was almost as if they were in an invulnerable trance as they surged towards an enemy. They'd already rampaged through townships, firing on commuter trains and paralysing parts of Joburg.

Brandishing their traditional weapons, they attacked Shell House, the ANC headquarters. They were driven by the fear that the Zulu national and cultural identity would be lost if their deadly rivals, the ANC, won the election and ruled the land. This was a political and a tribal statement. And, once again, it left blood on the streets. We spent the day dodging behind cars and buildings, filming the firefights as the central business district turned into the OK Corral.

Soon afterwards, Chief Buthelezi told me he wanted to find a way for his people to participate in the ballot – but he left it late. It was just a week before polling day when his brinksmanship ended. De Klerk and Mandela called his bluff, leaving him facing political isolation if he didn't join in. It wasn't the only threat to the election. Now it was white South Africa's time to 'cry freedom'. Hardliners saw the only solution as an independent *Volkstaat*, a people's state. The irony was that they were proposing a white homeland in a black majority country, in effect reverse apartheid.

Some just talked big, but others built barricades and bombs. Eugène Terre'Blanche, the firebrand leader of the Afrikaner Weerstands-beweging (AWB), the Afrikaner resistance movement, warned that his people were willing to use violence to stake their claim in the new South Africa.

It all came to a head in the tribal homeland of Bophuthatswana just six weeks before the election. When its President, Lucas Mangope, threatened to boycott the ballot, there was a popular uprising with demonstrations and labour unrest as his people demanded they become a fully integrated part of South Africa. Civil service strikes and army mutinies led to violent protests and looting. The scale of theft from the major supermarket chain Pick n Pay earned it the nickname 'Pick, Don't Pay'.

Things were made even more complicated by the unlikely sight of white extremists from the AWB coming to Mangope's rescue. It all went horribly wrong when three AWB militants were shot dead at point-blank range by a black Bophuthatswana police officer right in front of TV news cameras. The cop said he was enraged when he saw white extremists driving through the streets of his homeland recklessly firing at black citizens.

It was a PR disaster for the AWB. They were left humiliated and demoralised, forced to withdraw from Bophuthatswana, with tails firmly between their khaki-clad legs.

I sensed that much of this blundering bravado from the white right was borne out of fear. About the same time I went deep into rural Free State to meet Eddy von Maltitz, a proper Boer farmer, whose family had worked this land for generations. Normally he'd have been tending his prize dairy herd, but in the run-up to the election, I found him down in the woods by his dam running a boot camp for his teenage sons and his neighbours' youngsters. Armed with guns, knives and a zeal for Boer independence, these boy soldiers were training for guerrilla warfare. Eddy called them his 'Resistance Against Communism group'.

Now Eddy was a charming and amiable fellow. But he was deadly serious when he told me that whites might have to fight for their very existence. He painted a vivid, if slightly exaggerated, picture of South Africa's nightmare scenario – tranquil farmlands transformed into battlefields. It all seemed rather extreme. But it merely underlined the anxiety and uncertainty felt by those who'd long been protected by apartheid.

As well as disquieting moments, militant Afrikaners provided some comical twists in the tense final weeks before polling day. Lydenburg is a stunningly beautiful town in the Drakensberg Mountains, built by the Voortrekkers, who'd come here in wagons pulled by oxen a century and a half before. The Boers had tamed the hostile bush, turning it into lush farmlands, threaded with trout streams.

Now I'd come to listen to their fears that a Communist ANC government, as they saw it, would destroy it all, taking back their land and turning the country's bread basket into a basket case. Lydenburg had become a symbol of Afrikaner nationalism. And right-wingers had declared it part of the *Volkstaat*, the white Boer homeland.

So cameraman Rolf Behrens, producer Pearlie Joubert and I arranged to meet some of the more militant locals. We were instructed to wait in a lay-by on the outskirts of town. After a while a bunch of large men in khaki drove up in a *bakkie*, a pick-up truck, and told us we'd have to be blindfolded. They made it all sound very hush-hush and hugely important, like they were going to take us into a top-secret intelligence bunker. But there really wasn't a lot of intelligence to be found here.

They drove us round the small town of Lydenburg several times, with black scarves over our eyes, presumably to confuse us. Then we stopped under cover. When they removed our blindfolds they told us with great pride that we were in their *Volkstaat* 'nerve centre'. Frankly, it looked more like a garage with some extra shelves along the walls stacked with essentials: sugar, flour, tea, coffee and toilet rolls. And, of course, cases of the Boer's favourite tipple, Klipdrift brandy. We dutifully filmed the stockpiles that were apparently going to sustain the white homeland.

Later, as the light faded, these AWB stalwarts, who now saw themselves as freedom fighters guarding the values of their ethnicity, took us on manoeuvres in the hills outside town. For a while, they wielded their weapons and played out some battle scenarios. But it wasn't long before they'd got the *braai* lit and were serving up sizzling *boerewors*, washed down with Klipdrift and Coke.

It couldn't have been a more Afrikaner scene. I almost felt sorry for these so-called militants, full of bluster and Boer nationalism. These relics of apartheid, with their beer guts and guns. They talked tough, but really they were just confused. At heart they were farmers who felt betrayed by Afrikaner leaders like F. W. de Klerk, who'd encouraged them to profit from apartheid, but were now preaching multi-racialism.

These Boers portrayed themselves as an endangered species, under siege, making plans for a last battle to save the land they'd helped to build. They'd never been fond of the British. The reasons stretched back to the Boer War. So, after a long night keeping up with the AWB boys drinking Klipdrift, I took it as a compliment when their local leader, Faan Fourie, said: 'Ja nee, you're not that bad,' adding after a dramatic pause 'for an Engelsman.'

I knew Pearlie despaired of her fellow Afrikaners when we covered these sorts of stories. Although she deprecatingly referred to herself as a *boeremeisie* (a farm girl) from the Cape winelands, she was one of the brightest and sharpest journalists I'd ever worked with. She was also a fiercely independent and liberal woman who had learned her trade as a reporter on *Vrye Weekblad*, the first Afrikaans-language anti-apartheid newspaper. She had no time for the heel-dragging white resisters. A wonderful character and a great friend, Pearlie spent many a long hour explaining to me the subtleties of the Afrikaans language and the Afrikaner's mind.

We were soon to see a nastier side of white extremism. The Iron Guard, the AWB's elite corps, made one last bid to scupper the election with a bombing campaign that targeted Joburg's international airport, black businesses, election offices and pipelines. But to no avail.

Against the backdrop of violence and political turmoil, a nation-wide education campaign was being rolled out to teach millions how to vote. Nearly 80 per cent had never had a chance before. We drove up to the remote, rural homeland of Venda on the Zimbabwean border to find out how it was going.

It's worth bearing in mind that at the time most of Venda's 400,000 population didn't have access to newspapers let alone television. Radio and word of mouth were the main methods of communication. It led to some surprising results as they took part in mock elections to get the hang of the ballot process.

At one polling station where we filmed, the victorious candidate was none other than General Constand Viljoen, the last of the Boer army generals and one of the founders of the Afrikaner *Volksfront*. He couldn't have been more white or more conservative. Bear in mind the ballot paper presented you with nineteen different parties to choose from, each with a photo of their leader to help the less literate pick the right party. When questioned about their choice, the black voters told us that their tribal elder had advised them to put a cross beside the picture of the nice old man with white hair. He meant Mandela. Confusingly, General Viljoen also had a shock of white hair and his picture was above Mandela's.

On Tuesday 26 April 1994, somehow it all came together. The long road to freedom and democracy finally arrived at the polling station door. I was in the heart of Soweto on that historic day. As the sun rose in a hazy shroud over the vast, sprawling township, there was an autumn chill in the air and a shiver of excitement. They'd begun arriving hours before the 7 a.m. opening time, anxious to be among the first. Senior citizens and the disabled were given priority.

Neither age nor infirmity could keep them away as they shuffled up the slope to the ballot boxes in Holy Cross Church. Simon Kunene, a blind man of eighty, held my arm as I guided him towards the polling station. There were tears in his unseeing eyes as he whispered to me: 'I never thought I would live to know this day when we would finally be allowed to vote.'

Nearby an elderly woman was clutching her identity document. 'I couldn't sleep a wink last night thinking of this moment. I just held onto my ID,' she confided to me. 'I was so scared that I might lose it and they wouldn't let me vote. I have waited all my life for this day. Now I am here,' she beamed. 'Can you imagine what this day means to us – black people being allowed to vote in our own land? At long last I feel like a complete human being.'

It was impossible not to be touched by the joy of these elderly voters, the feeling that they had finally been made whole by having a say in their country after all the years of repression. I felt myself welling up as I listened to their stories.

Over the next couple of days, my Sky colleagues Peter Sharp, Alex Crawford and James Forlong filed similarly moving reports from ballots across South Africa. Though it wasn't without incident. Sharpy told us later of the chaos at the polling station at Inanda in KwaZulu-Natal when Mandela voted.

The throng of media trying to capture pictures of the historic moment of Mandela's very first vote was so deep and so desperate that it turned into ladder wars. Dozens of aluminium steps were erected by TV cameramen and newspaper photographers keen to get the shot. Inevitably there was jostling for the best position. And in no time at all ladders were being pushed over and punches traded among the harassed hacks. Luckily Mandela didn't witness the uglier side of election day. Though, as he passed near the press phalanx, one cheeky reporter shouted out: 'Who are you voting for Mr Mandela?' With a laugh, he shot back: 'I've been agonising over that choice all morning.'

For many foreign reporters this was their first taste of Africa. At times it was pretty obvious. Like the day an American TV correspondent arrived at our media base and asked if it was safe to travel to the nearby Sandton City Shopping Centre.

Pearlie and Rolf, seeing a golden opportunity for a wind-up, advised him to wear his flak jacket and helmet. The sight of this naive journo going shopping in full combat gear was priceless. He didn't see the funny side of it when he got back. Ag shame! as they say in South Africa. I always remember the scene as a famous US TV anchor stomped off to the airport two weeks before the election insisting: 'This story has no traction.' Two bombings, the Bop uprising and a riot later he was back, looking slightly chastened.

The voters themselves were far better behaved than the media: patient, proud and positive as they waited their turn. I'll never forget the footage of Zulus walking many miles through the Valley of a Thousand Hills in KwaZulu to reach a polling station. Or the voters who queued patiently for hours in the Highveld heat to have their say. The desire for democracy had overcome all the stumbling blocks of South Africa's past.

CHAPTER 22

RAINBOW NATION

There are moments in a journalist's life when the story is so big it clouds your judgement. Sometimes it affects everyone.

||||||||||||||||||||

Just picture the scene at the TV news centre in Johannesburg during the election as newsmen and women from around the globe filmed and edited their reports marking the end of apartheid.

Suddenly, a panicky producer emerged from the throng, yelling: 'Has anyone here got a white person voting?' For a moment, the hubbub in a hundred edit rooms fell silent. We all began looking at each other guiltily, as the embarrassing truth sunk in. We'd all been so caught up in showing non-whites voting for the very first time, we'd completely forgotten the whites. We'd got hours of footage of blacks, Cape Coloureds (a minority ethnic group in South Africa) and Asians voting – Xhosa, Zulus, Sotho, Venda, Tswana, Tsonga, Swazi and Ndebele by the thousands – but no whites to mark the end of 350 years of white rule.

Sky cameraman Rolf Behrens arrived just in time to save the day. 'I've got a white man voting,' he said, looking a little sheepish, 'but it's actually me.' Rolf explained that while he was out filming polling station queues he'd taken the opportunity to cast his own ballot. He'd given his camera to my youngest son, Adam, who was getting some work experience while on holiday with us, and told him to film him voting. And that's how my son's footage of my cameraman voting came to be used by news networks round the world. Allegedly it was the only known video of a white South African voting in the '94 election. It didn't alter the result, thank goodness.

My favourite election pictures were of Bushmen balloting in the remote Kalahari. Southern Africa's first inhabitants ended up having to queue like everyone else. But it gave me licence to get away with the script line: 'They didn't mind a short delay. After all, their tribe has been waiting 23,000 years for a chance to vote.'

The most telling images were of Mandela's victory dance and de Klerk's generous admission of defeat. The delight on Madiba's face as he did that iconic jig for victory was unforgettable. As was the sight of the outgoing President fighting back the tears as the lights literally went out while he paid tribute to his successor, the man he had set free.

Even more remarkable were the reports of peace superseding violence as people lit fires of liberation in the townships to celebrate their emancipation. Like many people of my era, I'd grown up thinking some things wouldn't change in my lifetime. I thought I'd never see the end of the Cold War or the Troubles in Northern Ireland or apartheid. Well, the Berlin Wall had fallen and the Eastern Bloc had become unblocked. Now for another miracle of mankind.

On a glorious May morning in Pretoria, the old executive capital of South Africa, the leaders of the world gathered to witness the swearing-in of the country's first black leader. I stood in the grand sandstone amphitheatre of the Union Buildings watching in wonder as Kings and Queens, Presidents and Princes, friends and foes mingled together, finding their seats. I saw Fidel Castro and spoke to Al Gore. I interviewed Douglas Hurd, Britain's Foreign Secretary, PLO leader Yasser Arafat, UN Secretary-General Boutros Boutros-Ghali, Benazir

Bhutto, Bishop Trevor Huddleston, the great anti-apartheid activist, and many more from this roll call of global influence.

Alongside them, the black freedom fighters of the ANC filled this bastion of white power. But above all it was a day for the ordinary people of South Africa, coming to pay their respects to the man who'd led them to liberation. The park around the Union Buildings was packed with people who never dreamed they'd live to see this remarkable day.

I was broadcasting the build-up to Mandela's speech live on Sky when a traditional Xhosa praise singer, an *imbongi*, took centre stage. Zolani Mkiva, dressed in animal skins and beads, wielding a knobkerrie, began to extol the virtues of the nation's new leader in the rhythmic cadences of Xhosa verse.

Good old Bob Friend, the presenter in London, could never resist an opportunity to put a reporter on the spot. With a twinkle of a smile and a tone of ill-disguised innocence, Bob asked me what the whirling, tongue-clicking praise singer was intoning. Xhosa was never one of my strongest languages. So I improvised – just a bit.

'Well, Bob, he's saying what a great day this is for South Africa. And what a magnificent President Nelson Mandela will be.' Raising my voice above the drumbeat, I added: 'And, of course, he's welcomed Sky News to this great gathering and says he always likes to watch Sky News when he's not busy praise singing.' There were no further questions from London.

Back to more serious matters, just yards from where I stood with microphone in hand, Mandela rewrote history at the stroke of a pen on goatskin parchment. Then he swore allegiance to the country that had tried to crush him and vowed it would never be allowed to happen again. His 'Rainbow Nation' speech set the tone for a land of reconciliation where black and white would stand tall together in a peaceful society.

Mandela finished with this pledge: 'Never, never and never again shall it be that this beautiful land will again experience the oppression of one by another and suffer the indignity of being the skunk of the world. Let freedom reign.'

It was a bold promise.

Planes from the new Defence Force roared overhead saluting the rebirth of a nation with smoke trails in the colours of South Africa's freshly designed flag. As I moved into the huge crowd, I heard a black woman look up at the fly-past and say to her friend: 'That's our army now.'

But Mandela's great day was far from done. Next stop was Ellis Park Stadium in Johannesburg where South Africa's football team were playing Zambia and were 1–0 down at half time. Mandela made a rousing speech to the crowd calling for national teamwork. As if to prove his magic touch, no sooner had he shaken hands with the home side than they went out and scored two quick goals to rack up their first ever win against Zambia. It was a perfect image to go with his call for South Africans to work towards a common goal.

I wondered how much South Africa would change under new management. For the next year I tried to chart the progress on delivery of those promises to free the country from poverty, deprivation, suffering, racial and gender discrimination. My reports were snapshots of the successes and the failures.

In Ramotse township in the rural north-west, we filmed the first efforts to power up the country. They were wiring up homes at over forty a day. In a country where two thirds of the population were without electricity it was going to be an awfully long job. But the Levumo family, who let us into their simple shack to film their first light being switched on, left us in no doubt that this was a miracle from Mandela. Nearby they were digging pipelines for water. If all went well, it would still take seven years for all South Africans to have access to clean drinking water and proper sanitation.

The new government promised to build better homes and schools for a populace, 10 million of whom lived in squatter towns and had precious little education. The scale of what was required to rebalance the iniquities of the past was monumental.

I came across some intriguing aspects of this new South Africa. In Zwide township outside Port Elizabeth, I met Nceba Faku as he left his rented matchbox shack for work. It didn't look like much had changed for him, until he was picked up at his front door in a shiny black limousine driven by a white chauffeur. This one-time liberation fighter, Communist and Robben Island prisoner had just become mayor of Port Elizabeth, the country's fifth largest city. He was the first black mayor to break into the white world of local government. Jenny O'Rourke, secretary to the last eleven white mayors, said the new leader was a 'breath of fresh air'. The mayoral driver, Monty Uren, found himself driving round black townships for the first time in his chauffeuring life.

It was all change at the town hall.

Down in Orange Free State, I came across Willy Pretorius, a middle-aged white man who had been brought up to believe Afrikaners were a superior race. At the time of our chat he was cleaning floors for a black family. When Willy fell on hard times the Mekhetla family were the first to offer him work and a roof over his head. Now he was their domestic worker and grateful for their kindness. It was the ultimate in role reversals.

White beggars were becoming more commonplace on the streets of Johannesburg. I learned that close to 2 million people, over a third of all white South Africans, were now living well below the breadline. Apartheid had been created as a safety net for whites to underpin their standard of living. Without that job protection and racial privilege, a white underclass was developing. But their numbers were still only a fraction of the non-white population who suffered from poverty and privations in the rainbow nation.

There were plenty of positive stories. I went back to the Free State to see AWB hardliner Eddy von Maltitz, whom I'd last filmed training Boers to resist the black regime. It seemed Eddy the farmer had had an epiphany. By chance he'd spoken to Nelson Mandela on a radio phone-in show and been converted. Caught up in the peaceful euphoria of the new South Africa, Eddy had promised to lay down his arms and give the new government a chance. He'd even taken his black farm workers to the polling station to vote for the ANC.

In KwaZulu-Natal, I reported on white staff at a paper mill volunteering to learn Zulu. They told me it had really helped to cut across racial and social divides. The atmosphere at work was friendlier and more productive. And they'd had a warm welcome when they went to visit black colleagues in their township homes.

But white extremism wasn't going away. We filmed AWB leader Eugène Terre'Blanche, mounted on his black stallion, leading a parade through Heidelberg to mark the founding of his resistance movement in that town twenty-one years earlier. In his usual manner, he leaned down from his horse to bellow at me in response to my questions. He was as defiant as ever, attacking the new ANC government, but now his fiery rhetoric was in English not Afrikaans – a significant concession. And his threats no longer seemed to hold much fear for black South Africans.

Mandela told me he didn't care if Terre'Blanche refused to talk to him. The election success had already cast the white supremacists into the political wilderness. However much Terre'Blanche huffed and puffed, he wasn't blowing anything down. Times were changing. Even the names were changing. Heidelberg, once in Afrikaner Transvaal, was now in the renamed province of Gauteng, Sotho for a place of gold. The AWB had been left behind.

In August I flew to Cape Town to interview Mandela about his first 100 days. We walked in the ornate gardens at Tuynhuys, the President's office beside Parliament. As we chatted he seemed completely at home in this long-held preserve of white South Africa. Jan van Riebeeck, regarded as a founding father of the nation, had built the house and garden in the late seventeenth century.

Three hundred years later, South Africa's first black leader told me he was more optimistic than ever about his country's future. Madiba felt his government had made a solid, if unspectacular start in redressing the iniquities of apartheid. He acknowledged the huge challenge of providing better housing, health, education and more jobs. Then he went on to remind me that he was a serious Anglophile, a great admirer of the Queen and Winston Churchill, though not Margaret Thatcher. Playfully he praised Britain, while chiding it for its role in supporting apartheid.

The next time I spoke to Madiba it was in the more informal setting of his home at Houghton in Johannesburg's northern suburbs. We'd arranged for a live interview by satellite for Sky News. I'd arrived with the brand new edition of his book *Long Walk to Freedom*, which was due to go on sale the following month. I'd been sent a copy to review, hot off the presses.

Madiba was late, delayed on his flight back from Morocco. When he eventually strode into his sitting room where Ian had set up his camera, Madiba, courteous and charming as ever, said: 'Hello Jeremy, how are you and how's your family?' Then he shook hands with Ian.

That's when he spotted my copy of his book on the coffee table.

'Ah, is that my book?' he asked me. He picked it up and looked with great interest at his face on the cover. I explained that it was a review copy sent to me that very morning.

'Haven't you seen it before?' I asked, intrigued.

'No,' said Mandela. 'I've been a bit busy, so it's the first time I've seen the book. It looks rather good doesn't it, Jeremy?' he said with a big smile.

I couldn't resist. So I asked: 'Madiba, would you mind signing this book for me?'

'With pleasure,' he replied and wrote carefully inside the front cover: 'To Jeremy, Compliments and best wishes. N. Mandela. 29.11.94.'

Hardly believing my luck, I checked again with the president whether this really was the very first copy of the book he'd ever seen or signed. When he confirmed it was, I asked, perhaps rather cheekily, if he would mind adding that fact.

'No problem,' he said. And he wrote on the facing page: 'This is the first copy of this edition that I have signed. N. Mandela. 29.11.94.'

I thanked him for his kindness and we conducted the interview down the line to London. As we left his home, I carried the signed book as if it were a box of golden Krugerrand. I still have it at home, undoubtedly my most precious memento from fifty years of reporting. I never opened the book in case I damaged the spine. So I bought another copy to read.

I wasn't the only one wanting to talk to Nelson Mandela in those heady early days of post-apartheid South Africa. British Prime Minister John Major was one of a host of world leaders flying in to court him. But I sensed the visit Madiba enjoyed most was that by the Queen.

It was forty-eight years since she'd last been to South Africa, accompanying her father King George VI as he became the first reigning British monarch ever to set foot in the country. Then General Jan Smuts was Prime Minister and the crowds were mostly white.

This time the Queen was to see a very different South Africa as we followed and filmed her in shanty settlements and townships, seeing the privations of apartheid, warts and all. There was plenty of pageantry too. A meeting of monarchs as the Queen of England shared the spotlight with the King of the Zulus. I remember the roar of approval from his people, as the Lion King paid her the highest compliment by presenting her with a lioness.

But the footage we all wanted was the Queen with Nelson Mandela, the world's two most famous and recognisable people. In Soweto they walked side by side, cheered by huge crowds. When I talked to the spectators, I discovered some didn't know much about the Queen. It was clear most had just come to see their hero, Nelson Mandela. But when I stopped him briefly to ask how the royal tour was going, he was the model of modesty. 'Hello Jeremy. How nice to see you,' he said as always. Then he added: 'It's going very well, thank you. They've all come here to see Her Majesty.'

I found out later that, far from referring to the Queen as 'Her Majesty', Madiba called her 'Elizabeth'. As far as we could ascertain, he was the only world leader ever to use her first name in conversation – a sign of the fondness and admiration they had for each other.

Around this time, my old mate Mike Nolan, now deputy head of Sky News, flew out to Johannesburg with a proposition. Over dinner in Rosebank he told me Sky were keen for me to open up a Washington bureau to cover North America. I was flattered to be asked, but I was torn. I liked the idea of a new venture, a fresh challenge, but I loved working in Africa. Though in reality, I knew the '94 election had been a watershed moment.

The story in South Africa would never be quite the same. It would never be a chart-topper again, never lead news bulletins for month after month. I knew I might become frustrated by the anti-climax. So I told Nolan I would move to Washington, but on one condition. That I could stay on in South Africa to cover the Rugby World Cup in May and June of 1995. We agreed and shook hands on the deal.

I was delighted. Rugby was my big sporting passion and I suspected the World Cup could have a major influence on South Africa. And so it turned out.

But none of us had a clue what was going on in Mandela's head as he planned to harness rugby to create a nation-defining moment for his new South Africa. As he said after the tournament: 'Sport has the power to change the world.'

But few believed he could do it through rugby. It was the ultimate white man's sport, loved by Afrikaners, loathed by most black South Africans. The green and gold Springbok shirt had long been a symbol of apartheid. When the Springboks played, black people invariably cheered their opponents. The international boycott of rugby had deeply hurt Afrikaners. It was hard to imagine how this image of rugby could be transformed into something positive.

When I first interviewed the newly appointed Springbok captain, Francois Pienaar, I sensed he was already starting to believe that his team really was playing for the whole country. Francois, who's become a good friend, told me later how Madiba had invited him to his office and explained why the World Cup was so important to South Africa.

When we filmed Mandela flying in by helicopter to meet the team at their training camp in Silvermine Bay before the opening match, it was clear he was sending a message to his people that he was personally backing the Boks. I remember the players shuffling about a little awkwardly as Mandela walked to meet them. Then fly-half Hennie le Roux presented him with a Springbok cap. The President popped it on his head and the team applauded. A bond had been formed that would embolden them all the way to the final.

The management came up with a compelling slogan: 'One Team, One Country.' They also persuaded this very white team to learn the new national anthem, 'Nkosi Sikelel' iAfrika' (God Bless Africa), once a song of the black resistance. They began to belt it out with gusto.

It seemed to be working. As I reported on games around the country, from Rustenburg to Bloemfontein and Port Elizabeth, it was noticeable that non-white support was growing.

At the Sunnyside Hotel in Johannesburg, there was a real effort to make the Irish squad feel at home. Few of the staff knew anything about rugby. So the manager decided it would be a good idea to teach them the basics. We filmed some exuberant training with chambermaids scrumming down against receptionists and chefs whipping out passes to switchboard operators, who, needless to say, said 'try again'. All good fun and a sign that the country was beginning to embrace the sport.

As the Boks sang the Struggle song before each match and kept on winning, the sense of racial bonding began to grow. By the day of the World Cup Final on 24 June the momentum was unstoppable.

High in the stands at the huge Ellis Park Stadium in downtown Johannesburg, Lynn and I watched in disbelief as Mandela stepped out onto the pitch wearing a green cap and a Springbok jersey buttoned to the top. On the back, a gold six, captain Pienaar's shirt number. There was silence. Then the crowd of 60,000, most of them white, began to chant: 'Nelson! Nelson!'

To add to the tumult, a South African Airways jumbo jet swooped low over the stadium, with 'Good luck Bokke' painted under its giant wings.

Pienaar told me later it was like playing with a sixteenth man, if not more. The Boks went on to beat the mighty New Zealand All Blacks 15–12. And there was no doubt who was man of the match – Nelson Mandela. After the final whistle, Mandela emerged again to even greater cheers as he presented Pienaar with the trophy. As they shook hands, he said: 'Thank you Francois for what you have done for our country.' Pienaar replied: 'No, Mr President. Thank you for what you have done.' They remained firm friends for the rest of Mandela's life. Madiba even agreed to be godfather to Francois's two sons.

Up in the stands, Lynn and I wept for South Africa. There was hardly a dry eye around us. It confirmed just how much this country had come to mean to us. How much we had become emotionally involved in the drama of its democratic evolution. How much we shared the joy of the people at this euphoric moment. Looking back on that day, I think it was perhaps the pinnacle of reconciliation, the ultimate hour of racial harmony and goodwill.

For South Africa, it would prove hard to capture, distil and repeat that intoxicating moment. Though the amazing story was immortalised in the Hollywood film *Invictus*.

It was based on the excellent book *Playing the Enemy* written by John Carlin, whom I got to know well when he was *The Independent* correspondent in South Africa. John told me later that Madiba confirmed he had come up with a deliberate strategy to reconcile blacks and whites using rugby as the tool. He did it through charm and persuasion. As John put it, the cup final was the climax of 'the most unlikely exercise in political seduction ever undertaken'.

For Mandela, that Rugby World Cup final marked South Africa's emergence from isolation. Job done. Game over. Hearts and minds were won.

A few weeks later, I went along to Gold Reef City outside Johannesburg to cover a special party to celebrate Mandela's seventy-seventh birthday. It was to be my last report in South Africa before leaving for my new bureau in the USA. I'll never forget the children who gathered round Madiba, telling him how much they loved him. One said: 'Please, Madiba, promise me you will live for ever.'

A small boy said: 'Madiba, I hope you live another 100 years, so I can vote for you when I am eighteen.' Three little girls chanted: 'Madiba, we love you.'

I managed a moment with the old man. I told him I was off to Washington to set up a new Sky bureau. I bade him farewell and thanked him for always being so long-suffering with us ever-demanding members of the foreign media corps.

'Good luck, Jeremy,' he replied, as courteously as ever. 'I wish you well. I shall miss you.'

I would miss him too. He was by far the most impressive man I'd ever met. It was more than a decade before I was to meet him again.

CHAPTER 23

RWANDA

Genocide. I'd grown up hearing the horror stories from the
Second World War.

But I never thought I'd witness it myself.

|||||||||||||||||||||

The news of Rwanda's terrible tragedy broke early on 6 April
1994. Reports started coming through that a plane carrying the
leaders of Rwanda and Burundi had been shot down as it prepared
to land in Kigali.

As Sky's Africa correspondent, I was soon called up for a situation
report.

The details were still sketchy as I went live on our breakfast programme *Sunrise*. 'From what I hear so far, on board the plane was
the President of Rwanda Juvénal Habyarimana and the President
of neighbouring Burundi Cyprien Ntaryamira. We don't yet know
how or why the plane came down, but there are already fears that
it could have been a hostile act. And there are signs of considerable
unrest in the two countries.'

It became clear that the crash was a deliberate act of assassination.
The killing of these two Hutu leaders, probably by Hutu extremists

within their own governments, was the catalyst that sparked the genocide. Within hours, there were reports of massacres across Rwanda as Hutu soldiers, civilians and militias, known as the Interahamwe, began the slaughter of their rival Tutsi tribespeople. An age-old feud between the two races had reignited, but in a more terrible way than ever before.

A core political elite within the Hutu government had been planning the genocide for months. Fearing that President Habyarimana was negotiating a power-sharing agreement between Hutu and Tutsi, they came up with the idea of a 'final solution' – killing every Tutsi in Rwanda.

The genocide was systematic and savage. In the rolling, rural hills of Rwanda, the slaughter was largely carried out by local Hutu villagers, using nothing more than machetes. They'd been taught to see Tutsi as dangerous enemies and they'd been brought up to believe in an unbending obedience to authority. When the orders came down from the Hutu hierarchy, they killed friends and neighbours, often without question. Those who did refuse were executed by their own people.

Over the following weeks, we witnessed the ghastly aftermath. The hacked-up corpses of thousands of victims piled high in churches and schools, where they'd tried to hide. There were bodies at the roadside, bodies in homes and gardens, bodies in rivers that, quite literally, flowed red with blood. It was brutal murder on a staggering scale. It was later estimated that up to 1 million people were killed in 100 days – 90 per cent of them Tutsi. And many of the women who survived the death squads were subjected to rape and sexual violence. The majority became infected with HIV. I remember the desolate words of one missionary in this God-forsaken place: 'There are no devils left in hell. They are all in Rwanda.'

Eventually, the Tutsi-backed RPF, the heavily armed Rwandan Patriotic Front, led by Paul Kagame took control of the country. Now it was the Hutus' turn to suffer. Fearful that they would become the targets of revenge killings, hundreds of thousands began to flee into neighbouring countries. Emotionally it was like falling off a cliff. One moment I'd been reporting on the euphoria of South Africa's first democratic election, the next I was plunged into this hell on earth. From great highs to the lowest of human horror stories. At times like this I found it hard to get my feelings straight, to set aside the disgust, the anger, the fear and tell the story how I saw it.

After all, many of these Hutus, whose plight we were now narrating, had probably been involved in the massacre of Tutsis only weeks before. It was difficult to have sympathy no matter how desperate they now looked. But, as always, my job was to be a neutral observer. However tough it was, I had to leave emotion out of the equation. Just keep telling myself: 'Be objective, be fair, be accurate. Let the viewer decide on the rights and wrongs. Just give them the facts.'

At the border post in Goma, Ian Robbie and I filmed as wave after wave of terrified Hutus trekked into what was then Zaire, now the Democratic Republic of the Congo. Border guards stripped them of their weapons and most possessions before allowing them to pass to the relative safety of Zaire. Huge piles of rifles, AK47s, handguns and ammunition rose up beside the frontier post. Among the weapons were machetes and even bows and arrows – the instruments of genocide.

Such were the numbers that the UN and other aid agencies were overwhelmed. They tried to set up camps, but they had neither the space nor the equipment. The refugees simply flopped down exhausted wherever they could find space. Some had walked barefoot for weeks, driven on by the advancing army of the Patriotic Front. Over 1 million flooded into Goma alone.

As I reported at the time: 'There were columns of refugees as far as the eye could see. The tragic tide of humanity was unceasing. Desperate, frightened Rwandans pouring across the border – thousands every hour. They carried and dragged what remained of their lives.'

The camps were squalid and grossly overcrowded. Even worse, they were pitched on a wasteland of rock-hard lava beneath the great Nyiragongo volcano. So there was no way people could dig latrines or any other means of sanitation. And there was nowhere to bury the dead. Within days the camps were rife with disease. Epidemics of cholera and dysentery seemed unstoppable.

Many others camped by the shores of Lake Kivu, hoping the waters would offer them a better chance of survival. But such were the levels of pollution in the lake where they bathed and drank that they were dying just as quickly.

In another report I observed: 'It has become a wasteland of wanting. Mile after mile stripped bare by scavenging hordes – as thick on the ground as locusts and equally destructive in their desperate struggle to survive. They've taken every scrap of food from the fields and torn down almost every tree for firewood.'

The United Nations staff sent to coordinate the humanitarian effort seemed beset by inertia and bureaucracy. As I'd seen so often on my travels to the world's trouble spots, the UN dithered and delayed over security worries. They appeared unwilling to act until their fleets of white Toyota Land Cruisers had been flown in. Even then the clipboard-wielding agency members looked more intent on checking their vehicles at Goma airfield than in saving lives in the camps of misery less than a mile away.

The cholera had taken a fatal grip. The epidemic enveloped the refugee camps. The dead and the living were crammed in side by side. There was no escape. From first symptoms to death could take as little as five hours.

At a hastily erected medical centre, volunteers from Médecins Sans Frontières (MSF) tried to keep hundreds alive. All they needed was fresh water and basic drugs. But the aid planes flying into Goma simply couldn't keep up with the demand. As Ian and I picked our way through the field that had been turned into one vast open-air ward, we saw people expiring as we filmed. MSF told us one refugee was dying every minute. It was heartbreaking to witness. Victims were wailing at their impending doom. A baby girl sat lonely and confused beside the body of her mother – now wrapped in a bed mat ready for collection.

We heard the diggers before we saw them. When we went to investigate they told us they were excavating trenches to bury the dead en masse. Starving refugees camped out among the headstones watched listlessly as this mass grave was dug for their fellow countrymen and women.

The cholera was spreading like a medieval plague. The death toll was running into the thousands. The victims, wrapped in mats as a token of dignity in death, were laid out like kerbstones along the roadsides ready for collection by the body wagons. We saw some crushed flat by careless lorry drivers. At the mass grave they were burying them by the truckload. Soon more trenches were being dug, bigger and deeper. The stench of death was stifling.

French soldiers, who'd come to this place to save lives, now found themselves carting away corpses. But it wasn't only disease they had to deal with. One night the RPF, the Tutsi army, fired mortars over the border from Rwanda. It was too dangerous for us to move in the hours of darkness. So, as daylight came and the firing faded, Ian and I followed a team of French army medics to a grove just yards from the frontier.

It was littered with bodies. The medics checked for signs of life in this field of death. There were precious few. The mortars had landed in the midst of a huge cluster of refugees, blowing them to pieces. It was carnage. We saw several tiny babies among the body parts. Ian and I thought we had become almost inured to the atrocities of conflict. But this was one of the most horrific scenes we'd ever witnessed. One we would never forget.

They were grim days filled with gruesome scenes. But at least the pictures made it onto Sky News and other TV channels in those days – the world witnessed the full horror of it all. Looking back,

I realise we were far bolder and braver about telling the story as it was. Two decades later, I wouldn't get a fraction of that footage on air.

British TV and its audiences have become ever more squeamish. News bosses and broadcast regulators have grown increasingly sensitive over what pictures should be allowed on air. We now self-censor to a point where I believe we barely tell the tale any more.

I've spent much of my career going to difficult places to tell tough stories as fairly and accurately as I can. Powerful pictures make strong points. My aim has always been to provide viewers with the raw material, give them the full facts, so they can decide what they make of it. It was never up to me to determine what people think. In my view, redacting some of the most telling images from a story was short-changing the public, taking them for fools, depriving them of the full facts. That approach has shades of George Orwell's Big Brother, the intrusive protector from Orwell's dystopian novel *Ninteen Eighty-Four*. If you really can't stomach the reality, there's always an 'Off' button on your TV.

One day Ian, Pearlie and I were filming in a vast refugee camp when it became enshrouded in thick, black ash from the volcano above. It gave the place a primordial feel, with humans reduced to the activities of cavemen. Then out of the murk emerged a man peddling a bizarre bike made entirely of wood. We stared in disbelief as he clattered and careered downhill, with no sign of brakes. A fellow hack shouted: 'Look, the Flintstones on acid!'

Back in Goma, as the sun rose, hazed by choking campfires, the aid agencies were doing their best to feed the starving masses in this miasma. It was a task of biblical enormity. Ian filmed a multitude gathered on a hillside queuing for the food trucks. I remember thinking it was like the parable of the loaves and fishes. The Red Cross were trying to feed the 5,000, but seventy times over. They were attempting to stretch their relief supplies to feed 350,000 refugees – and that was just one day's rations. There still wasn't enough clean water to stave off the cholera and some didn't even have the strength to make it to the feeding station. We saw a mother collapse and die amid the relentless tramp of feet. Her baby abandoned at the roadside. It was an all too familiar sight.

One day I was wired up ready to do a live cross with CBS's *This Morning* show. In my earpiece I could hear we were on a commercial break. All the adverts seemed to be about food. The last one promoted a whopper burger that purported to be 'flaming tasty'. In the next breath, CBS anchor Paula Zahn asked me how things were at refugee central in Goma. As I began answering, a woman on the road just behind me collapsed and died from starvation. A mother leaving another orphaned child. The terrible irony of it all.

The contrast couldn't have been starker between the overdeveloped world of plenty and the barely developed, bedevilled world of Rwanda, with over 40 per cent of its population now displaced. The First World peering in at the Third World.

The orphans of cholera were the hardest aspect to deal with emotionally. Several orphanages had been set up to handle the spiralling numbers. The conditions were awful, the orphanages woefully understaffed and underfunded. In one we found 2,500 little, lost souls. Cots filled with newborns. Many were already on their last legs. Cholera was no respecter of age. The sounds we caught on tape were haunting. All around us babies were crying – empty, hopeless howls. Most had drawn their first breaths in the cholera-infected camps. And would probably draw their last breath here in this compound of despair.

The only doctor, Dr Minet Lalani from Oxfam, was at her wit's end. She told me the odds of keeping these foundlings alive were insurmountable. The children's dry, white lips were the telltale signs of dehydration.

We came across Kevin Noone, an aid worker with the Irish charity Goal. In his arms, he was carrying a baby girl he'd called Amina. He'd found her all alone in one of the camps. Her parents had perished. He hoped the orphanage could take care of her, but his doubts were growing.

In one room he saw Banzubazi, a little girl he'd brought to the orphanage only the previous day. He said she already looked much sicker. Her life appeared to be draining away. Kevin choked back tears as he held her tiny hand and mopped her brow. He admitted a feeling of total helplessness.

Outside we saw three trucks arrive bringing 300 more tiny children found abandoned on the streets of Goma. Many of them were clearly sick. By now Kevin was wracked with guilt at the thought of leaving Amina in a place where even the staff admitted the baby was almost certain to die.

'You've crossed the line, haven't you, Kevin?' I asked him. He slowly nodded as a tear rolled down his cheek.

'Yep, that's it. I've done it now. That's probably my life as an aid worker over,' he admitted. 'But I can't leave her here. I can't just watch her die.'

The last we saw of Kevin he was walking back to the Goal office, with Amina still wrapped in his arms, to explain to his boss why he'd lost all objectivity in the name of humanity. Other children at that orphanage weren't so lucky. They had no Kevin to save them.

A few minutes later some UN staff arrived, in a convoy of flashy white Land Cruisers, with their offer of assistance – a large bag of footballs for the kids to play with. It was inexplicable. Ian, Pearlie and I couldn't conceal our anger. I muttered in my usual booming whisper: 'Oh yes, that's exactly what the kids need – footballs.' It could hardly have been less appropriate in this place where sickness and starvation were rife, where most of the orphans barely had the strength to stand, let alone kick a ball.

Things were no better at Goma's General Hospital. This sanctuary of medicine had been turned into a bedlam of sickness. Its 150 beds had long ago been filled. Now more than 700 patients were strewn along the corridors and out in the gardens. It wasn't just cholera that was killing them. There were chronic cases of starvation, diarrhoea and dehydration. With nobody to remove the bodies, they lay where they died side by side, sharing beds with the living. We wrapped scarves round our faces to filter out the stench of death. The diseased were left amid their own waste. Most of the staff were sick or had fled. The last drops of intravenous fluid were spent. We saw one man die at the gate before he could even make it inside the hospital. Though it's doubtful he would have been saved in that place. A baby still suckled at the breast of her dead mother.

It was as if Goma was gripped by an ancient curse. Residents were told to bring out their dead for the wagons to collect. Sick refugees filled the churches. People fought over scraps of food in the death camps. We recorded a child drowning in mud as he tried to scrape up a cupful of dirty water. By now the number of refugees had swollen to more than 1 million. As we drove away from this charnel house, Pearlie ducked down in the back of our car as she grabbed a bite from an energy bar, consumed by the guilt of being seen to have food.

That night I pondered Kevin's dilemma – crossing the line. How many times had I had that debate in my own head, whether to get involved or not? Faced with reporting the horrors of our world – the wars, the violence, the famine, the disasters, both natural and man-made – most journalists will have a moment when they are torn. Do they intervene or intercede or interfere – whichever way you'd like to put it – or do they stay at arm's length? You often wonder whether saving one baby's life or handing out a small offering of food to a starving person is the right thing or the best thing to do. I have come to terms with the view that getting these people's stories to an international audience will, in the end, be of greater good to a larger number. My skill was as a storyteller, a communicator, not an aid worker or a medic. Help where you can, even if at times you feel helpless.

Gradually the relief effort began to catch up with the demands. But not before we'd filmed a few ill-judged airdrops. The Americans, aiming to parachute forty-four palettes of food onto an airstrip, managed to miss the runway and hit a coffee plantation. Many of the sacks split open, spilling a cargo of cheese and chocolate – a curious choice of nourishment for starving Rwandans. The French were in the air as well. They hit a house with one food drop.

Eventually, some of the displaced began returning home to Rwanda. We followed and filmed several families as they tentatively travelled back. They told us what awaited them couldn't be worse than the hell on earth of Goma's camps. Their fear of the RPF, who now controlled most of Rwanda, seemed to recede as soldiers offered them food and a safe passage.

In the village of Jenda we met Celestine Kabanda, a Tutsi who had every reason to fear the Hutus returning from Zaire. He showed me the homes where his entire family had been slaughtered three months earlier – his wife, parents, brothers and sisters – ten of them in all. The Hutu militiamen had rounded them up, locked them in their homes and thrown grenades in after them.

Soon after, his old Hutu neighbour Augustin arrived from Goma with his family. They told me they had seen Celestine's family massacred, but amazingly there seemed no ill will between these Hutu and Tutsi neighbours. Perhaps it was a first sign of hope for post-genocide Rwanda.

It was another fifteen years before I returned to the country. This time it was as a tourist, taking Lynn to see the silverbacks, the mountain gorillas, who survived in the volcanic mountain range high above the massacres and mayhem of their close human relatives.

Travelling through the Mille Collines, the land of a thousand hills, known as Africa's Little Switzerland, it was still hard to comprehend how such brutality had been inflicted in a land of such beauty. It was lush and green, densely populated and intensely farmed. And full of the warmest and friendliest of folk.

Yet driving through the countryside, there were regular reminders of Rwanda's moment of madness. In almost every town and village there were signs pointing to Musée Jenocide. In Rwamatamu, a small village in the rural west of the country, I asked our young Tutsi guide Jimmy to stop and find out more from the local residents. The place was little more than a hamlet straddling a dirt road. He chatted to an old man sitting on a bench outside a wooden shack of a coffee shop. His name was Gombaniro Anselme. He told us he was a survivor. He showed me his machete scars to prove it. He pointed to their genocide museum on a ridge overlooking the village.

We walked up to take a look. At first sight it was macabre; it was like a single-storey brick-built shop, but the only things on display in its windows were bones – human skulls staring out empty-eyed. Beside them, neatly stacked, were the bones of arms and legs – hundreds of them, packed behind the glass. You could see the bones from every corner of the village – a constant reminder of Rwanda's recent past.

Old Gombaniro told us sanguinely: 'Over 20,000 of my neighbours are buried beneath that memorial.' He went on: 'But we're leaving the past behind. We've not forgotten and forgiving is hard. But we are a united nation now. We have to teach our children where it all went wrong.'

Driving on to the provincial town of Kibuye on Lake Kivu, Jimmy showed us the football stadium where 10,000 victims had been rounded up and killed. On the hill above was the Catholic church, where another 11,400 were hacked to death as they sought sanctuary under God's roof. Even priests had been among the killers. Yet Rwanda seemed to be dealing with the truth and reconciliation process in a remarkably positive way. Almost a model nation determined to make a fresh start.

In every community we saw happy children packed into little schools, waving enthusiastically at passing tourists like ourselves. It suggested Rwanda was repopulating fast with a new generation full of hope, instead of hate.

CHAPTER 24

USA: TWO NATIONS DIVIDED

I'd never really fancied America. It held no great attraction for me. But as a foreign correspondent it was the must-have, must-do posting. I knew my education as a journalist wouldn't be well rounded without a stint in the States. But after Asia and Africa it was strangely unsatisfying. I guess it was because what I liked were big, single-issue stories you could really get your teeth into, like Mandela and the end of apartheid, Somalia, Rwanda and Tiananmen Square.

||||||||||||||||||||||||

The USA turned out to be a patchwork quilt of news, a multitude of mismatched panels, rarely sewn together. More like scatter cushions. The upside was that an endless stream of pictures came pouring into our new Sky bureau in Washington DC. It was manna from TV heaven. You were never going to miss much around the US, but it did mean you could find yourself stuck in DC churning out a production line of packages on anything from school shootings to the Oscars, without ever leaving the office. The tough part was getting out of DC to report on the rest of America. It was such a vast country that, by the time you got to Kalamazoo or Kissimmee, the story was often over.

It was a curious mix of tales to tell, from Bill Clinton's campaigns and scandals to quirky cowboys and chain gangs. There was a rich diet of Brit-related stories. And far more overseas travel than I'd expected. I reported from Cuba, Peru, Kuwait, Ireland, a volcano on Montserrat, the Hong Kong handover and the Blair election in the UK. But inevitably it was US crime that played big.

I arrived in the US just in time for the climax of the O. J. Simpson trial. Straight to the courthouse in Los Angeles as judgement day approached. Retired American football star O. J. was being tried for the murder of his wife Nicole and her friend Ron Goldman in one of the most widely televised cases of all time. This was America in all its technicolour, larger-than-life gory glory. A sporting icon, a double murder on Hollywood's doorstep, rogue cops and a court so full of overpriced lawyers it looked like a scene from *12 Angry Men*. If you thought it was a circus inside court, it was even more bizarre outside. The surrounding streets had become a soapbox for every whack job and barrack-room lawyer in California. I bought an O. J. watch from a singing salesman. There were cross-dressers, mime artists, jugglers and sword swallowers, all with a view on the outcome. You could buy T-shirts, wall clocks, bumper stickers and even flowers to give to your favourite lawyer. I felt like I'd been bashed by the full US silly stick.

As this crazy soap opera unfolded, the live pictures from inside the court attracted the biggest audiences Sky News had ever had – peaking at more than 1.2 million. There were so many camera crews that a precarious fifty-foot-high riser, a set of wooden terraces, had been built opposite the court to serve the massive media demand. I was reporting live from about halfway up the gantry when the jury delivered their verdict, sensationally acquitting O. J. of murder. Suddenly there was a thunderous trample as news teams scrambled up the riser to man their live shots. The temporary planking leapt and quivered. Sky viewers must have wondered why I was bouncing up and down on their screens like a mad trampolinist while trying to tell them such serious news.

Two years later another trial was to attract even more viewers. This time the central character was a young English girl: Louise Woodward, a nineteen-year-old au pair, was accused of killing an eight-month-old baby in her care at the child's family home in Boston. Again it was all live on TV and Sky News covered every moment of the case. It was compelling viewing.

When Louise Woodward gave her dramatic evidence, talking of 'popping the baby on the bed', 'being a bit rough with him' and 'dropping him on the floor', our UK audiences rocketed to a record 1.6 million, with millions more watching around the world. I was in the courtroom when the jury found her guilty of second-degree murder. The tension was incredible. I remember reporting on how Woodward doubled up in anguish as she absorbed the verdict. She was shaking and sobbing and cried out: 'I didn't do it. I didn't do anything.'

Days later she walked free, her conviction reduced to voluntary manslaughter on appeal. Cameraman Mick Deane and I were in the media melee back-pedalling madly as she took her first stroll along the Boston harbour side. She never spoke to us despite our best efforts. But those two trials set new broadcast benchmarks for Sky, proving there was a huge viewer appetite if we were bold enough to stay with one, big, compelling live story.

I sat in a Denver courtroom watching Timothy McVeigh, impassive as always, as he was convicted of killing 168 people in the Oklahoma bombing, the deadliest act of home-grown terrorism on US soil. A former army veteran who'd turned into a 'hate-filled monster' according to the prosecution. I found it hard to imagine what had driven him to commit the atrocity and hard to comprehend just what it meant for the victims' families as they wept and cheered, hugged and applauded as they left court. Most of us never have to face such ordeals. I was always searching for the right words to do justice to their emotions.

School shootings were starting to become a theme. The Colombine massacre was still a couple of years away, but Westside Middle School at Jonesboro, Arkansas, Pearl High in Mississippi and Thurston High in Oregon were signs of worse to come. Maybe some were young McVeighs in the making. Despite the awful scenes we reported of children being gunned down, the gun lobby remained implacable, always hard for most Brits to understand. So too was the death penalty, dished out to McVeigh and many more.

I went to the small Texas town of Huntsville, known as the execution capital of America, to witness the capital punishment of Karla Faye Tucker. She was set to become the first woman put to death in the state since the Civil War 135 years ago. The story was that Karla Faye, portrayed by prosecutors as a drug-crazed hooker, had been convicted of hacking two people to death with a pickaxe fifteen years earlier and had then found God behind bars. Such an American tale.

As she waited, strapped to a gurney in the 'death house', as they so sensitively call it, a grim circus was being played out beside the prison gates. The condemned woman's last message appeared on a giant TV screen as a passionate debate raged over whether or not she deserved to die. Local radio reporter Wayne Sorge chatted to me on his way in to witness his ninety-ninth execution. He said it had just become part of the job.

It wouldn't be America without the occasional celebrity murder. Fashion designer Gianni Versace was gunned down on the steps of his stunning Miami South Beach mansion by a random nutter-cum-serial killer. Cameraman Allen McGreevy and I thought it in keeping to base ourselves at the nearby News Café to cover the manhunt. The FBI and police weren't doing too well, so it did them a favour when the gunman topped himself. As we weaved between the usual South Beach parade of musclemen in tight T-shirts and bikini-clad rollerbladers, Miami, the 'glamour capital', did Versace proud with a totally over-the-top outpouring of emotion, glitz, fashionista tributes, mega floral displays and cloying messages.

There were times when the stories I covered felt more like movies than news. But I guess they were among my favourites. Like the day the Governor of Alabama brought back chain gangs in his jails. We knew it was a publicity stunt, but it was irresistible. It was also pretty remote. McGreevy and I flew to Birmingham then drove north to Athens, near the Tennessee border. We'd been travelling all day. It was hot as hell and we were parched. We chucked our bags into the end-of-the-earth motel and asked the lady at the desk where we could get a cold beer. 'Boys,' she said, slightly sanctimoniously. 'This is a dry county.' First time we'd come across this blight to humanity. 'Well, where's a wet county, madam?' I pleaded as politely as I could. 'Thirty miles away,' she replied, pausing to add pointedly, 'if you're that desperate.'

We were. So we drove to the next state. Just fifty feet over the state line there was a folksy little bar with very cold beer. We weren't the only travellers in need. Early next morning at the Limestone Correctional Facility the sun rose over an idyllic scene. Well, idyllic, if you're filming, not doing time. Barbed-wire fences with watch towers rising high above them, manned by guards in Stetsons, the blazing sun reflected from their prison-issue Ray-Bans. Perfect. Beneath them 200 inmates trudged in, knelt to have their chains locked on and then resignedly started a twelve-hour shift breaking rocks. Crashing sledge hammers and clinking chains – the sights and sounds of the bad old days of Dixie.

The prison governor admitted to me it would be cheaper to buy crushed gravel than truck in rocks for the convicts to crack. It was just a stunt to show the state was tough on crime. The cons told me it was all 'bullshit' and no deterrent. But when I asked them if they'd sing, these hard nuts kindly obliged, filling the yard with the sound of spirituals and soul music. It was pure TV magic.

Back at the White House, President William Jefferson Clinton was dealing with his own problems. Allegations of wrongdoing and scandals plagued him through the '90s. Rumours of sexual affairs and peccadilloes had hovered round Bubba Bill since his days as Governor of Arkansas. Paula Jones, a state employee who sued him for sexual harassment, brought a case that rumbled on for years and led to his impeachment.

There were more grand juries than public holidays. Investigating Clinton was a Washington sport. It felt like I was reporting more prosecutions than politics. Bill and Hillary got drawn into a real estate controversy, known as the Whitewatergate Scandal. There was Travelgate, Fostergate, Filegate and Zippergate. They'd nearly run out of gates. And gas. But Bill kept going and governing.

It was Monica who really messed him up. I was in Havana, reporting the visit of Pope John II to Castro's Cuba, when the bombshell dropped. The story broke that a 22-year-old former White House intern called Monica Lewinsky was claiming an affair with the President. It was one of the first scoops to emerge online in the new internet age. Clinton launched a vigorous defence on TV, with Hillary at his side, insisting: 'I did not have sexual relations with that woman.'

The story was as juicy and salacious as it gets and kept the media munchies away for months on end. Every day there was a new twist, a fresh allegation, a grubby blue dress. Even British Prime Minister Tony Blair got dragged into it at a White House press conference a few days after the scandal erupted. I asked Blair if he was sticking by his buddy Bill even when the President faced impeachment. Blair and Clinton glared at me with leadership lasers of an intensity usually reserved for dangerous dictators. It was another seven months before Clinton became the first sitting President to testify before a grand jury investigating his conduct. He later admitted an inappropriate relationship with Lewinsky. And he was eventually impeached. Inevitably he ended his second term as a 'lame-duck' President. Though a pants-round-his-ankles President was probably more accurate.

None of this could distract from the fact that Clinton was a wildly charismatic and compelling personality. I felt he was the first man who looked like he was born to be US President. For all his faults and foibles, he was a very bright guy and a consummate communicator. I never asked him something he didn't know the answer to. When it came to politicians marketing their policies, persuading voters and selling dreams, he was the best I'd seen.

Whether from two feet or 200 yards or 20,000 miles away via TV, Bill could grab and hold people's attention. He had that skill that made everyone feel like they were the only one he was addressing, whether they were face-to-face or just part of a vast campaign throng.

During the 1996 election campaign, I spent a day with Clinton in Detroit, watching him address a whole series of rallies. His schedule was relentless. First it was the toughest of all blue-collar crowds on the shop floor of a car plant. They were soon cheering for Bill. Then a gathering of religious leaders of all faiths. Within minutes they were captivated, chanting: 'Hallelujah'. Next captains of industry – more Republican than Democrat – but soon buying the Clinton party line.

Finally, a huge town hall meeting packed with regular voters was swiftly beguiled by the Clinton factor. In between he spoke to every small child, old lady and passing punter like he was their best friend. He had people spellbound. It was like he tapped into the mains when he walked into a room and was energised by the power of the people within. He could change his tone, his mood, his words for every different scenario. Part-politician, part-preacher, part-storyteller.

On the plane home, a typically tough female TV news veteran, sceptical of Clinton's legendary charms, admitted her surprise at going weak at the knees when he sat down with her for a quick chat. He was good with the personal touch. He even found time to talk to foreign correspondents like me, keen to pick our brains about UK politics or, one of his passions, Ireland and the Good Friday Agreement. Until Monica, that is. Then Bill suddenly grew rather distant.

In November 1996 I was in Arkansas to see the 'comeback kid' do it again, as he was re-elected for a second term and set Little Rock a-rocking. I'd always had a theory that Bubba Bill was a product of his own enormous appetites. He had a huge thirst for knowledge, a passion for power, a well-developed weakness for women and a voracity for food. Downtown at his favourite Little Rock diner, Doe's Eat Place, the head chef showed me how the President liked his steaks cooked. As we filmed, I commented that it looked a very big T-bone. The chef said casually: 'And not just one. The President sometimes eats three at a sitting.' My point proved, I thought.

The best thing about Tony Blair getting elected, from my side of the Atlantic, was the appointment of a new British ambassador who actually liked the media. Christopher Meyer was great. He invited the British journos round for lunchtime briefings, grand dinners and functions. We got to watch Five Nations rugby at the Embassy Club – for me one of the biggest perks. He even asked me to join him when comedian Bob Hope received an honorary knighthood.

He was the most helpful ambassador I encountered on my travels. His guidance helped me understand just how Washington worked.

There were always British news angles to cover, from the US reaction to Princess Di's death to British political decisions. There was Jump – Eddie the Eagle's attempted skiing comeback at Lake Placid; Thrust – a Brit land speed record attempt in Nevada's Black Rock Desert; and Punch – my ringside seat in Nevada to see Frank Bruno whacked by Mike Tyson in a one-sided world heavyweight showdown in Las Vegas. If Tyson didn't like Bruno, he liked the media even less. He hadn't muttered a word all week. Instead of going to the press conference, I tried a different tactic and waylaid him as he walked through the gardens at the MGM Grand. When I boomed out in my abnormally loud voice: 'A word for your British fans, Mr Tyson?' the champ walked straight over to me and McGreevy. He was a fearsome-looking monster, but, to my surprise, he started rabbiting away in his light, lispy voice, calling me 'Sir' or rather 'Thir' all the time. I suggested that Brits had been supportive when he'd been in jail for rape. 'Yeah, they were great,' he said. 'I love the Brits. Hundreds of them wrote to me in prison. That's why Liverpool is my favourite country.' Lucky he stuck to boxing.

There's an old saying that Britain and America are two nations divided by a common language. And there were plenty of times I felt the wisdom of that aphorism in the backwoods and byways of the good old US of A.

Americans can be quaint and quirky, a bit like us, but different. Like down at the Cowboy Poetry Festival in Elko, Nevada. Below the snow-clad Pequop Mountains, Larry Schutte sang the lonesome lyrics of the West as he rode the range rounding up his cattle. In an Elko hall, folk in Stetsons, bootlace ties and buckaroo boots listened in rapt silence as Waddie Mitchell read out his mournful cowboy poetry. I interviewed cowboys and Native Americans in the same room. There were comics and crooners and painters all determined to keep their cowboy culture alive as the Wild West galloped to keep up with the World Wide Web.

Half a country away on the Atlantic seaboard I got another glimpse of pure Americana. Wild ponies swimming the narrow channel between the wonderfully named Assateague and Chincoteague islands, herded by firemen on horseback dressed as cowboys. Legend had it the ponies' ancestors had been shipwrecked here on their way from England to the coal mines of West Virginia three centuries back. Now some were auctioned each year to fund the local volunteer fire service. As Allen McGreevy and I filmed aboard a small cruiser, the elderly owner chatted to us in an accent still burred with the West Country tones of his forefathers, who were early English settlers. Extraordinary to find a place in the US so remote that a voice could be almost untouched by the New World into which he'd been born.

Lynn, who'd come along to watch this romantic and historic spectacle, was rudely shaken from this rustic idyll when a leering local in dirty dungarees walked up to her and said: 'Hey ma'am, you're real purdy.'

When we left the US a few months later to return to London, our American friends insisted we had a yard sale to get rid of anything we didn't need to take home. Among the first customers to arrive were a hillbilly family in a rusty old shooting brake. They doffed their hats politely and prodded about in our leftovers for a while. As they walked away empty-handed, they nodded bashfully to Lynn and said: 'Sorry ma'am, but your stuff's too good for us.'

CHAPTER 25

OLYMPICS

'Over the moon and way, way over the top.'

That was my final script line at the opening ceremony of the 1984 Los Angeles Olympics, as a rocket man, powered by a jet pack, flew above us at the Coliseum. And the Games just got ever more bizarre. By the closing ceremony, we'd had a UFO and an alien invasion.

|||||||||||||||||||||

It started badly. As ITN sports correspondent, I was despatched to LA three months before the event even began. Fourteen Eastern Bloc countries announced they were boycotting the Games in retaliation for the US-led boycott of the Moscow Olympics four years earlier. Then Iran pulled out over 'US interference in the Middle East'.

When Libya said they too were boycotting the Games, accusing the US of numerous offences, I was left in a half-finished Olympic Park racking my brains how to illustrate the story. All I could think of was the flag. Surely they'd haul it down from the impressive rows of member flags. But what did the Libyan flag look like? I couldn't come up with the right answer, and neither could my crew. And in those pre-Google days there was no quick search. Then I spotted a

Games volunteer in her distinctive blue uniform. She was a sweet, young Japanese-American girl who offered to find out. She came running back ten minutes later and uttered triumphantly: 'It's a prain gleen frag.' Ah! Almost lost in translation. 'A plain green flag?' I checked.

Just before the Games started, ITV cancelled its coverage after a long-running dispute with the technicians' union over the cost of working overseas.

That left me with a long-running job, the only ITV reporter still on air. In effect, I was the network. I covered everything, commentating on the 100 metres, rushing off to film the Great Britain hockey team and Steve Redgrave winning the first of his five rowing golds.

I interviewed the ever controversial Daley Thompson when he won his second decathlon gold, who told me rather colourfully: 'I haven't been this happy since my grandmother caught her tit in a mangle.' Before long I was racing round the hospitals of LA with my ITN crew, Seb Rich and Rob Bowles, trying to track down the ailing Steve Ovett, who'd collapsed at the end of the 1,500 metres final. It almost eclipsed Seb Coe's gold medal.

But the biggest story was the clash between America's golden girl, Mary Decker, and a shy eighteen-year-old barefoot runner from South Africa named Zola Budd, who was now racing in GB colours. When Decker stumbled in the 3,000 metres and crashed to the track, dashing her hopes of gold, she blamed Budd. Soon the entire ITN team was in Olympic action, sprinting round the stadium trying to get shots and interviews with Decker, Budd and anyone else involved. In the days that followed the celebrated collision we must have run a marathon tracking the athletes. My colleague Terry Lloyd was sent on a now-legendary 'Wild Budd Chase' to Disneyland, a 160 acre theme park with 30,000 visitors a day. Needles. Haystacks.

My favourite memory was of ITN sports editor, Mervyn Hall, a man at the opposite end of the physique spectrum from the string bean Zola Budd, graphically demonstrating to us how the Decker trip might have happened. It was a cameo performance worthy of a medal in its own right.

There was more controversy four years later in Seoul, when 100m champion Ben Johnson was stripped of his gold after a positive drug test for anabolic steroids. As a result, Britain's Linford Christie moved up to silver, but not before he'd faced a disciplinary hearing over traces of a banned stimulant. He told me he'd taken 'nothing more serious' than ginseng tea.

I covered several GB success stories – another gold for Redgrave, wins in swimming, shooting and sailing, and a surprise gold for Britain's hockey team, with its even more surprising South Korean women cheerleaders.

But, as ITN's new Asia correspondent, I found myself covering more hard news than soft sport in Seoul. Student demos were back in fashion. The last time I'd been pepper-sprayed they were calling for democracy. In 1988 they wanted reunification with Communist North Korea. It was the usual rules. The students threw firebombs, the police replied with tear gas. The government flooded Seoul with security just in case the North's nutty leader, Kim Il-sung, chose the Olympics as a good moment to invade.

I did stories on shanty towns, sweatshops, crackdowns on fake goods and the sex trade, and, of course, dogs. Westerners had always been queasy about the Korean tradition of eating dog meat. So, predictably, the news desk asked me for a report. It wasn't easy. South Koreans were sensitive about the subject and knew what we were up to. We did some discreet filming in the market where dogs were sold, then set out to get shots in a restaurant.

After my cameraman wired me up with a hidden mic, I headed into the café with my trusty Korean driver/fixer Mr E. B. Lee. As planned, EB ordered a full lunch of dog. When it was served I whispered into my mic and in came the crew with camera rolling to capture the moment. But the husband and wife who owned the place reacted very swiftly and were soon hurling empty beer bottles at us.

I fended them off, allowing the crew to get a few more shots. Then I said: 'Come on, let's get out of here.' As we headed out of the door, I looked back to see EB contentedly tucking into his dog meat lunch. I hauled him out before he embarrassed us any further. I told him they didn't do doggy bags.

It was eight years before I covered another Olympics. This time it was in Atlanta and I was now Sky's US correspondent. Sport barely got a look in. I'd just filed the usual pre-Games stories on drugs, security, the heat and politics, when there was a catastrophic plane crash. When the Olympics began two days later, I was still camped out on a Long Island beach looking out at the spot in the Atlantic where flight TWA 800 had gone down, twelve minutes out of New York's JFK airport, with 230 people on board.

It was the USA's third deadliest aviation accident. There was plenty of speculation that it had been a terrorist attack. The FBI took sixteen months to decide there was no evidence of a criminal act.

No sooner had I flown back to Atlanta than a pipe bomb exploded in Olympic Park. It killed one person and injured over 100. The blast happened at 1.25 a.m., rousing some of us from our beds and the rest of the Sky crew from a nightclub. Sports presenter Mark Saggers, now a talkSPORT radio legend, and I remained on air over the next seventeen hours, with the assistance of some colleagues, who steadily sobered up.

Richard Jewell, the security guard who found the bomb and moved people to safety, quickly went from hero to potential villain when the FBI named him a 'person of interest'. In one of the less edifying moments in journalism, the media pack, me included, tracked Jewell down and laid siege to his home. Fuelled more by figments than facts, there was a trial by media, with some news outlets branding him the main suspect. It was several months before he was exonerated. Seven years later, fugitive Eric Rudolph, a domestic terrorist with an anti-abortion and anti-gay agenda, was arrested in North Carolina and admitted to having carried out the Atlanta bombing.

It was a very strange Olympics, not enhanced by our digs at a desperately mediocre motel on the Atlanta ring road. The only place to eat was at the nearby IHOP – International House of Pancakes. Every day was the same. The Sky gang would file in for breakfast and I'd order: 'Full breakfast, please. But no pancakes.' To which the waitron would always reply: 'But sir, we're the International House of Pancakes. You have to have pancakes.' To which, I'd answer: 'No I don't. I don't like pancakes, thanks.' After several exchanges they'd reluctantly get the message. But, just like the film *Groundhog Day*, we'd go through the whole routine again the next morning. And, in fact, every morning. I won, but it was a battle over the batter.

The Beijing Olympics in 2008 took me back to the Chinese capital for the first time since I'd covered the uprising in Tiananmen Square nineteen years earlier. What a change. The drab grey city with its legions of bicycles powered by riders in Mao jackets had morphed into a shiny metropolis full of cars, driven by fashionably dressed shoppers heading to malls packed with global luxury brands. The only thing that hadn't changed was the air pollution and the dismal human rights situation. The authorities still weren't keen on me filming in Tiananmen. The 'open media access' didn't seem very open.

So what had really changed since the massacre of 1989? There was no doubt the lives of millions of Chinese had been improved by a booming economy and greater freedoms. But I talked to plenty of people who thought the Communist Party would use the Olympics to strengthen its grip on power.

The futuristic stadiums – the Bird's Nest and the Water Cube – were spectacular. Like the breathtaking opening ceremony, a glimpse of China's aspirations. The message was: 'China wants to be friends with the world.'

There were problems like pro-Tibetan protests, swiftly shut down by security squads, and reporting restrictions, fiercely defied by foreign correspondents. But Beijing was far more friendly than I remembered as we filmed dragon dancers on the Great Wall, Olympic torch bearers at the Forbidden City, Peking Opera shows and parades in the parks.

As for the sport itself, we only got brief snatches. What most viewers never realise is that TV networks without Olympic broadcast rights have no camera access to any event. So for a channel like Sky News the only action footage we receive comes from the host broadcaster and we're usually limited to showing two minutes of footage at a time. Any athlete interviews or other footage has to be filmed outside the Games' official venues. So when a TV news team tells you they covered the Olympics from a car park, they almost certainly mean it. I had none of those worries when it came to the London Olympics of 2012.

For once, I wasn't working. I just went along with my family and enjoyed the action and the emotion. We'll never forget that second 'Super Saturday' as the sheer volume in the stadium seemed to lift Mo Farah over the line in the 5,000 metres for his second gold of the Games. Then we roared as the Mobot and the Flash of Usain Bolt put on a superhero show to delight the crowds.

I had just as much fun interviewing many of Team GB's sixty-five medal winners as I jumped on and off floats on their victory parade through the streets of London. Though float-hopping doesn't quite give me Olympian status!

CHAPTER 26

KOSOVO

'Oh, no, we still haven't been to Alaska,' was Lynn's first comment when I told her Nick Pollard wanted me to return to London as a presenter. As an afterthought, she added: 'Oh, and how do you feel about that?'

In our time posted overseas in Asia, Africa and now North America, we'd always used our holiday breaks to explore the continents. And we certainly hadn't been to every corner of the USA.

|||||||||||||||||||||

I flew back to London for a chat with Nick. I told him I'd like to give presenting a crack, but felt it was a waste not to use all my experience as a correspondent. And I warned him, as a mate, that I might get a bit restless just stuck in a studio all my working life. So we hatched the concept of a field presenter. I'd work in the studio much of the time. But when the big story broke, I'd be despatched with my own crew so that I could anchor on location. Nick and I agreed that it might add weight to our coverage, take viewers to the frontline with a familiar face to guide them and allow our reporting teams greater freedom to tell their stories.

So Lynn and I returned to London. It was to be the beginning of a new phase in my career.

Sky had pioneered the 'Breaking News' brand, with bright-coloured straps and screen crawls to alert our viewers. We'd also hammered home the concept of 'owning the story'. 'Monstering it' was the usual phrase. Committing enough news troops to dominate the story, so viewers were left with the feeling that there was only one place to follow the event – and that was on Sky News. My maxim was: 'Be first, be fast, be factual. Get in early, get out early.'

Sky News had already made an impact on big stories from Tiananmen Square and the fall of the Berlin Wall to the Hillsborough disaster and the IRA mainland bombing campaign at home, as well as on foreign stories like Mandela's release and the O. J. Simpson trial. But it still seemed to be struggling for public and industry-wide recognition.

Nick stepped it up a gear, making some quick, brave calls to send news teams on stories, even when he couldn't be sure how big they'd be. As he used to say: 'If you're early and you're wrong, you can always pull out. But if you're late, you'll always come second.' And being runners-up wasn't an option for Sky News.

What we needed was a big story to roll out our latest project – field presenting. The testing ground turned out to be Kosovo.

The Balkan Wars had been raging for eight years, as post-Tito Yugoslavia fragmented into factional and ethnic fighting. By the late '90s the focus had moved to Kosovo, where Serbian forces under nationalist leader Slobodan Milošević were busy persecuting Kosovo's largely Albanian population. This led to the rise of the KLA, the Kosovo Liberation Army, an ethnic-Albanian paramilitary force bent on counter-attacking Yugoslav Army units in Kosovo.

It was a nasty conflict, based on guerrilla and mountain warfare, with claims of war crimes, massacres and ethnic cleansing from both sides. By March of 1999, NATO had intervened with a ten-week campaign of airstrikes designed to drive Serbians out of Kosovo and fill the vacuum with peacekeepers.

When Milošević signed up to an international peace plan in early June, we realised it might not be long before NATO peacekeeping troops, under the banner of KFOR (the Kosovo Force), would be ready to enter the beleaguered territory.

Sky's own forces – reporters, presenters, crews, engineers and producers – had been gathering in anticipation in the Macedonian capital of Skopje. The key factor was Nick Pollard's decision to give us the right backup to mount our own rapid reaction unit. With Sky's operations chief, Jackie Faulkner, running logistics, Nick sent four mobile satellite trucks – SNGs as they were known – on a 1,600-mile journey through Europe to meet up with us in Skopje and on the Albanian border with Kosovo.

We were still negotiating with the British military contingent of KFOR for places in a media pool that would drive in behind the peacekeepers, well behind we suspected. Their plan was to offer a single flyaway uplink portable satellite dish on a flatbed truck, providing us with a series of pool feeds. The large number of British media meant it would soon descend into a dogfight. And it would enable the military to decide the timing and possibly the content. The army clearly wanted to control the message and the media on this operation. They had no idea we had our own satellite trucks hidden out of sight in Skopje. And neither did the rest of the British media.

In fact, many were still arguing the toss with the army about pool places, when my team rolled across the border into Kosovo. It was early on the morning of Saturday 12 June. During the night we'd heard a whisper KFOR might soon be on the move. So we camped out by the frontier and sure enough, as dawn broke, the first NATO vehicles rumbled past us. We simply drove out behind the convoy and crossed into Kosovo. In the post-war fog we found the frontiers wide open, with nobody in charge. Anarchy was ideal for opportunists. We just piled on up the road.

Within minutes we were in the village of General Jankovic. I asked the crew to stop and rig up the satellite. Within minutes engineer Pete

MacDonald had a signal to London and we were broadcasting live from inside Kosovo – the first British TV station on air by several hours. The planning had paid off.

'You join me live on Sky News from inside Kosovo.' It was hard to hide my excitement and nervousness. It was barely 6.30 a.m. on a sun-sharp summer morning. 'Until a few hours ago this village was under Serb control. Now it's held by British Gurkhas.'

The village was deserted as I took viewers on a guided tour. With British tanks and armoured cars churning by us, cameraman Anthony Whiley and I wandered into deserted homes. We found fresh bloodstains on the walls, hastily discarded family photographs, the wreckage of homes and lives – a chilling first glimpse inside Kosovo for Sky News viewers. Just yards from us, Gurkha infantrymen patrolled the streets, marking homemade booby traps for the bomb disposal squads to dismantle later. I checked with them live on air. The booby traps were still armed and primed. It was clear the Yugoslav forces had left only hours before.

Then we saw KLA soldiers emerging from the surrounding hills and walking towards us. They were heavily armed. I had no idea what to expect. Would they be hostile or friendly? I took a chance. Anthony and I walked through the village to meet them with our camera still rolling. Luckily Pete had a long cable on the truck allowing us to roam. The KLA guys seemed unsure what to make of us. One of them knew just enough English to tell us they were pleased to see the British NATO troops. They saw them as a liberating army. But they still made it clear they'd come down from the hills to reclaim their villages and weren't planning to give up their weapons.

Way beyond our expectations we were inside Kosovo and going live.

By now I'd got word from the executive producer in London that our second satellite truck was in position to go live. Andrew Wilson took up the story several miles farther up the road leading to the capital Pristina. With fellow correspondents Keith Graves and David Chater also on the ground, we were able to chart the progress of the peacekeeping forces. My truck and team moved past them to find a new location. Throughout that historic day we leapfrogged each other, passing the broadcast baton and keeping Sky News on air all day from inside Kosovo.

At one stage Wilson's vehicle blew a tyre. For a moment the crew thought it was gunfire. Fortuitously, they'd been forced to stop beside a deserted house where some KLA fighters showed Andrew where fifteen people had been massacred, evidence of a mass grave – the first of many to be discovered.

After all the months of hearsay and speculation about what had gone on in Kosovo, we were able to give the world a first-hand, rolling account of the destruction. We traced the telltale signs of this latest Balkan tragedy. Eerie, empty villages, looted shops, shattered homes and burned-out cars.

A third satellite truck crossed the Albanian border from Kukes, allowing Ross Appleyard to report live from another location in Kosovo. Emma Hurd, with our fourth truck, provided moving live stories of Albanian refugees from around Prizren. It was comprehensive coverage. At one stage we had a British Army spokesman on air, who admitted that Sky News seemed to have a better idea of what was going on than the men from the military. Not a bad compliment. Ahead of us in Pristina itself, correspondent Tim Marshall was using a flyaway dish to report the retreat of the Yugoslav Army as we headed towards him.

By late afternoon my team had reached a ridge on the outskirts of Pristina. We set up to present *Live at Five* and were well into the programme when hot news got even hotter. Deputy head of news Jim Rudder was gamely operating a portable, but cumbersome teleprompter for me while sheltering from a hailstorm under a bin liner. He shouted that he'd seen sparks on the roof of our satellite truck.

Then we heard the distinctive pop and fizz of small arms fire. It was very close. We could see tracer rounds above us. A warning that the Yugoslav troops weren't quite ready to quit Kosovo. We ducked behind our vehicles, threw all the gear in the truck, jumped into our battered old Merc and cleared out double quick.

Over a beer that night in Pristina's ghastly Grand Hotel, we all knew we'd been part of a little bit of television news history. The speed, the flexibility and the immediacy of our coverage was at a level we'd not been technically capable of producing before. It was Sky News's most ambitious project to date. The new, more portable satellite equipment allowed us to be even quicker on our feet than usual. We'd always seen ourselves as David in a battle against Goliath. With fewer people and resources, we'd long ago learned we had to be nimble to match or outwit the big, traditional news networks. This time we'd left them trailing in our wake.

The Grand Hotel was anything but grand. A thirteen-storey brutalist lump of Soviet-era concrete, in which little worked from the sewers to the staff. Entering the lobby we were greeted by the gagging stink of drains and urine. The toilets didn't flush and there was no running water, mainly thanks to the RAF, who'd bombed the water treatment plant a couple of days before. My handy hint of striking a match over a toilet bowl to burn off the stench came in useful. Apparently sulphur in the match head masks smells. It wasn't long before we got stuck in the only working lift, trapped in total darkness ten floors up for half an hour.

The hotel had been the base and the fiefdom of the Serbian warlord and war criminal Arkan, whom I'd the dubious pleasure of interviewing two days later. He denied everything I put to him – the massacres, the torture, the assassinations. Apparently he'd never laid a finger of anyone. Funny that. The maimed, the witnesses and the mass graves suggested otherwise.

For several days we broadcast live from the roof of the Grand watching out for Arkan's snipers.

I was amused to read Robert Fisk's take in *The Independent*: 'Sky's coverage was by far the most independent-minded. Jeremy Thompson's sergeant major approach to all interviewees had Serb killer Arkan squirming in his shoes.'

Jaksa Skekic, our Belgrade bureau chief, gathered the Sky News team to offer some advice: 'Welcome to the Wild West. Don't go out after dark and don't use the restaurant. And it's worth remembering they watch Sky News here. Not the BBC or NBC or CNN. If you're not 100 per cent for them, then you're against them. You're the enemy.' And NATO hadn't yet reached Pristina.

Then good old Jaksa pointed at me, Andrew and Tim in turn and added disconcertingly: 'And they recognise you ... and you ... and you.' Oh well, I guess we'd chosen to be in front of the camera.

The hotel was still a base for Arkan's Serb paramilitaries and Yugoslav Army officers, who seemed reluctant to leave Kosovo. They were armed and clearly intent on intimidating the media and running us out of town. Jim Rudder was on his way to get some bags from our car when a window opened above him and a soldier sprayed the street with rounds from his Kalashnikov. In fact, Pristina rattled with gunfire throughout that first night. It felt like we were under siege. Few of us got much sleep – not surprising with twenty Sky News staff crammed into three tiny bedrooms, temperatures in the 30s Celsius, no air con and no water.

There were seven of us in my room. Six of us restless. But links engineer Pete MacDonald, a former Royal Navy signals man who'd learned to sleep anywhere, anytime while at sea, was out like a light under a chair. My 11 p.m. two-way to Sky on the satellite phone was conducted against the ambient background sound of Pete's snoring and much gunfire.

Early next morning the team was hugely entertained by the sight of Keith Graves and I both trying to shower sharing a litre bottle of water. Nothing amused the troops more than grumpy talent arguing over water rations. At $5 a bottle that water was a precious commodity.

When he wasn't showering, Graves could be heard booming his latest bon mot at any passing hack: 'Never trust anyone in a uniform.'

I had to trust them a bit, as I was to spend the next couple of nights camped out with a British Army unit, who were holding a frontline position in the local bus station. KFOR may not have been in the Grand Hotel, but they were all round town trying to persuade the remaining Yugoslav soldiers to leave without a gunfight.

As I huddled behind a sandbag late into the night, I hoped Lynn wasn't too worried about me. I'd managed to get word to her that I was OK. But I knew, however calm and supportive she might sound, that she would worry until I was safely out of the danger zone.

Like many other nights in my career, the sound of small arms fire made me wonder why I was doing this crazy job. It was always a question of weighing risk against reward, deciding whether the story was big enough and important enough to push the limits. As a journalist you always want to be there, at the sharp end, where it matters. You have to go for it.

This time I was in no doubt. I'd been part of a Sky News team that had set a new benchmark in broadcast news. We'd taken our viewers with us on an unprecedented real-time, moving journey into a war zone. It was not just breaking news, but quite literally rolling news.

Sky had enjoyed plenty of big story moments before Kosovo – from its early days covering Tiananmen Square and the fall of the Berlin Wall to the death of Princess Diana and the headline-catching trials of O. J. Simpson and Louise Woodward. Some of Sky's viewing figures in the 1990s were huge and rarely surpassed. But somehow Sky News had never been given much recognition for the quality of its reporting. Industry awards had proved elusive. Many insiders felt the TV news old guard simply didn't take this upstart channel seriously.

Kosovo changed that. Even the British Foreign Office praised Sky's 'first-class coverage', adding 'I have rarely seen a better piece of straight-to-camera reporting than Jeremy Thompson's piece on arrival in Pristina.'

After ten years on air it was a defining moment. BBC, ITN and other news networks around the world were forced to take notice. On this story, we'd left most of them on the starting line as we roared off towards Pristina. Media commentators in the national papers, who'd largely ignored us for a decade, gave us credit for our coverage. And the Royal Television Society finally conferred a major award. Our peers in TV news judged our Kosovo Liberation Day coverage the best news event reporting of the year.

Within two years, the RTS had even created a News Channel of the Year award – recognition of Sky News's place among TV's big beasts and the creation of rival news channels at the BBC and ITV. We won the award that first year and many more times afterwards.

For several years before we started winning gongs, Nick Pollard had put on a highly entertaining 'Not-the-TV-News-Awards Night' party for the Sky newsroom. It was a raucous alternative awards night to celebrate our outsider status and cock a snook at the TV news establishment. In an Isleworth pub far from the glitzy RTS ceremony in the Hilton Park Lane ballroom, trophies were handed out for all manner of achievements, not always involving excellence. Mirth, booze and morale were all boosted. There was no doubt it reinforced the remarkable team spirit that drove Sky News. We still relished the underdog role as we continued to take on the big dogs.

I well remember the last of those parties. Another great night of goodwill about to become even more unforgettable. Awards and ales were being handed out aplenty when I got a phone call from Lynn informing me that our first grandchild, Isabella, had just been born. It was 26 May 2000.

I was a granddad. And, like me, Sky News had just entered a new phase of adulthood.

CHAPTER 27

VOLCANOES AND TSUNAMIS

What is it about me and volcanoes?

I've seen them erupting. I've seen them dormant and extinct. I've flown over them and into them. I've walked on cooling lava flows and backed away from molten spumes. I've seen the destruction caused by undersea eruptions called tsunamis. And I've even appeared in a movie called *Volcano*.

So Montserrat was a must.

||||||||||||||||||||

When the Soufrière Hills volcano exploded into life on this small British overseas territory in the Caribbean I started plotting how to get there. When it really went ballistic, or maybe stratospheric, in the summer of '97, I persuaded Sky News boss Nick Pollard to ship out a flyaway satellite dish so we could cover it live.

Cameraman Mick Deane and I flew down from Washington and teamed up on the island with my old producer pal, Nick Toksvig, and links engineer Steve Peters. We rented an abandoned house with an ash-filled swimming pool and magnificent view of the venting volcano.

It was a spectacular sight as we reported live from beneath this smouldering, spouting mountain. Each eruption filled the horizon with grey clouds of ash and rock crushing the sky into a kaleidoscope of blues from slate to aquamarine where it touched the Caribbean.

But smoking Soufrière was both beauty and the beast. We arrived in the wake of a huge explosion that had killed nineteen people, blanketed the capital Plymouth in ash, closed the airport and seen 8,000 residents – two-thirds of the population – flee the island. Most of Montserrat was now uninhabitable, a ghost island coated in pale grey ash, its economy buried beneath volcanic debris.

The remaining residents were crammed in the north of the island, staying with relatives or stuck in transit camps waiting for the ferry out. Soon it wasn't only the mountain that was rumbling on this normally tranquil outcrop. The grumblings of fear and discontent erupted into riots, with burning barricades eclipsing the volcano's fires. Protesting locals marched on the governor's office demanding to know what Britain, the colonial ruler, was going to do for them. A hastily organised aid package offered some compensation and a free passage to the UK.

It was one of those rare stories when we seemed to have the place to ourselves. It felt like we'd got to know almost everyone on the island and we'd become their mouthpiece, their megaphone to the outside world. Residents almost queued up at our base to tell us the latest news, or more often gossip, to seek our advice or ask us about faraway London. It was more like being on a local paper than an international news channel. It was hard not to feel an affinity for these gentle island folk whose carefree lives had been blasted to bits.

Our 'exclusive' island in the sun was inevitably invaded by other networks. NBC correspondent Mike Boettcher, an old mate from Gulf War days when he was with CNN, turned up with a crew and a helicopter, but no means of feeding out his reports. Our networks weren't affiliated, but we worked out a local deal. He used our satellite dish. We got rides on his chopper. Then ITN arrived and objected strongly because they were linked to NBC, who shouldn't be talking to us. Mike and I swiftly explained the facts of TV life on the road. The OPA, the Old Pals Act, takes precedence over network niceties when you're out on location.

So, ITN were left seething like a geyser as Mick and I flew off in NBC's helicopter for a closer look at the volcano. With the door open I could feel the intense heat as I filmed a piece to camera close to the smoking summit. Mick, with a big grin on his face, was urging me to lean out further and further. It was scary. Looking down it was like a huge sulphurous furnace. Beneath me great claws of lava had gouged out canyons of destruction in the sloping landscape.

We landed at Bethel. The ruins of the church stood like a headstone to a village that had died, its people chased away by the fire-breathing dragon looming above. The graveyard was encrusted in magma. We walked out onto the lava, now just cool enough not to burn our boots. Deep beneath us were the bodies of villagers who'd failed to escape the pyroclastic flows.

My report ended: 'The idyllic island life now just a memory for the villagers who thought they lived in paradise, but woke up in hell.'

Two days later our mission to Montserrat came to an abrupt end. The Sky team had been out for a Saturday night treat to the only inn still open. It was more of a shebeen than a gastro pub. The menu offered a choice of goat water stew or mountain chicken, the nickname for their local delicacy, the giant ditch frog. Goat or frog? Yum. But after two weeks we'd got used to it, as long as there was plenty of beer and rum to wash it down.

We got back to our cinder-covered billet feeling quite mellow and didn't really take in the brief message from London about a car accident in Paris. Early next morning we got the message loud and clear: frantic calls from HQ on our satellite phone to inform us that Princess Diana had been killed. 'Just get that satellite dish back to London soonest,' was the order.

Before we started packing up, I thought we should try to put together a reaction piece from Montserrat. After all it was a British territory. So we headed down to St Patricks Church, now housed in someone's bungalow. We got permission to film the service expecting plenty of mentions of the princess's tragic demise. But not a word from the avuncular Irish priest. As they left the service, I attempted to vox pop some impressive-looking women in their flowery summer frocks and wide straw hats. I asked the first lady if she'd heard the news: 'Oh yes,' she replied. 'Very sad. She seemed a nice young girl.' Another told me matter-of-factly: 'Oh well these things happen, dear.' A third was rather more indignant. 'Well, young man, you think we've got time to worry about things like that when we've lost our homes and our island's in crisis.' I'd been told in no uncertain manner.

Reluctantly I gave up on my mission to inform. We packed the gear and sipped a beer on the jetty as we waited for the ferry to Antigua. And a plane home.

Natural disasters are part of a reporter's portfolio. I've found myself covering avalanches and earthquakes, hurricanes in the Gulf of Mexico, monsoons in the South China Sea, tornadoes in Oklahoma and floods from York to Bangladesh. And I'd reported from the slopes of Mount Etna as it erupted. But I'd never before seen the sheer destructive power of an undersea volcano, like the tsunami of 2004.

I was enjoying a great family Christmas, with sons and grandkids, lots of presents and too much to eat. Then came that call early on Boxing Day. 'There's been a tsunami in the Indian Ocean. How soon can you get to Heathrow?' said the foreign desk. Most of my family hadn't seen me in full-on work mode. At the double, I packed a bag, kept an eye on Sky News, made notes and was out of the door in minutes, as the kids looked on in startled amazement.

Next stop – Phuket, Thailand. The scene that greeted us was staggering. The seafront had been ripped away. Palm trees torn from the ground, roots and all. Houses smashed flat. The beaches had been scoured, tons of sand thrown around like a child's play pit. Yet the damage was strangely skin-deep. The seismic sea surge had trashed the low-lying land, excoriating the seashore. Our hotel just fifty feet above the beach was untouched.

Less than twenty-four hours after leaving my own family safe in England, I was standing on a Phuket beach all too aware that this was a family tragedy on an epic scale. More than 60,000 people were already reported dead and the toll was rising. Around me were bereft tourists searching for their loved ones. Thailand was a favourite haunt for thousands of European families coming to enjoy Christmas in the sun. Now their dream holidays had turned into nightmares.

And it wasn't just Thailand. A dozen countries had been hit all around the Indian Ocean. The tsunami was so powerful it had made the entire planet vibrate. In one of the most audacious operations Sky had ever mounted, presenting teams were flown in to three main locations. Julie Etchingham joined me in Phuket. Kay Burley and Martin Stanford set up in Sri Lanka and Chris Roberts headed for Banda Aceh in Indonesia. For the next week we anchored our main programmes eighteen hours a day from the field, the first time it had ever been attempted on TV news. It was pioneering stuff, recognised by many in the media.

The Guardian quoted a BBC senior producer, who told him in a weary tone: 'When Sky's Jeremy Thompson started broadcasting live from Phuket the day after it all happened we knew the game was up.' Always good to live up to our motto: 'First for breaking news.'

MediaGuardian reported: 'Sky and ITN had swiftly despatched their star presenters to the region, the BBC's big guns were held back in the studios.'

Not only that, but we had a cast of top correspondents reporting across the disaster zone.

At the local town hall, they'd erected message boards so that tourists could pin up photos and descriptions of the missing in the hope that someone might have found them alive. It was heartbreaking as I listened to the stories of countless holidaymakers, from Britain and Sweden and beyond, as they described how they lost touch with families and friends as the tsunami swept ashore. I walked down the avenue of boards, showing the photos and reading out the names and messages live on air. I just hoped it would help.

Sky put new technology to good use, developing a brand new ticker-tape message board on screen allowing survivors and families to get in touch and send messages. We learned later it had helped many people link up with those thought to be lost.

But many were never found. At the five-star resort of Khao Lak I understood why. The paradise beach had dissolved into pandemonium as the wall of water engulfed the seafront hotels. This volcanic force of nature had destroyed a tropical playground, smashing the packed hotels, crushing the guests and sweeping many back out to sea. Half a mile inland rescuers came across a fishing boat lifted from the ocean and dumped in a forest. As we filmed they were still finding corpses washed up along roadsides and hanging in trees. A local Buddhist temple sequestered as a temporary morgue was overflowing with body bags.

Around a quarter of a million people died in the tsunami, though the final death toll from the killer waves remained uncertain. For me, witnessing the devastation and the torment of the disaster in Thailand that Christmas was another reminder of the force of nature.

CHAPTER 28

MILLENNIUM TIMES TWO

We want you to cover the millennium.
But we'd like you to do it twice.
Well, they don't come along very often. So, why not.

⁣⁣⁣⁣⁣⁣⁣⁣⁣⁣⁣⁣⁣ⁱⁱⁱⁱⁱⁱⁱⁱⁱⁱⁱⁱⁱⁱⁱⁱⁱⁱⁱⁱⁱⁱ

Late December 1999 I set off for stage one – New Zealand. With me were producer Nick Toksvig, cameraman Jonathan Scarratt, and my wife Lynn. She bought herself a round-the-world ticket, as we figured we were never going to witness another new millennium and there was no way she was going to miss this trip.

It was to turn into a travel marathon, done at a sprint.

We piled off the plane in Auckland after a 28-hour flight and went straight to work. Nick, Jonathan and I had to film a build-up piece on the eve of the millennium. So we hoovered up every bit of relevant footage we could find: Maori war canoes and their crews practising for the regatta, cultural dance groups, hakas, choirs and parade floats. The New Zealand capital was a buzz of excitement as the clock counted down to the end of the year.

But by the time we'd edited and fed the package to London, Team Sky News had run out of zing. Not long after we sat down to dinner, half the crew were asleep at the table. Jet lag collided with lasagne. And the next day was 31 December.

Revived by a night's sleep, we set up for the big moment – the new millennium. They only come around every 1,000 years. So you really don't want to blow it. And we'd been given the honour of opening the batting, so to speak. We were to anchor the last sunset of the past 1,000 years, and the first midnight and first sunrise of the next 1,000 years.

Our live position on Auckland Harbour was spectacular, with views across the city and the waterfront. Sadly, as we got ready for a twelve-hour stint of live television, the rain started. And never stopped.

Luckily the first pictures I had to commentate on were being beamed into Sky from the world's most easterly landfall of Kiribati, where there was a wonderful sunset as the lights began to fade on the past 1,000 years. Dancers on the newly named Millennium Island chanted farewell to the past and heralded a new age of unity as the clock touched midnight.

It was to trigger a chain of celebrations across the South Sea Islands. Then in Auckland a huge firework display. A slightly damp squib, bedraggled in the downpour. But New Zealanders are hardy and optimistic folk. So there were enthusiastic cheers as 1999 clocked out and the new millennium clocked in. On a small TV monitor, wrapped in several bin liners to resist the rain, I could just about make out what was happening elsewhere as the rest of the world followed suit, time zone by time zone.

As the first sunrise emerged, there were more events across NZ to herald the dawning of a new age. A flotilla of 2,000 craft – waka war canoes, Pacific Island outriggers and dragon boats – came ashore at Okahu Bay as the first rays of daybreak lit up the beach. A burst of flares banished the night. From the beaches of Gisborne, Dame Kiri Te Kanawa greeted the new millennium with the Maori love song 'Pokarekare Ana'. It was hauntingly beautiful as her words drifted across the waves.

It was hugely uplifting after a long, damp night of commentating in the rain.

But, for us, that was just part one of our millennium mission. We swiftly derigged, dried out the gear, repacked and headed straight for Auckland airport.

By nine in the morning local time, we were flying east from the city in an Air New Zealand jet – heading backwards in time, or was it back to the future?

Now, do you remember the millennium bug? It was a growing fear that computers might malfunction as their internal clocks misread the oos of the new millennium date and go haywire. By the final months of 1999, concern escalated into near panic. Experts prophesied drought, famine, thousands of deaths, accidental nuclear war and billions wiped off the markets. Some predicted that planes would fall out of the sky.

That was the bit that caught our eye. And the eyes of thousands of other air travellers too, no doubt. As you can imagine, at 30,000 feet above the earth's surface, we had a vested interest in whether the bug or the Y2K problem, as the boffins dubbed it, was clever science or conspiracy theory, bulging brains or bullshit.

It wasn't just us who were having a few irrational fears. It was estimated that governments and multinationals had spent up to £500 billion countering the Bug.

Airlines were taking no chances. So, as we flew back in time across the International Date Line, and midnight on 31 December loomed again, our Air NZ captain told us his orders were to land in Fiji until the potential 'Bugging Hour' had passed.

So we disembarked at Nadi International Airport just before midnight GMT – midday local time – and waited for the witching hour. It was reported from around the globe that there were no planes in the sky at that moment. We hung about in the terminal for an hour not knowing quite what to expect. When it was eventually apparent that the plane was still in one piece and nothing had gone ping or bang or done whatever millennium bugs cause planes to do, we trooped back on board, took our seats, crossed our fingers and took off into the clear Fijian sky without a missed beat. The great millennium bug had not caused the computer meltdown so many had feared. So from Y2K it was back to Operation Sky2K – our millennium mission times two.

Six and a half hours later, we touched down in Honolulu. It was 9 p.m. on 31 December 1999. Again. We'd crossed eighteen time zones in three days. I'm not sure whether we were wired or weird or just plain whacked. But no time to waste. Straight into a cab and down to the exotic Waikiki Beach on the southern shores of Hawaii's Oahu Island.

What a sight. One of the world's most famous beaches decked out in its party finery. Fairy lights, lanterns and garlands strung from every palm tree. Thousands of people in traditional Hawaiian dress, swaying to the music of the islands. Every hotel and bar along the mile-long sandy strip was hosting a *luau* – a feast and a fiesta. It was spectacular.

And parked in behind the palm trees was the ugliest satellite truck you've ever seen – just for us. It was owned by an American husband and wife team of engineers, Frank and Kay, who'd shipped it all the way from the USA, at Sky's behest, just so I could anchor the world's last midnight of the old millennium and Hawaii's first sunrise of the New Year 2000.

They were great. Despite the hassle of getting their truck to Hawaii, they were up for the gig. They loved each other, they loved satellite technology and they loved news. So putting us Brits on air was just 'a real pleasure' for this unlikely Mom and Pop team.

I quickly slipped into a garish Hawaiian shirt, was garlanded in *leis* by the Mayor of Honolulu and stepped in front of the camera for my second millennium night. And what a night. Fireworks by the thousand. And this time they were dry. No rain. Just a clear Hawaiian sky. Waikiki partied all night. We had music and *hula* and *kalua* pig roasts and fun. It was colourful and joyful. You don't get too much joy in television news. So, when you do, make the most of it and put it on air.

We saw another sunrise – our last in the world on this New Year's Day – as it appeared over Diamond Head Mountain. And I ended one of the great double marathon broadcasts of my life on a sun lounger, in dazzling sunshine, on Waikiki Beach, wearing a shocking shirt and sipping champagne – all live on TV. Another first. Sky, a champagne news channel for the twenty-first century! It was midday on 1 January 2000. Or so I was told. By then I didn't know my *aloha* from my *hula*.

We'd been up so long, we'd mislaid the concept of sleep. So Jonathan, Nick, Lynn and I went for a splendid seafood lunch to revive ourselves. And then did the tourist bit and visited Pearl Harbour. On this strange and historic day, we virtually had it to ourselves.

CHAPTER 29

9/11

I was having lunch at home before heading to the Sky studio when the first plane struck. It was 1.46 p.m. in the UK, 8.46 a.m. in New York. For a moment I stared at my TV screen in disbelief. 'What the hell's going on here?' I said to Lynn. It looked, for all the world, like a ghastly accident.

I'd just put on my suit and tie when the second aircraft ploughed into the South Tower of the World Trade Center. Now I knew this was no mistake. I rushed out of the door, calling to Lynn: 'Not sure when I'll be home. This could be a long day.' I ran to my car.

It was 11 September 2001.

|||||||||||||||||||

Twenty minutes later I was at work and racing straight into the studio. I sat down next to Kay Burley, who'd been presenting her programme when the first dramatic pictures reached us of that plane careening into the North Tower. We looked at each other and raised our eyebrows. A shared feeling of disbelief. Then we settled in for one of the toughest shifts of our careers.

Like millions of people around the world, watching the events unfold on TV, we too were almost lost for words. How do you describe the indescribable? How do you relate the unthinkable? My impulse was to let my jaw drop and just stare at the images in horror. But somehow, Kay and I managed to keep our composure and find the words to bear witness to the unfolding calamity.

When the South Tower collapsed just under an hour after it had been hit, I remember taking a long pause to let viewers absorb the enormity of what was happening. Words would have been a trite irrelevance when everyone could see the crumbling skyscraper.

Eventually I said: 'Everyone around the world will surely never forget this day – 11 September 2001. The loss of life, the devastation.'

Hearts racing, adrenalin pumping, it was hard to stay cool and calm that day. Kay and I had seen and reported a lot of strange and awful things in our working lives. But nothing like this. We were struggling with our own feelings of shock. I think we both felt the huge responsibility on our shoulders, not to mess up, not to lose the plot, not to get emotional and not to make matters any worse. Stay professional. Stick to facts. Don't speculate.

As the 110-storey North Tower began to tumble, I instinctively reached out and held Kay's hand for a moment. Like me, she was obviously shaken. We swallowed hard and ploughed on with our grim task of transmitting this tragedy to a watching world, transfixed by the images.

We could see what was happening, but the big question was: why? Our executive producer fed us all the latest facts through our earpieces, while Kay and I searched websites and news resources on our laptops for clues as to who might have been behind these events and with what motive. On my screen, I had aviation websites, terrorism background, US news online, anything that might give us verifiable information about the causes.

No sooner had the Twin Towers been hit, than there were stories about the White House being a target. Then reports filtered in that the Pentagon had been attacked and another flight had crashed in Pennsylvania. All US flights were grounded.

We were told by the gallery that it could be hours before any of Sky's correspondents in the US reached the scene in New York. The place was in lockdown. It was down to us to keep going. It was a challenge staying on top of all the sources, sifting reliable reports from wild rumours. It was tough enough being the messengers relaying all this dreadful news without adding to the sense of panic.

Looking back at my notebook I'd jotted down: '3.11 p.m. explosion at Pentagon. Act of War? Explosion on Capitol Hill. Uncertain. Unchecked. One of WTC Towers collapsing. Phone lines in NYC gridlocked. All US flights in the air diverted to Canada. All US internal flights grounded. 2nd Tower collapsing. Planes in UK grounded. Corner of Pentagon collapsed. Plane reported crashed S. E. Pennsylvania.' And so it went on for hours.

I vividly remember the footage of US President George W. Bush hearing the news. He was in a classroom at an elementary school in Florida when his chief of staff leaned down and whispered in his ear. Bush sat there looking dumbstruck for what seemed an age as the kids sat around staring at him. It summed up the day: one of disbelief.

Slowly, it became clear that the planes were part of an orchestrated attack. The implications were enormous. Soon, Kay and I were interviewing intelligence experts on who could be behind this strike against the USA.

My notepad reads: '"17.21 US seals its land borders." Later: "Surreal. Nothing moving in Manhattan apart from rescue workers." Blair says at 18.55: "Full horror becoming clear. Carnage and terror."'

The hours flew by. I'm not sure we knew exactly what time it was.

It was gruelling, but unbelievably gripping. Around 9 p.m. the boss decided we'd had enough and replaced us with a fresh team. I'd been on air more than seven hours. Kay had clocked up at least nine hours. Even then they almost had to drag us out of studio. I think we'd have gone on all night, given the chance. Stories like that are once in a lifetime.

In the newsroom, Kay and I let out a long sigh and hugged each other. We'd held it together in the studio. Now the emotions could show. We'd been through a day like no other.

I felt an overwhelming need to see my family. It was almost like I had to check that they were safe and all the world wasn't under attack. I dashed home to be with Lynn and called my two grown-up sons, James and Adam. Like everyone else, they were bewildered and slightly scared at what had taken place. Then I poured myself a large malt whisky and stared into space. It took a long time to unwind. The thought I kept turning over was what it would have been like that day at Ground Zero. As a reporter I always wanted to be on the story and at the scene.

When Sky News later won a BAFTA for that coverage, the *New Statesman* observed: 'Sky's presenters maintained not only technical assurance throughout, but the command of tone that eluded their BBC rivals.'

That day of 9/11 was to have a major impact on the rest of my career. We didn't know it then, but it was to be the start of the War on Terror. I saw it as the new Cold War. Like the Soviet–Western Bloc tensions of the past, it was to form a threatening backdrop to our lives. It was an event that changed the world.

Before long I would find myself reporting on a new war in Iraq and heading for the terrorist launch pads of Afghanistan and Pakistan. Soon the war would come to us, with terror attacks on the streets of Britain. The Arab Spring was triggered, fomenting terrible conflicts in Syria and Libya, unleashing a fresh refugee crisis. Al Qaeda and the so-called Islamic State were the new enemies of the West. In time other European cities would become the target

CHAPTER 30

IT'S NOT ABOUT ME

You would have thought being a lead presenter on the main evening news would be a pretty big ego trip. Well, there's no doubt there is some ego involved. But as I've always reminded myself: 'It's not about me.'

⁣||||||||||||||||||||

I've always seen the role of the reporter or the anchor as a medium, a cipher – someone to bring you the news without getting in the way. And, trust me, ego can be a major impediment. If it's too big, it eclipses the story.

If you think of a news team like an orchestra, then each reporter is an individual instrument, with their specialist part to play. The presenter is the conductor, bringing in the reporters to deliver their piece on time and, hopefully, in tune. Done well, the presenter should pull everything together to create a well-balanced opus, a good programme. That's in a perfect world, of course.

So what can go wrong? Well, just about anything and, sometimes, everything.

TV news is all about teamwork. Let's work backwards. First there's the presenter, in the studio, stuck in front of the camera, a hostage to human error. In his or her ear, talking from the nearby gallery, a windowless control room, is the director, who calls the shots and tells the presenter what's coming up next. Next to the director is their assistant, who's a bit like the accountant, keeping the books, calling out the order and the timings. Then there's the programme producer, the person who dictates editorial content, changes the running order, rewrites scripts and gives the presenter the latest news lines.

Behind them are all the technical folk, who make sure the machines are working, roll the pictures, turn up the sound, operate the microphones, scroll the teleprompter and link in all the outside sources. Then there are the teams who make all the graphics and the text, which furnish the screen: editors in booths cutting the pictures and audio into shape. Out in the newsroom a host of producers are compiling anything from a single news story to an entire programme. And beyond them, loads of people are racing around the world filming and reporting the day's news.

Back out front, presenters are being paid the reasonably big bucks because they've managed to acquire the curiously brain-splitting talent of being able to speak out loud while listening to multiple voices in their ear.

These voices are, often conflictingly, giving instructions, passing on the latest news-wire copy, telling you to keep talking or to shut up, asking if you want a cup of tea, or telling you that make-up is coming to the studio because you look too shiny. Sometimes, they're asking if you had a nice holiday or if you've heard who just got the sack, or if you knew old so-and-so had split up from his girlfriend.

The idea is for the presenter to keep all the verbal plates spinning while absorbing a baffling array of detail. And keeping eye contact with the viewer, who's blissfully unaware of the minute-by-minute mayhem of a TV news studio or the inside of an anchor's head. Pitfalls? I've had a few. They ranged from my microphone not working to my computer freezing, meaning no scripts and no running order, my earpiece becoming blocked, my chair collapsing, the director having a coughing fit, the producer losing track of what's coming next, no pictures to go to, a technical meltdown, the teleprompter crashing without a hardcopy script to fall back on, or general hysteria in the gallery. And that was just Monday!

Then there's 'pilot error' or presenter's foot-in-the-mouth syndrome. I remember saying to an unassuming Hezbollah spokesman called Osama: 'Thank you very much, Osama bin Laden.' It just tripped off my tongue before I'd engaged my brain. It's never a good idea to mistake a Shia for a Sunni. He wasn't amused and stormed out of our Beirut studio. And for some reason I always managed to mistakenly call the One Direction pop band 'One Dimension'.

Seriously, you ask anyone in the business and they'll tell you it's a miracle programmes get out on air. But, even more seriously, I've spent over forty years in TV news working with scores of great professionals, who make sure we stay on air, despite all the potential problems.

As we say in the trade, content is king, but delivery is the Household Cavalry. Get to the story, stick with it and make sure it's compelling viewing.

'Sky News – horribly addictive, even before 9/11', was the *Mirror's* comment in its 2001 TV awards. The key thing at Sky was identifying the right sort of story that would turn into compelling viewing.

One such event was the disappearance of three-year-old Madeleine McCann in Portugal in May 2007. After the impact of the Soham murders five years earlier, a missing child in mysterious circumstances raised an immediate alert. Sky correspondent Ian Woods was sent to Praia da Luz on the Algarve in the first few hours. He quickly realised it had the makings of a major story and called for reinforcements. Woodsy was joined by crime correspondent Martin Brunt, along with Emma Hurd and Amanda Walker. The story was that Madeleine had vanished from her bed in a holiday apartment just yards from where her parents were having dinner with friends. A day later Anna Botting and I flew in to share presenting duties.

The Sky theory was that anchoring on location gave added focus to the story. It allowed the correspondents to pursue news angles and gather information while the presenters held the fort. They would offer live reports or edited packages on merit.

The Madeleine story quickly grew into one of the most heavily reported missing person cases we'd ever been involved in. There were several key factors. A pretty three-year-old girl, the willingness of her parents, Kate and Gerry, to open up to the media, a family holiday drama – all set in an attractive seaside village. On top of that there was the suspicion that all was not as it seemed and the fact that this was every parent's worst nightmare – the child who disappears when mum and dad let their guards down. Rightly or wrongly, everyone had a view on the McCanns' parenting skills.

As the search went on, new twists emerged. There were reports of sightings of the missing girl, church vigils, emotional appeals for help and huge rewards offered for Maddy's safe recovery. Her fourth birthday came and went. Next day a local resident was taken in for questioning by police. It wasn't the media's finest moment, as some journalists all but named him as the guilty man. It turned out he was completely innocent, just a touch eccentric. Nothing more came of it. The McCanns vowed to stay on in the Algarve until their daughter was found.

Then four months after Maddy went missing, Kate and Gerry McCann were declared *arguidos*, formal suspects by the Portuguese police. It took ten months before prosecutors dropped the status through lack of evidence. Years later the hunt for Madeleine goes on.

For all of us on the story the most difficult aspect was how to cover such a sensational case with sufficient sensitivity. We'd become well aware of the growing number of child abduction and murder stories we were covering. Not just the Soham murders of Holly Wells and Jessica Chapman, but those of eight-year-old Sarah Payne, who was abducted in West Sussex in 2000, Milly Dowler, a thirteen-year-old, whose body was found six months after she went missing in Surrey, and April Jones, aged five, who went missing and was murdered in Wales in 2012.

They were among the most harrowing stories I covered, all innocent children snatched from the heart of their families. With the exception of the unresolved McCann case, they all ended with the prosecution of sick men with paedophile tendencies. Some called it the Jimmy Savile Syndrome.

I found the key thing to remember was tone. It was almost impossible to present stories like these child abductions without upsetting people. They were upsetting stories and viewers were bound to get emotional when hearing the news. So I tried to concentrate on not sensationalising the story. They were already horrifying enough. The thing was not to overdo it in the other extreme. In other words, don't go dirge-like and make it sound funereal. Just try to keep an even tone, stick to the facts and avoid being dramatic. The story invariably has sufficient drama without ramping it up.

Yet I've come across a lot of reporters in my lifetime who played fast and loose with the truth. Newsmen and women who thought it was OK to bend the facts to fit the story. I lost count of the calls I had from my own newsdesk telling me how a rival reporter had come up with a great news line and asking why I didn't have it in my story. 'Because it's not true,' I'd often reply. 'Because I was there and it didn't happen. They made it up.' Even then I could sometimes sense the doubts in the news editor's mind. In my view, reporting was about using the facts effectively, not twisting or distorting them.

The trial of Oscar Pistorius was another case that divided views and stirred emotions. In South Africa, the 'blade runner' as he was known, had been a national hero until the night when he shot his girlfriend, Reeva Steenkamp. From then on the public either backed him or despised him.

The story had all the elements of a Shakespearean tragedy. A handsome hero with the world in his grasp guns down his beautiful girlfriend, claiming it was a dreadful mistake – and all of it on Valentine's Day.

This controversial case opened up many of South Africa's social scars – racial tensions, violence against women, celebrity and entitlement, money buying justice. The South African Department of Justice, perhaps bravely, decided to televise the trial, opening up its courts to global scrutiny. It turned out to be a blockbuster.

With Sky special correspondent Alex Crawford and our crime man Martin Brunt, I covered the trial from start to finish. Alex got great access to Pistorius's home, showing the scene of the crime, and footage of the accused shooting melons on a firing range. It all added to the drama of the courtroom.

This was a news event made for the multimedia age. Not only did we have live coverage from inside the trial, but the correspondents could use social media to tweet minute-by-minute reports from inside the court, describing how Pistorius was looking and behaving, adding colour to the atmosphere, the lawyers and the public gallery.

Outside court, I used any breaks in proceedings to discuss legal developments with our analyst, Llewellyn Curlewis, a very experienced prosecutor and judge in Pretoria. As a reporting team we provided online stories and commentary on the case and filmed special programmes to round up each day in court. It was another reminder that news has moved into a multiplatform age and that means TV journalists have to be all-rounders.

So back to the business of presenting. Is it still relevant in this new media age? Or has self-selecting social networking obviated the need for a guide? Not yet, I would argue. I still see presenters as the sales force. Scores of people have spent the day crafting great picture packages, preparing live reports and creating smart graphics. Now someone's got to be out front to sell the product – on television at least. And, for the moment, I still see TV news as being the main content generator for a channel like Sky News. Online, social media and mobile apps all need moving pictures, action, interviews and reports. TV remains the most effective engine for gathering that quality content.

When I switched from being a foreign correspondent to a presenter I thought it was a natural step, an easy transition. It surprised me. I reckon it was a year before I really felt at home in the studio. It was a big leap to go from a two-minute live report on location to holding together a four-hour-long programme. The key thing is to know who you are and how to be yourself. You've got to be comfortable in your own skin, otherwise the viewer will never feel comfortable watching you. Don't try to be somebody you're not.

I learned a good tip on a BBC training course when I was in local radio. Imagine your mum or your granny sitting in an armchair about the same distance from the microphone as you are. Then, without a script, just tell them the story of the day in a way they'd understand. Don't shout, don't hector or holler. Just look them in the eye and explain what's going on. It stood me in good stead for forty-five years.

Keep it simple. Over my career I've seen all the latest fancy technology, the newest gizmos, clever graphics, stunning studios and mega news-walls. In the end it all comes down to having a good yarn and telling it well, well enough that the viewers don't want to turn off.

It's also about knowing when to turn yourself on and off. When I won the Royal Television Society Presenter of the Year Award in 2005/06, the judges noted my 'unique ability to capture the moment, to know which tiny little things really matter and, crucially, he knows when to shut up and let the pictures do the talking'.

I don't think storytelling has changed that much since the days of town criers.

They'd stride into a town square shouting 'Oyez, oyez, oyez' with no more than a bell, a strong voice and a way with words. TV has just added pictures. It's all down to the way you tell them. If you haven't got a good story and a manner to match, the crowds will simply drift away.

CHAPTER 31

THE DAY I MET A MURDERER

Soham. It sounds so innocuous.

A quiet little market town of 10,000 people, winding through the Fenlands of Cambridgeshire.

I remember it well from my days as a cub reporter on the *Cambridge News*. I'd often been sent out to cover the local council or report on a Soham Town Rangers match. In mid-winter their pitch was one of the most marrow-chilling places to watch football anywhere.

'When the wind blows, there's nothing between us and the Urals,' hardy spectators used to tell me with a knowing wink as they huddled on the touchline.

Now I was back. Thirty-five years on. The cub reporter had become a TV news presenter, though still a reporter at heart. But sadly, the reason for my return was nothing so mundane as local politics or sport. This time it was about trauma, possibly tragedy.

||||||||||||||||||

In Soham, two local girls had disappeared. Were they lost? Had they had an accident? Could they have been abducted? Or worse? Nobody could explain it.

Holly Wells and Jessica Chapman had simply vanished. Police posters of these two pretty ten-year-olds in matching red Manchester United shirts stared out from every front window and lamppost in town. It was a photo taken the afternoon they disappeared. Above their faces the one word: 'MISSING'. An image no one could forget. Two cute kids who'd just popped out for some sweets. Surely no harm could come to them?

The haunting images and the uncertainty soon began to unnerve Soham.

When I arrived with a Sky News team to cover the story two days later, residents quickly stopped us in the High Street to check if we'd heard any fresh information. It wasn't just Holly and Jessica's parents who were desperate with worry. This was a close-knit, rural community that shared a common concern. It was becoming a town in trauma.

Cambridgeshire Police were still treating it as a missing persons inquiry. Though local officers we spoke to didn't seem altogether convinced. They'd searched everywhere – backyards, bushes, drains and ditches. You could sense their anxiety as the hours passed with no sighting of the girls.

The idea that they'd simply lost their way was starting to look less plausible. Abduction was becoming a very real fear. But by whom? And where? And how? The investigators seemed to have few answers.

The story led our news programmes all week. They were the dog days of summer. A sweltering hot August. Not much was moving in the air or on the news front – apart from this.

Sky kept a team of correspondents on the case, chasing leads and reported sightings. The public appetite grew by the day. The photo of Holly and Jessica was on every front page and in every TV news bulletin. Soham was suddenly a place everyone had heard of. The missing girls had become virtually the only story in Britain. Each new development was followed closely by a concerned country. Some stories simply have that pulling power, a lure, an awful fascination.

Collectively Britain seemed to be willing them to come home safe and sound.

But a week on there was precious little progress. The police seemed stumped, their inquiry running out of steam. Leads were dwindling, possible sightings drying up.

At an editorial meeting back at Sky News, I suggested we should head back up to Soham for a concerted day of news presentation. My idea was 'to see if we can revive this flagging investigation and get the public to refocus on the case'. We agreed that the story of the missing girls was the only one anybody cared about that week. Putting our best resources on the case might just stir up a fresh lead.

So, on Thursday 15 August, I began a full day's broadcasting from the centre of Soham. It was eleven days since Holly and Jessica had mysteriously vanished. Our idea was to jog people's memories about their last movements. We set about filming a reconstruction to run on *Live at Five*, the early evening programme I presented.

We knew the girls had been enjoying a family barbecue at the home of Kevin and Nicola Wells, Holly's mum and dad, on Sunday 4 August when they decided to pop out to buy some sweets. Our camera crew filmed their likely route from the Wells's home in Redhouse Gardens, down into the town, over the main road and to the tuck shop at Soham Village College, the local secondary school. A walk of a few hundred yards at most.

We knew from the police that the last person believed to have talked to the girls was the school caretaker, Ian Huntley. One of our producers checked if he was willing to do an interview. Huntley agreed, though he said it would have to be pre-recorded. He was busy later. We set a time. He suggested we talk to his girlfriend Maxine Carr, a teaching assistant at the girls' school, St Andrew's Primary. Obligingly, Carr said she'd she talk to me live on my programme at five.

At 4 p.m. we met up with Huntley outside his staff cottage on the Soham Village College green. Cameraman Nathan Hale rolled his camera as I walked towards Huntley, introducing him as the last person to see Holly and Jessica before they disappeared.

'How do we know the girls were here?' I began. 'Because we have an eyewitness. Ian Huntley, the school caretaker, a familiar figure round here. The girls would know you.'

'Well I don't know the girls,' Huntley quickly replied. 'I was stood on my front doorstep, grooming my dog, and they just came across and asked how Miss Carr was. She used to teach them at St Andrew's. I said: "Not very good as she's lost her job there."'

We all agreed later that he set off no alarm bells. Huntley was a slightly awkward man, with dark, deep-set, tired-looking eyes. But there was nothing to suggest he was lying. He looked at me throughout the short interview. He was fluent and seemed sympathetic. I still had no reason to suspect he was a murderer.

He went on: 'They said "please tell Miss Carr we're very sorry" and they walked off in the direction of the library. They seemed fine, cheerful, happy, chatty.'

And Huntley added: 'I didn't see anything untoward, nobody hanging around. They just seemed like normal happy kids.'

Yet within thirty-six hours, Huntley had been arrested on suspicion of murder.

The same man who told me on camera, without a twitch, that their disappearance was an 'absolute mystery'. And the same man who looked me in the eyes and said: 'What people around here are saying is that when there's no news, there's still a glimmer of hope. That's what we're all hanging on to.'

You always tend to think you'd be able to spot even the slightest sign of guilt in someone who'd committed such a heinous crime. But experts say these psychopaths or sociopaths are skilled liars and deceivers. It turned out Huntley's words were simply the callous falsehoods and fabrications of a killer.

As one analyst told me later: 'Huntley probably got a real kick out of talking to you on television. Of feeling like he'd fooled the world.'

But his deception would last only a few more hours.

Meanwhile, back on the High Street, it was 5 p.m. We began broadcasting our timeline of the day when the girls had gone missing – as well as that now infamous interview with Huntley.

His girlfriend Maxine Carr had joined me for a 'live' interview. She was a slip of a girl, dressed in a blue football top, with a cross on a chain round her neck. She'd worked as an assistant in the girls' class until losing her job at the end of the previous term.

She told me how Holly and Jessica were 'lovely, bubbly, kind girls'. She said they'd 'never run away' because they very close to their families. Then she showed me a card Holly had written to her on the last day of term. There was a poem inside and a message saying how much she'd miss Maxine at school.

'This is something I'll keep for the rest of my life, I think. Holly was very upset I didn't get my job.' Then Maxine Carr went on: 'That's the kind of girl she was. She was just lovely, really lovely.'

When I asked if she had a message for the girls, she said: 'Just come home. Or, if somebody's got them, just let them go.'

As Carr walked away, producers Cait Fitzsimmons and Ed Fraser said to me: 'That was a bit strange, wasn't it, her talking about the girls in the past tense?'

We all agreed and decided we should mention it to the police. Though it seemed the police had soon picked up on this paradox. And on some other potential clues. Maybe our reconstruction really had stirred things up.

Events began to accelerate at a dramatic pace.

Next morning Cambridgeshire detectives held a news conference at Soham Village College. It was another heartbreaking appeal from Holly and Jessica's parents. We were all struck by the courage and dignity shown by Leslie and Sharon Chapman and Kevin and Nicola Wells. We could barely imagine how tough it was for them to face the cameras as calmly as they did, when inside they must have felt a turmoil of emotion.

They pleaded with whoever might be holding the girls to allow them back home safely. It was an anguished appeal from four people who had been going through hell for nearly two weeks now. Even the most hardened hacks in the room found it difficult to hold back the tears. We carried the whole media briefing live on Sky News.

At least one person in Soham knew that appeal was in vain. As yet we didn't know his name.

Soon police called another news briefing. There was hardly time to draw breath. We raced back to the assembly hall at Soham Village College. Detective Chief Inspector Andy Hebb revealed that two people were voluntarily helping with their inquiries – a man of twenty-eight and a 25-year-old woman. He mentioned no names. I caught Ed Fraser's eye and mouthed the names – Huntley and Carr. He gave me a discreet thumbs-up. Instinctively we knew it was them.

As the conference ended, I picked up my live broadcast in the school hall with this piece of breaking news. Fraser was on the phone trying to confirm the names. Within minutes he let me know that he'd learned the two people being questioned were Huntley and Carr. But I was told not to report the information until it had been cleared by our lawyers. Sensible advice. The police still hadn't confirmed the names. So the information we had amounted to no more than hearsay. And the age-old journalistic adage we stuck to was – check it at least twice, if not three times before you publish or broadcast.

So I kept presenting. Our highly mobile Sky News mini-link meant the crew could follow me out onto the Soham Village College green, nimbly staying focused on me as I walked backwards across the greensward, ending up outside No. 5 College Close – Huntley's home where I'd interviewed him less than twenty-four hours earlier.

I still couldn't broadcast any names. Just that the police were questioning two people in their twenties. Not suspects, I stressed on air, just a man and a woman 'helping police with their inquiries'. It was a subtle but important difference. They hadn't been arrested or charged.

Luckily I had a team of great reporters to add texture to the story. Crime correspondent Martin Brunt, David Bowden, David Crabtree and Michelle Clifford were around Soham gathering information and adding to the picture we were providing for the viewers.

It still felt like an eternity, telling a story, but keeping a secret. Suddenly the voice of the executive producer in the gallery at Sky Centre came into my ear. 'JT, our lawyers have cleared it. They say we can now go with the names.'

'We have some very dramatic breaking news for you,' I said into the camera.

'We can now tell you the names of the two people helping police are Ian Huntley, the caretaker here at the college, and his girlfriend, Maxine Carr, who worked until recently as a classroom assistant with Holly and Jessica.'

Moments later we played out the interviews I'd done with Huntley and Carr the previous afternoon. I told viewers that I was outside Huntley's home. I was able to go into more detail about that interview and my thoughts at the time. As I was talking, police in blue overalls began arriving and entering the cottage. It was obvious they were about to search the place. It really was breaking news as it happens.

We presented live from Soham late into that sultry summer's evening. I'd just come off air when we heard the latest development: Huntley and Carr had been released by police after more than seven hours of questioning.

'Didn't Maxine give us her mobile number yesterday?' I said to my team. 'Yes, I've got it,' said Cait. 'Why don't you give her a call?'

So I did. And after three rings, Maxine Carr answered. I asked her how she was and about the police interview.

She didn't say a lot. 'We're OK, we're fine, thank you for asking. We're pleased to be free.' All very polite. No alarm bells going off as she added: 'We've finished with the police now. We're going home.'

Then Huntley came on the line and said quite tersely: 'As Maxine said, we're fine. We've got nothing else to say. Cheers.' And he cut the line.

I went back on air to relay the news that I'd spoken to Huntley and Carr and that they were definitely no longer with the police. They hadn't had much to say, but it was pretty rare to talk to people in their position.

Finally, we had a very late supper and got to bed at a local hotel. It had felt like a long day. But what seemed like only minutes later, we were woken by a tip-off from colleagues that the police had carried out two arrests. Soon our engineers were firing up the Sky links truck and we were back on air. It was Saturday 17 August. Another day we'd never forget.

Detectives called an impromptu presser beside St Andrew's Parish Church. DCI Andy Hebb confirmed that they'd pulled Huntley and Carr back in for questioning in the early hours of the morning. Huntley had now been arrested on suspicion of abduction and murder, Carr on suspicion of murder.

It was clear the police searches of the Soham Village College building had recovered items of 'major importance'. It later emerged that clothes matching those the girls were last seen wearing had been found in the caretaker's lock-up. It was the first time the police had admitted they feared Holly and Jessica might be dead. It changed everything.

Now we were reporting a story not of two missing girls or an abduction, but a case of double-murder. This airless, August day of stifling heat seemed to grow ever more oppressive.

As I presented live from the town centre, Sky correspondents Bowden and Crabtree began to report on activity in the flat Fenlands to the east of Soham. Police cars, search teams and tracker dogs were seen in the surrounding countryside. Officers on sentry duty guarded taped-off lanes, preventing our camera crews getting too close.

The day stretched slowly into a humid afternoon of tension and apprehension. It was hard to keep conveying hope and positivity to viewers, who probably already feared the worst.

Finally the news broke. Police, tipped off by a local gamekeeper, had found two bodies in a ditch near the fence of RAF Lakenheath, some twelve miles from Soham. There was no immediate confirmation. It took four days to formally identify the girls. But from the first report, everyone seemed to know that this was it.

Holly Wells and Jessica Chapman had been missing for thirteen days.

The next day the church of St Andrew's was filled to capacity as the community came together to share the families' loss and grief. Then, just as swiftly as they had welcomed us two weeks earlier, the people of Soham shut their doors. The media, who'd brought them news and sometimes hope, the news crews they'd brewed tea for and swapped theories with, were no longer welcome. To them, the news vendors had turned into vultures, reminders of the horror and violence that had descended on their once quiet little town.

And so we left, knowing it was one of the saddest stories we would ever cover.

Like everyone in Britain who had followed this tragic tale, we were invested in it and, like so many others, had our fingers crossed for a good outcome. In the end it turned out to be what every parent fears most. But, for me, it wasn't to end there. A few months later detectives on the case called me up and asked to take a statement. It turned out they might want me give evidence. And so it turned out that in December the following year I was called to the Old Bailey as a witness for the prosecution. That was a first for me.

I'd reported enough cases there, including the trial of the Yorkshire Ripper, but I'd never been in the witness box. It was a daunting prospect, amplified by the anxiousness of fellow witnesses in the waiting room. The truth is journalists much prefer asking questions to answering them.

At last I was called to Court One. I stepped up onto the impressive stand that allows you to survey the whole of the great, wood-panelled court, from the judge's bench across the well of the court to the accused seated to my right.

I was sworn in and asked by the prosecuting counsel to verify my television interviews with Huntley and Carr. He wanted to know if I had suspected anything at the time. Then the defence counsel, in time-honoured fashion, did his best to trip me up and put his clients in a positive light. Then they ran those now infamous TV interviews.

It didn't last long. I looked down at the prisoners several times and tried to make eye contact with Huntley. Carr just seemed to be fiddling with her hands. Huntley was scribbling notes. He was a lot less willing to look me in the eye than he had been sixteen months earlier – just hours before it became known that he was a murderer.

Years later Martin Brunt recalled that, unlike most nervous witnesses who are asked to speak up in court, the booming Thompson was actually asked to turn down his volume while giving evidence.

It could've been true!

For the record, Huntley was sentenced to two terms of life imprisonment for murdering Holly and Jessica. It turned out that Carr had been in her hometown of Grimsby, visiting her family, when the killings took place at the Soham home she shared with Huntley. She was given three and a half years in jail for perverting the course of justice.

As the trial ended and those verdicts were announced, I delivered the news live on Sky from the streets of Soham.

CHAPTER 32

IRAQ WAR 2003

To embed or not to embed, that was the question of the war.

It was nothing new. They'd been doing it since the Crimean War, 150 years ago, attaching news reporters to military units so they could get closer to the action. Some media liked the idea. The military certainly did.

It meant they could control the message and the messengers, 'dominating the information environment', as one general put it. It was always controversial because embeds could easily be mistaken for inbeds, journalists spoon-fed by the military, drawn into the propaganda machine.

‖‖‖‖‖‖‖‖‖‖‖‖‖‖‖

To me, embedding was anathema. I was a self-proclaimed maverick and proud of it. I liked my independence. I was curious to the point of being nosy, a wild card and a pain in the butt. I valued my freedom. I always believed a journalist's natural state was to be independent and unilateral. I liked to make my own decisions. I liked not conforming. I liked not being too reliant on others.

Embedding was an uncomfortable compromise. Reporters end up being dependent on the military for transport, food, water, fuel, security, access and, above all, information. Their sheer proximity to troops puts them at risk of being seen as combatants. Then there was censorship. If things went wrong you could bet your life the information officers would shut down your ability to broadcast.

When the Iraq War began there were 767 embeds with the US and 138 with British forces. The rest of us were mavericks, doing our own thing. Looking back, I'd admit the mix worked pretty well. The embed teams got some great stories and the unilaterals, as we called those not embedded, added colour and perspective. The result was live TV war coverage as never seen before, courageous and high-quality reporting.

As the 'shock and awe' bombing of Baghdad began, I was presenting it all live from the rooftop of our Kuwait hotel, talking to David Chater, Sky's correspondent in Baghdad as he vividly described the aerial bombardment. Several times I was forced to spit out my words through a gas-mask filter, as Saddam buzzed us with a few of his ancient Scud missiles and the sirens squealed. We were still being told he had lethal weapons of mass destruction.

My old pal Alastair Campbell, author of the infamous dossier on WMD, who was watching it all on Sky News in 10 Downing Street, even phoned me during one broadcast to offer 'some guidance' from the PM's office. Good old Alastair, always trying to massage the message.

My plan was to move forward as soon as possible. An old uplink truck, which had rarely seen action outside the M25 before, had been shipped out to us in Kuwait. We kitted out the truck and two jeeps with extra fuel, food, water and supplies and headed north to the Iraqi border. After an overnight stay in a nearby cottage, we decided to cross the frontier. As we weren't accredited, we knew we were seen as 'illegals' by the local authorities. So we drove discreetly through a hole in the frontier fence, over some sand defences and into Iraq. We turned left, a crucial decision.

Within an hour we were broadcasting live from the Iraqi border town of Safwan. It wasn't long before I was surrounded by bemused and hostile Iraqis. In a mix of pidgin English and my woefully inadequate Arabic, we struck up a conversation. As British and American armour started pouring up the road beside us, I asked them what they thought of this liberating force. They sort of shrugged and grunted. Some were still giving Saddam a thumbs-up. But when I mentioned Blair and Bush they blew raspberries of disapproval.

Then, in my earpiece, I heard the Sky gallery in London say they had Defence Secretary Geoff Hoon on a live link from the MoD. I shouted down the line: 'Give him to me.' Moments later I was asking the minister responsible for sending in these British tanks to explain their presence here to these bewildered Iraqis, who didn't seem that keen on being liberated. The Defence Secretary seemed thrown and struggled for a convincing answer.

It was a long, hot and highly emotional first day in Iraq. I'll never forget the date, Saturday 22 March 2003. A day on which we'd illegally entered Iraq, been mobbed by local citizens, been shot at – and the day on which my younger son Adam was getting married in rather more tranquil Surrey. I'd sent a message. But it was never enough. Not for the first time, my job had got in the way of a big family event.

Then, as the light faded across the desert, came the terrible news that Terry Lloyd, my old mate from our ITN days, had been killed a few miles to the east of us. We were in shock, hardly knowing what to say to each other. The information was sketchy. Terry, with his two-man crew and an interpreter, had got caught in crossfire between Iraqi militias and US troops.

It was only a few days before that I'd flown into Kuwait with Terry. We'd known each other twenty years. We'd had a long chat and a chuckle about the 'good old days' and all the stories we'd covered together, right back to the Los Angeles Olympics in 1984 when we'd dubbed Terry 'Reggie' because he'd got maudlin over not getting on air enough (a jokey reference to Reginald Maudling, former Tory Home Secretary in the 1970s).

Looking ahead to the conflict we were about to cover, I'd said:

'Hey, Terry we're getting too old for this stuff, aren't we?' We were both over fifty.

'Well, maybe,' said Terry, with a wistful smile. 'But it's still a helluva good story. And I'd rather be covering it than not covering it.'

'Fair point,' I said, adding that ancient hack adage: 'And it's way better than working for a living!'

We shook hands, wished each other the best of luck and promised to meet for a beer at the end of it.

Now Terry was dead. I couldn't believe it. He was one of the best. A top-class reporter and a great bloke. We'd come up the same way, the long way – local papers, agencies, regional TV and eventually network news. It appeared that we'd entered Iraq around the same time, same day and not far apart. By chance, I'd turned left and Terry had turned right.

His death certainly changed our thinking and our mood. If there was any gung-ho it had now gone cold. I got the Sky team together – producer Ed Fraser, cameramen Andy Brattan and Pete Milnes, and the links truck engineers. I told them that if any of them were worried we'd get them back to Kuwait. For the moment, they all decided to stay with the team. But security had become an even bigger issue.

Up the road we found the Desert Rats, the 7th Armoured Brigade, setting up camp to the west of Basra. We ducked in alongside them and asked if it would be OK for us to take shelter. They seemed pretty relaxed and said help yourselves. Reporting war was all about minimising risks. We certainly felt safer within sight of British squaddies. Not embedded, just in touch.

For the next two weeks we reported on the Battle for Basra, up to twelve hours a day. Every night I'd present my own programme, *Live at Five*, from different locations. A strict blackout was in force, so we had to be inventive, resourceful and hidden. On different nights, we set up temporary wartime studios under the barrel of a Challenger battle tank covered in tarpaulin, inside an armoured car and the back of a signals truck, from the army post tent on Mothering Sunday, a MASH-style field hospital, Saddam's secret underground bunkers and several sweaty squaddies' tents.

Not only did we cover the fight on the frontline, but also won our own battle for hearts and minds, mainly the army's. The Desert Rats weren't allowed to phone home. So we set up a live show so they could send messages to loved ones. Occasionally we lent them our phones for a sneaky call home. One Saturday, the Sky engineers fixed a satellite downlink so the soldiers could watch Ireland vs England in the Five Nations Rugby Championship. That went down well.

By now the lads liked having us around and the colonel in charge told me: 'You're proving very good for morale. So you can stick around.' Then he added with a knowing wink: 'I just don't want to see you, officially that is.'

True to his word, the colonel gave us all the help he could. He allowed Sky to stay on the edge of camp, let me slip into his briefings, told me what was happening in the war and even warned me about attempts to evict me.

The MoD had set up its much-vaunted Forward Transmission Unit, dubbed the Hub, a sort of super embed for top reporters, who were promised unrivalled access to the frontline. In fact, while I was reporting freely in Iraq, they were still stuck in the sands of Kuwait, not seeing any action and growing more frustrated by the day. Sky's Emma Hurd, Alex Thomson from Channel 4, the BBC's Caroline Wyatt and many other excellent journalists just couldn't persuade the MoD to move the Hub up into Iraq.

I got word that the Hub's military spokesman had become 'almost obsessive about Jeremy Thompson's roaming maverick operation'. Later I heard that MoD war planners at Northwood High Command were 'determined to remove Thompson from Iraq and repatriate him to Kuwait. Then tell him to apply as an embed.' I was seen as a 'thorn in the side of the Hub'.

If the embed system was working so well, surely they wouldn't have been so bothered about evicting me.

Friendly Desert Rats gave me the tip-off that officers from the Hub had come looking for me. The Sky team melted into the desert for a day, avoided 'capture' and even came up with a good story on the Black Watch visiting a memorial where regimental comrades had died in 1914 on a previous British Expeditionary Force into Iraq.

The embeds versus unilaterals row rumbled on. A few weeks later, in *The Times*, Brian MacArthur noted: 'The swashbuckling war correspondent, symbolised by Jeremy Thompson on Sky, preferred to move where he wished and fend for himself, occasionally seeking shelter and sustenance from the military.'

He went on to report that some embeds felt trapped and were envious of our greater access. They were heard describing us as 'blisters', 'embed sores' and much, much worse.

One MoD media officer told me later: 'You really buggered up the embed system, but hats off to you. You got some great material and I admit we watched Sky all the time.'

There were several major alerts that had squaddies and hacks alike scrambling into NBC (nuclear, biological, chemical) suits and diving for cover under trucks and tanks. The officers had been told to expect Saddam's weapons of mass destruction to hurtle their way. But nobody seemed very convinced. The 'Dodgy Dossier' hadn't hoodwinked the Desert Rats. Off the record most of the British Army lads and lasses we talked to were struggling to understand the justification for this whole operation. They felt Blair's government simply hadn't made a convincing case for war.

There was far more justification for the soldiers' moan that they were underprepared. We saw many young squaddies being sent out on sentry and checkpoint duty without any body armour. They admitted being highly envious of our issue. They had no local interpreters and were soon borrowing Sky's man Nial to talk to the locals. Before long they'd offered him a contract. It swiftly became clear that the Brits were being dragged into a type of warfare they hadn't expected. Instead of traditional tank battles with Saddam's Republican Guards, they faced urban-guerrilla fighting against the Fedayeen. But we were impressed to see the Brits learned fast.

Eleven days in, Andy Brattan and Ed Fraser were overlooking Basra filming a fierce exchange across Bridge Four between the Irish Guards and Iraqi militias defending the city. Suddenly a mortar exploded nearby and shrapnel hit Ed in the shoulder. When I got to the field hospital at Shaibah air base, Ed was being patched up by the medics. As he said, it could've been worse. Former soldier and thoroughly gutsy bloke that he was, Ed insisted that he wanted to stay on the story with the Sky team. But this was no place for the wounded. A couple of days later we bade him a fond farewell and he was medivacked home. Like a good hack, Ed was just pissed off that we'd tracked down Chemical Ali's country house and done a story on it without him. A proper trooper. He healed nicely and went on to become managing editor of *Channel 4 News*.

After more than two weeks anchoring around Basra, I heard that the Hub was finally on the move in our direction. Andy Brattan, producer Roger Protheroe, who'd come in to replace Ed, and I agreed it was time to shift.

We'd now been joined by two security men sent in by Sky to look after us, probably at the insistence of the company's insurers. I'd never had security before and was sceptical about their value. The last thing I wanted was gun-toting cowboys turning us into targets. But Jock and John, both ex-SAS, were good guys and didn't get in our way. We left the SIS link truck behind. It would never make the 300-mile journey north to Baghdad. Our plan was to stay ahead of the media pack and link up with our Sky team in the Iraqi capital. Without decent maps and before satnav, it was to be quite a trip. Two days of sandstorms, wrong turns, flat tyres, gunfire and scary escapades, including a night camped out on a filling station roof with a squad of tobacco-chewing US Marines and James Mates from ITN. Funny who you bump into in the gritty clouds of war.

We emerged from the swirling dust to find producer Nick Purnell and engineer Des Jenkins at a US Marine Corps encampment on the southern outskirts of Baghdad. The commanding officer Colonel John Pomfret lent us his command tent. Des got a signal on his flyaway and, with just seven seconds to go before *Live at Five*, I heard director Jon Bennett say: 'Hi, JT. Seeing and hearing you. And we're ready to go in – five, four, three, two, one, cue.' Wow, that was tight.

I said: 'Good evening, we're presenting live on Sky News from Baghdad. It is day twenty of the war in Iraq.' A little bit of TV history. And what a line-up of Sky talent I was able to talk to. David Chater was still in the heart of Baghdad, Colin Brazier with US forces in the desert to the west of me, Stuart Ramsay with the US 101st Airborne Division in Hillah, Greg Milam with the Royal Irish Regiment to the south and Lisa Holland with me and the US Marines. Emma Hurd, with the Hub, had finally made it to Basra. It felt like Sky had it covered.

The next night I presented from Saddam's Special Republican Guard base in Baghdad, now deserted. Our two former special forces bodyguards told me: 'JT, we've never had so much fun before. You TV guys are crazy.' They told me they'd spent the last Gulf War, twelve years before, hunkered down in the Iraqi desert, too far from the action. They'd finally made it to Baghdad, courtesy of Sky News. They still got us doing 'stag' guard duty in turns throughout the night. Early next morning we pushed on into central Baghdad as Chater was reporting the iconic images of Saddam's statue being toppled.

Later we linked up with Chater and his crew, who'd courageously manned the Sky bureau in Baghdad through more than three weeks of 'shock and awe' and hell. Our two teams shared a brief, war-weary, slightly manic celebration. A couple of beers, then most of us fell asleep. It had been an extraordinary and exhausting tour de force from Sky's news warriors, both in Iraq and back at base in London. I started my last live broadcast from Baghdad with the words: 'Iraq is a country in chaos tonight.' That was April 2003. Not much has changed.

When Sky eventually pulled me out, a gang of us made the return road trip to Kuwait, with more gunfire, sandstorms and fun and games along the way. But it was when we reached the Kuwaiti frontier post that the trouble really began. After the invasion of 1990, Kuwaitis viewed anything coming out of Iraq with suspicion. The guards found Saddam mementos stashed in media bags and, even worse, a bottle or two of Scotch. Instead of a well-earned rest, we found ourselves locked up in the border post cells for the next few hours. It took a lot of British diplomacy to win our liberation.

Andy Brattan, Nick Purnell and I decided to divert via Dubai for a few days to chill out. Lynn insisted I should take time out on the way home. 'Decompression,' she called it. 'Get the story out of your system before you come home,' she advised, all too aware that after previous 'big stories' I'd been hard to live with for a while, wired and not ready for normal social gatherings. These days, you probably get counselling for it.

It had been a great team effort and we felt Sky had won another big battle of the news channels, with bigger audiences than BBC News 24 or the ITV News Channel. Newer, better, lighter, more effective technology allowed us to provide live pictures from any area of the theatre of war and deliver them right into the viewers' front rooms. Never has war been so closely, intensively or relentlessly covered. We had literally taken our audience to the frontline.

The merits of that became a matter for much discussion. And the debate over embeds went on long after the war was over. Along with several other journalists, I was asked to give evidence before the Commons Defence Select Committee. I was not alone in telling MPs that I believed our job was to serve the public not the establishment, to beat the system and question it, not be part of it. I saw my role as a journalist to probe, not act as a propagandist. Being unilateral allowed us freedom of movement, giving us a broader perspective on the war. We'd policed ourselves, assessed our own risks, not compromised ourselves and never given away military positions or classified information.

A couple of weeks after getting back from Iraq, Nick Pollard and I were taken to lunch at the River Café by the boss of BSkyB, Tony Ball, a good bloke who'd worked his way up through the TV ranks to become CEO at Sky. He just wanted to thank Sky News for doing such a great job in Iraq. Though he did add, over the pasta course: 'Phew! I'm glad that's over, guys. You were costing us £22,000 a day in personal insurance alone.' You tend to forget the incidental costs of war.

Curiously, one of the main questions I get asked is how did I manage to stay looking neat and tidy in 45°C heat, sleeping in a tent in the desert. If you really want to know, I always took thick cotton shirts in colours that didn't show the dirt. Lynn would give me a short clothes line, a few pegs and some Woolite. After hand washing the shirts, I'd peg them up by their tails and put stones inside the shoulders to stretch them. It was as good as ironing them. The secret to my war wardrobe.

CHAPTER 33

US PRESIDENTS

It was ice cold.

A frigid draft was blowing under Washington's door, sweeping down the Mall, chilling Capitol Hill to the bone. On the steps of Congress they were preparing to crown America's first black President in a white-out.

Just to cover it we had to go on a polar trek.

||||||||||||||||||

As dawn broke on 20 January 2009, the secret service sent us on a two-hour route march in sub-zero temperatures carrying all our gear from the Sky bureau to our live position, less than a mile away. Officialdom!

Welcome to Inauguration Day for Barack Obama, about to become the 44th President of the USA.

It was also the day Sky had earmarked to try out HD to see if it was worth converting our news channel to the latest broadcast must-have – high-definition TV. We knew all the company's big cheeses would be glued to the box as we went on air. No pressure then, as I stood on our platform on the Mall, surrounded by 1 million people, hearing the countdown in my ear from director Jon Bennett at Sky in London. Then, the moment I started to present our inauguration special, all I could hear was silence. So many channels went on air simultaneously that the internet carrying all the presenters' talkback overloaded and crashed.

I just kept talking and talking and talking. It was lucky I had plenty of notes because I was broadcasting in a vacuum. It was five minutes until IFB, the interruptible foldback system, was re-established and I could hear the comforting words of Jon Bennett again. Trust me, five minutes on TV can feel like five hours when things start unravelling. We survived. The programme stayed on air, nobody noticed the glitch and the Sky bosses declared it was such a success that Sky News was soon in glorious HD.

It wasn't our only problem that day. To help guide me through the ceremony, we'd hired an inauguration expert to be my 'presenter's friend' as we call them. But it was so cold my producer Jamie Wood soon noticed this elderly academic was turning blue. With wind chill, it was around -10°C. We swiftly carted the professor away through the huge crowds to revive him in the warmth of our links truck. I was on my own for the rest of the day.

The impact of Obama's election was enormous. I'd never seen such a throng on the Washington Mall. The attendance was estimated at 1.8 million people. Among them were two young men, who came over to my cameraman position and said: 'Hi Jeremy.' A bit of a surprise as Sky News wasn't available in the US. It turned out they'd flown from Zimbabwe just to witness the inauguration of America's first black President. 'We simply couldn't miss such a historic day,' they said, explaining that Sky News was their favourite channel back home in Harare.

Mandela had hailed Obama as a 'new voice of hope'. We found others who prayed that was true. On the eve of the inauguration we travelled to a forgotten corner of Mississippi, to a town where a black American dream was born. Mound Bayou was the first community in the US built and governed by freed slaves. That had been only 120 years ago. Its population was still 99 per cent African-American.

We found a sad, dilapidated place. Time had been cruel to Mound Bayou. Collapsing cotton prices, political neglect and white indifference had hastened its decline. Religion was the only thriving business left in town. But in the churches, the schools, the shops and on the streets we found residents freshly inspired by Obama's election. His success had ushered in a new era of hope.

I started and ended that extraordinary election year numbed. By tradition, the Midwestern state of Iowa was the first to select presidential candidates. As Iowa was mostly famous for being very flat and full of farms, our US bureau chief Sally Arthy decided, for the sake of authenticity, that I needed to present from a farm for an entire day. It was early January, thick with snow and -20°C. My teeth chattered through twelve hours of programmes. And a farmer pulled his gun on me, but only to illustrate his right to bear arms. It still didn't warm me up.

But later I did get my first sight of Obama. He looked good, sounded eloquent and announced his arrival as a serious candidate by surprisingly winning the caucus, the local vote, beating John Edwards and Hillary Clinton. It was early in the campaign so we could still get close enough to him to throw a few questions. Later he'd be surrounded by security men. He was smooth and charming, though I thought he looked a little fazed by his success.

By Super Tuesday, the moment in March when many large states hold their primary ballot, I was in Dallas, Texas, talking to voters who thought Obama could be a new John F. Kennedy. In contrast, Hillary, who had been expected to walk the nomination, was struggling to attract crowds down the road at Fort Worth's historic stockyards district, known as Cowtown. Perhaps an unfortunate choice of venue, considering what many Texans thought about her. By the time Obama was getting a standing ovation across the state in San Antonio, pundits were already asking if this was Hillary Clinton's Alamo.

In fact she won the Texas primary, but it was to be her last stand. At the Democratic Convention in Denver, the party confirmed

Barack Obama as its nominee for President. He made his acceptance speech in the Mile High Stadium. It felt more like a rock concert as we watched Bruce Springsteen, Stevie Wonder, Sheryl Crowe, John Legend, will.i.am and Jennifer Hudson belt out songs for Barack.

Early the next morning we were packing up to leave Denver, when our mobiles started chirruping. Obama's Republican rival, Senator John McCain, had announced Sarah Palin as his running mate. Sarah who? There was a mad scramble for search engines as we all tried to find out who the hell she was, and then get back on air to tell the world all about it.

She didn't win, but she did provide plenty of amusement.

Fast forward to Tuesday 4 November. I presented Sky's election night special from the New York skyline on the roof of CBS News at West 57th Street. An Obama win looked odds-on. And by 11.10 p.m. local time McCain had conceded.

Executive producer Chris Birkett and I decided to nip down to Times Square, meet up with our crew and gauge the mood on the street. It was like New Year's Eve. Hundreds were already celebrating Obama's historic victory, some a little too much. Though in the US, passers-by always gave a polite and coherent answer even in the middle of the night, unlike the UK where you'd more likely get a drunken mouthful of abuse. I thought it would be fun to vox pop yellow taxi drivers on the move – a first for me. Cameraman Dave Prime, always the pro, followed me in and out of the Broadway traffic as I fired questions at unsuspecting cabbies. Like Obama, we just said: 'Yes we can.'

It seemed light years on from my first brush with a US President. Over thirty years in fact, since I'd interviewed Jimmy Carter in Washington. Not DC, but Washington, Tyne and Wear, ancestral home of America's first President, George Washington. Security was a lot looser in those days and my abiding memory as a callow BBC correspondent is of Norman Rees, my ITN rival, and me almost falling into the presidential limo as we scrapped to get the first question to Carter. He was very polite considering we'd got him pinned against the car. His secret service detail eventually prised us away. But we'd got our sound bite for the evening news. It was a reminder that the duel between the BBC and ITN, when there were only two news outlets, often turned into a daily dogfight.

It was a multichannel broadcast world by the time George W. Bush got elected in 2000. But his campaign seemed positively analogue compared to the digital crusade eight years later. Obama's team had harnessed the internet as never before, getting his message to every corner of the US, raising small donations from huge numbers, organising supporters and using social media to propagate campaign videos. Obama turned it into the first wired White House.

The 2000 election felt old-fashioned in contrast. Clunky, manual, slower moving. It wasn't a great choice either. George W., son of President George H. W., was seen as 'smiling, folksy and congenial', but lacking respect and experience. Or Vice President Al Gore, seen as 'cheesy, bland, too liberal, uninspiring' and overshadowed by President Bill Clinton.

In the end the star of the show was election night, with its catalogue of counting errors, its confused TV hosts and its 'hanging chads'.

With funds a bit tight, Sky News's 'Results Centre' was basically producer Chris Birkett and our camera crew in a bedroom at Washington's Hay Adams Hotel, with me presenting from the window sill so there was a backdrop of the White House behind. Not ideal. But in the chaos that followed nobody noticed.

I was fronting our show, chatting to Sky correspondents across America and cutting into US news programmes live. At 7.07 p.m. local time, seven minutes past midnight in the UK, CBS News anchor Dan Rather announced dramatically: 'We think this may be the closest election in forty years.' And so it proved.

As state after state declared for either Gore or Bush, it became clear that it could all come down to one state – Florida. At 7.50 p.m. at least one US network said Gore had taken Florida. Ten minutes later, CNN, NBC, FOX, CBS and ABC followed suit.

Less than an hour later, I looked towards the three old TV sets we had balancing precariously on a footstool and said, rather grandly: 'I can see from my bank of TV monitors that something is seriously wrong. It looks as if Republican lawyers are questioning the Florida result.'

Sure enough, over the next hour, the US networks began reversing their calls.

Cheers were heard from Bush's campaign HQ in Austin, Texas. The legal battle over the Florida count went on throughout that night. The election was to hang in the balance for another five weeks as lawyers argued over 'hanging chads', bits of card not properly punched out by voting machines. Bush won by 537 votes out of 6 million cast in Florida.

George W.'s re-election four years later was largely unmemorable as he brushed aside his Democratic challenger, John Kerry. But if Bush's 2000 win looked like a quirk born out of the Florida fiasco, his 2004 victory made him into a political fixture instead of a freakish footnote in American history. What struck me most about anchoring that night's election coverage from Washington was that, like me, two of the Sky correspondents I spoke to, Peter Sharp and David Chater, had been on the frontline in Iraq. In Bush's first term, 9/11 had led to his interventions in Afghanistan and Iraq. The War on Terror was now a major election issue, on both sides of the Atlantic.

That election saw a resurgent Republican Party, followed by an attempted takeover by the Tea Party, a group of grass-roots conservative activists, who made quite an impact in 2010. Sarah Palin was their poster girl, to give you an idea of their leaning. I was anchoring the midterm elections from California when I went to check out a Tea Party event in Modesto. They were a motley mix of angry and authentic, anti-establishment and anti-big government, not always strong on facts.

One woman in a rather dated bonnet told me: 'We love the Brits, but you know, if you guys hadn't adopted that Communist health system of yours, maybe we wouldn't have had to fight the War of Independence.' Interesting sense of history, I thought, and replied: 'I'm not entirely sure about your chronology, madam. But it's been really great talking to you.' Strange place, America.

The Tea Party had cooled off by the time Barack Obama won a second term in 2012. I presented election night from the banks of the Chicago River in his home city as the President saw off his Republican opponent, Mitt Romney.

Obama was reportedly playing basketball with friends as the polls closed. The height of cool and confident. It didn't bode well for Mitt. He'd conceded before midnight local time.

At the McCormick Place convention centre, we were waiting for Obama to arrive for his victory speech, when I spotted the rapper and singer will.i.am walking by. I waved him over. He agreed to do a live interview and was soon talking knowledgeably about Obama and US politics.

Out of the corner of my eye I could see a local American TV reporter called Blake staring at us and telling his studio anchors: 'Just to give you a bit of info. That's Wyclef Jean giving an interview next to me.' Wrong! I could see his cameraman waving frantically and mouthing at his reporter, who tried again: 'Sorry, it's Wale. I've got my artists mixed up. All these singers coming out for the President.' Wrong again! Blake from Channel 7 battled on, before his crew finally wrote it down for him: 'will.i.am, good grief man, I am tired,' he wailed. 'I'm mixing up my artists here.' Third time lucky. You just knew his colleagues were never going to let Blake forget that one. You can still see it on YouTube under will.i.am (local news blooper).

To rapturous cheering from his party followers, Obama arrived with a rallying cry: 'We are an American family and we rise and fall together as one nation.' It was a call for political unity that was to fall upon deaf ears. Four years later the US was to look more divided than ever as President Obama handed the reins of power to President Trump. Not something he could have imagined in his wildest dreams.

CHAPTER 34

SAINTS AND SINNERS

It was a delicious irony. We were in Cuba – the ultimate island of idealism – all eyes sharply focused on the epicentre of communist kookydom. Here was Castro's crazy experiment in the Caribbean and there was America having its worst little scandal in a decade. The USA had become the USE – the United States of Embarrassment.

|||||||||||||||||||||

Castro had seen off ten American Presidents. Most of them had tried to assassinate him – by poisoning his cigars, burning his beard, strangling his economy or flying in exploding pigeons. But Bill Clinton had probably caused more mirth in Cuba Libre than any President since Kennedy hogtied the Bay of Pigs invasion. Humiliation by Havana. Take one Oval Office, one round Cuban cigar, one oversexed President and one well-rounded intern – and bingo! You have the Monica Lewinsky scandal. Another US President who got blown.

I happened to be in Havana because Pope John Paul II was about to make the first papal visit to Communist Cuba. It was described as a clash of faiths. The day Christianity met Marxism. It was to prove one of the last gasps of the Cold War era. Castro still standing resolute while Communism was imploding around the globe.

Right now I was watching the big, bearded El Jefe, unusually dressed in a suit instead of a uniform, pacing impatiently across the tarmac of José Marti International Airport as he waited for the late arrival of the Pope. The money shot was a frowning Fidel pushing back his sleeve and staring at his watch as John Paul II finally descended the steps of his Vatican jet 'Shepherd One'. Fidel didn't look like he was thinking very Christian thoughts.

Fidel wasn't the only one clock-checking. The Lewinsky story had literally broken minutes before. The entire US media corps had already forgotten about the Pope and were jigging from one foot to the other, just itching to get back to Washington or New York.

The US networks had spent a fortune erecting elaborate studios for their big-name anchors on the Malecón, Havana's seafront esplanade. But minutes after they'd fronted the evening news shows, Dan Rather, Tom Brokaw and Peter Jennings were winging their way home on executive jets for the 'Big Story'. My colleague Jonathan Hunt was back in Washington covering the breaking news, so I stayed on to finish the papal visit. Cameraman Mick Deane and I had already filmed several features to give some insight into Cuba circa 1998. We looked at the country's two success stories, education and medicine. Though with no more Soviet funding, even they were looking careworn. Wonderfully well taught kids, but with few facilities. And hospitals with great doctors and nurses, but a distinct lack of medicines.

It wouldn't have been Cuba without stories that included mojitos and daiquiris from Hemingway's favourite bars, vintage cars, boxing and baseball. We filmed in a famous cigar factory. The *puro* were hand-rolled, but disappointingly not on the lily-white thighs of virgins – yet another apocryphal tale unmasked.

At the museum to Che Guevara in Santa Clara, we interviewed an itinerant Marxist wanderer from Norway, who was so besotted with the hero of revolution he stripped off his T-shirt to reveal that iconic image of Che in his black beret tattooed right across his back. Now that was dedication to a fading ideal. And there was no doubt Cuba was fading.

With no support from Russia, the country looked close to bankrupt. In Havana, many people were living off tourism. Our interpreter was a university professor, who couldn't survive on his government salary. Like the cabbies, hookers, fixers and street vendors, he craved US currency. It had become a dollar economy, with thousands dependant on the country Castro so despised. It felt only a matter of time until Cuba became a virtual US state.

Back in the US, it was bedlam as usual with the Lewinsky story topping the headlines in all its lewd glory. But more on that elsewhere.

From the sinner Clinton, let's return to the saintly Pope John Paul II and my tenuous links to the pontifex. Now, I admit, I wasn't up to much on religion. Mum and Dad were keen churchgoers and I remember Dad would often try to win family debates by saying: 'I'm a Christian and so I'm right.' That meant I was usually wrong, in his mind. Ah! Fathers and sons. I ended my schooling at King's Worcester, a cathedral school, where Sunday worship in the big church was mandatory.

Those services always seemed interminable. As snotty, iconoclastic teenagers, we tried to tune out the religious rhetoric by secretly listening to pop music on transistor radios stuffed into inside pockets, with headphone leads fed up through jacket sleeves. We were caught and caned a couple of times a term. But that was a small price. I wouldn't say I ended up an atheist, but somewhere between ambivalent and agnostic.

Goodness knows how I got a gig as a holy-roller reporter. Yet here I was in the Holy Land following his Holiness on his historic pilgrimage to the 'Land where God chose to pitch his tent', as John Paul II so nicely put it. It was, of course, the 2,000th anniversary of the birth of Jesus. The year 2000 as we called it.

His seven-day trip to the Holy Land was known to be the highlight of all his papal pilgrimages. And bear in mind, by the end of his reign, he'd visited 129 countries, flying over 1 million kilometres during his twenty-seven years as Pope. For John Paul II it was seen as the climax of his papacy. For me, it was a big eye-opener into the complexities of this contentious corner of the Middle East.

I presented a half-hour special programme every evening that week, charting the Pope's historic journey and its impact. I talked to secular and orthodox Jews, Muslims, Catholics and Greek Orthodox priests – people of so many faiths and cultures crammed into this fiercely contested territory to the west of the River Jordan.

Together with correspondents Keith Graves and Emma Hurd we tried to explain some of the religious and political history that had made the Holy Land so controversial.

For Sky viewers it was like the best guided tour you could ever get as the Pope followed in the footsteps of Jesus. And we followed the Pope to Bethlehem and Nazareth, the Mount of Olives, the Garden of Gethsemane and Yad Vashem Holocaust Memorial, rounding off in Jerusalem at the Western Wall and Holy Sepulchre Church. It was an incredibly emotional week, with massive crowds everywhere he went. For me it was a bit like a Bible class come to life with moving pictures, context and real people – way better than anything I'd been force-fed at school.

John Paul II gave his own version of the Sermon on the Mount to 100,000 pilgrims in Galilee, he met PLO leader Yasser Arafat and kissed Palestinian soil, encouraged reconciliation between faiths and prayed at the holy sites of three major religions.

It was hard not to be moved. Though old sceptics like Graves and myself wondered if the Pope's visit would really resolve the differences in this divided land. I asked Keith how he'd managed to keep his sanity working in the region for nearly thirty years, mainly with the BBC and then Sky. He told me, with just a hint of irony: 'You know, I just disliked them all equally.'

Despite that, Sky viewers appeared to love our coverage. I received more plaudits than I'd had for years. Most said they were 'riveted by Sky's coverage', which was handled with 'charm, professionalism, enthusiasm and, above all, sensitivity'. One commented: 'In a secular age, it made very pleasant viewing.' My favourite came from a priest in Belfast, who wrote: 'Dear Jeremy, I don't know if you are a Roman Catholic, but, if I may be so bold to say, you ought to be.' I'm not, but I was very flattered by the kind thought.

Maybe on the strength of that, I ended up anchoring from Rome as Karol Wojtyla, Pope John Paul II, drew his final breath. They called it the long farewell. The Pope knew he was dying and so did the vast crowds who thronged St Peter's Square. But he wasn't in a rush. From a rooftop overlooking the great piazza we charted his condition with as much dignity as we could. I'd never talked or learned so much about electrocardiograms.

Reporting someone's last hours was never easy. At mass in the Vatican, a cardinal announced: 'The Pope is already seeing and touching the Lord.'

Some over-hasty Italian media outlets immediately declared his death. They were somewhat premature. But Calvary was mentioned a lot.

After three days on death watch, producer Tim Cunningham and I decided it was time to give our team a break and we headed off to a good Roman restaurant we'd had our eyes on. I was just chewing my first mouthful of a tasty *tagliata di manzo* when our phones went crazy. The Pope had died. It was 9.37 p.m. local time on a Saturday evening. We ran back to our live position and picked up the presentation. Below me St Peter's Square was awash with tears.

The world grieved. Its leaders spoke of their sorrow. Italy declared three days of mourning. And I started mugging up on the rituals and traditions dating back to medieval times that had now been set in motion – the crucial business of electing his successor.

A tide of pilgrims swept into the city to pay their respects as Pope

John Paul II lay in state. Rome had 'full up' signs. The city was saturated with mourners. Its population of 3 million had doubled. I remember seeing pilgrims sleeping on the streets. My colleague Anna Botting, one of the best presenters I'd ever worked with, travelled from the Pope's birthplace in Poland with a train full of devoted followers, some of whom knew him from his early days as a priest in Kraków.

The funeral was one of the biggest ever seen, watched by billions of television viewers. Bells were tolled and prayers intoned around the world in memory of one of the best-known Popes of all time.

After a three-hour requiem in the square, the Pope was buried in the Basilica in a simple cypress wood coffin near the resting place of St Peter. Nine years later he was canonised and declared a saint.

It was another ten days before the Conclave of Cardinals met to choose the new pontiff. This secretive and ritualistic process was much more exciting than any election I'd covered. The cardinals eligible to vote, 117 in all, were locked into the Sistine Chapel. We sat back and waited for the 'white smoke' – the famous sign of a chosen one.

The bookies were loving it. Paddy Power had Nigerian Cardinal Francis Arinze as its 3–1 favourite. German Cardinal Joseph Ratzinger was running a close second. William Hill had Ratzinger as favourite ahead of a Frenchman and an Italian. There was serious money being punted on the new pontiff.

When I say we sat back, we didn't exactly take it easy. It was thirteen hours into my shift on day one when black smoke emerged from the Sistine Chapel's chimney signifying a negative ballot.

So we returned the next day for round two. It was Tuesday 19 April 2005.

Ratzinger's name kept coming up. But there was talk of compromise candidates because the German might be too conservative for some cardinals. More black smoke. More false alarms. The chimney was working overtime in this rarefied religious world of stovepipe politics.

Finally, at 5.52 p.m., more smoke emerged. 'It's black again, I think,' I said uncertainly on air. Fellow presenter Julie Etchingham, always a delight to work with and something of an expert in Catholic matters, thought it looked paler. Seconds later we agreed it was 'sort of whitish smoke'. The Vatican kindly rang seven bells just to avoid confusion and the cry echoed around the square: 'Habemus Papam.' 'We have a Pope.'

High in the Vatican above St Peter's Square, the balcony doors swung open and out stepped the 265th Pope. It was Joseph Ratzinger, soon to be called Pope Benedict XVI.

One of my crew irreverently muttered: 'I knew it was going to be the German when I saw the beach towel hung over the balcony rail.' An old gag, but nicely reworked.

I must admit I was fascinated watching the Catholic Church at work, in all its majesty and mystery, keeping alive and relevant one of the most enduring institutions in the world, the papacy.

Nowadays my main contact with saints and sinners is an annual charity golf day of that name at Sunningdale. Well, it's in a good cause.

CHAPTER 35

MOVIES

I was running Sky's US bureau out of Washington DC when I got the call. The boss said I was needed in Hollywood. Fox Movies had asked him to lend them a Sky News correspondent to feature in their latest film, *Volcano*. So, all expenses paid, I flew to Los Angeles ready to become a movie star. It turned out it wasn't quite as glamorous as that.

|||||||||||||||||||||

I was told to report, not to Hollywood, but to a rather drab back-lot in Culver City. There I was handed a script and told to go to make-up. Over the next hour I was daubed in pretend volcanic ash, largely made out of grey papier-mâché. I looked a pretty curious sight, like I'd had bits of egg cartons stuck on me, but then so did everyone else.

I was directed to the actors' tent and told I'd be called when it was my scene. That was around six in the evening. Then the waiting began. There was food laid on, TV to watch and games to play. I joined several other bit-part players whiling away the hours until we were needed.

It was eight hours later, four in the morning, when I was finally called to record my bit. The rather ridiculous plot was that there'd been a volcanic eruption in Los Angeles and the La Brea tar pit was threatening to engulf Wilshire Boulevard, fancy shops and all. I found myself on top of a fire engine, as the LA brigade lined up, hoses playing and sirens wailing, for a last stand against the onrushing wall of lava. There were flashing lights, helicopter beams overhead and a glowing make-believe volcanic flow heading towards us. All quite convincing.

As I shouted out my lines to one camera, reporting the imminent demise of LA, the star of the movie, Tommy Lee Jones, was doing the big stuff to another camera a few yards away. It is the nearest I have come to Hollywood stardom. In the finished cut I'm seen on screen for less than ten seconds, though you can hear my voice for a bit longer, but it was an intriguing experience. I had to sign up to SAG, the Screen Actors Guild, in order to film. And I still get royalty cheques to this day. Though they've now dwindled to around $3.50 once every three months.

The director was Paul Greengrass, whom I remembered from his days on Granada's iconic current affairs show, *World in Action*. It was a series I'd always aspired to work on. But sadly it had faded away, like all too many good UK current affairs programmes, before I was grown up enough to apply.

Greengrass was to ask me to make another brief appearance many years later when he was directing the Jason Bourne films. I was called down to Waterloo Station where they were filming some great action scenes for *The Bourne Ultimatum* in the main concourse. My role was to be the TV newsman reporting that shots had been heard in the station. They allowed me to write my own script so it sounded authentic. To my surprise, more of my footage was used five years later in *The Bourne Legacy*.

That was a rare location shoot. Most of the time my brief film cameos were recorded during commercial breaks in my Sky News programmes. They were that short. Not very Hollywood; barely even Pinewood. That's how I ended up in *St Trinian's*, though sadly nowhere near the real stars: Rupert Everett, Colin Firth, Russell Brand and Gemma Arterton.

Anna Botting and I teamed up for a 'Breaking News' appearance in *Pixels*, a sci-fi action comedy, about a video-gamer becoming US President and then recruiting his old arcade pals to take down Pac-Man. We diss the Prez for cooking instead of saving the world.

For a few years I popped up regularly as a newsreader in the BBC spy drama series *Spooks*. Then I heard that several BBC News presenters had taken a dim view of a Sky man being on a BBC show. Before long the only newsreaders on *Spooks* were BBC types.

My biggest break in movies was *Shaun of the Dead*, wonderfully described as the world's first rom-zom-com – a romantic zombie comedy. The guys who wrote it, actor Simon Pegg and director Edgar Wright, asked if I minded recording a short news line. I understood why they were asking nicely when I received the script. They wanted me to say: 'The attackers can be stopped by removing the head or destroying the brain.' And repeat it several times while advising viewers to: 'Stay indoors for your own safety.' That was the moment Pegg and co-star Nick Frost woke up to the realisation that London was in the grip of a zombie apocalypse. After cursing me on their TV screen they rush outside to tackle zombies in their own garden armed only with household items and a vinyl record collection. Pegg liked my contribution enough to ask me to record my afterthoughts on the zombie invasion, which ended up as a solo on the movie soundtrack.

The upshot of *Shaun* was that I got as much recognition from that one film as I did from years as a TV newsman. And much more 'street cred' among younger generations. As one youngster said to me recently: 'Hey there, you're that news bloke off *Shaun of the Dead*. Go on say that line.' So I trot it out, with heaps of gravitas: 'The attackers can be stopped by removing the head or destroying the brain.' The young man says: 'Thanks. That was great. So what else do you do in life?' Ah! The joys of being a movie star.

CHAPTER 36

WAR ON TERROR

The War on Terror was to be a major thread throughout my years as a presenter. It was becoming our new Cold War; the constant tension from the threat of attacks now the backdrop to our daily lives. The Taliban, al Qaeda and the so-called Islamic State were a less conventional menace to the Western way of life. But no less dangerous.

|||||||||||||||||||||||

As I stood on the streets of Brussels in March 2016, anchoring Sky's coverage of the latest bombings, it was apparent that Europe was under attack in a way it hadn't been since the Second World War.

Intelligence was emerging that this terror cell, operating under the IS banner, was linked to those involved in the Paris terror attacks four months earlier. These terrorists appeared to be operating almost with impunity across Europe's borders, outwitting security forces. Brussels was in shock, just as the people of Paris had been only a year previously. Residents of Europe's big cities were now aware that no one could guarantee their safety.

The Charlie Hebdo shooting in January 2015 had struck at the heart of Western liberal values. Twelve people died when jihadist gunmen burst into the Paris offices of the satirical magazine who'd dared to print a cartoon of the prophet Mohammed. In the streets nearby, I spoke to Parisians in tears, horrified by such an assault on their city.

As we covered the atrocity round the clock, I could see the residents of the French capital gaining strength steadily through their shared revulsion and indignation at the attack. Soon thousands were rallying under the slogan 'Je Suis Charlie' in a show of national unity.

Meanwhile, we were also following a huge police manhunt for the killers. It ended with a dramatic siege in a village near Charles de Gaulle airport. I was anchoring live from our links truck parked beside the N2 motorway, while Sky correspondents Ian Woods and Joey Jones were sending reports from their locations within sight of the stake-out.

When French police tried to shepherd all the media off to a press conference, I told them my crew was staying put. I sensed they wanted us out of the way. Sure enough, within minutes there were several explosions at the siege site. The terrorists, who were brothers, made a run for it and were shot dead as they traded shots with police commandos. A few miles away in Paris, fellow presenter Kay Burley and crime correspondent Martin Brunt gave us a running commentary of a related hostage-taking at a kosher supermarket.

Ten months later I was back in Paris in the aftermath of an even more heinous wave of attacks, in which 130 people died. Nine terrorists in three groups bombed and shot their way across the city. Their targets ranged from a football match at the Stade de France to a rock concert at the Bataclan Theatre. It was mayhem as I arrived with my crew outside the concert venue.

There were still bloodied clothes and shoes on the pavement. At the police barrier a few yards from the Bataclan, a shrine was already taking shape. Parisians told me of their fear and consternation as they came to lay flowers and light candles. This was a city, if not a whole nation, in mourning.

One of the great dilemmas of reporting such awful events was conveying the scene and the mood to viewers without intruding on people's grief. It was a fine line. The media en masse can be an ugly beast. Being sensitive and discreet was not always easy when the streets were full of TV cameras and trucks. Getting the tone right was imperative, as was respecting people's feelings.

My great frustration as a presenter was the sense of being trapped or restricted. A reporter can roam free to gather information. I found, as an anchor, I might be stuck at one location for ten to twelve hours at a stretch, sometimes even longer, wired in to a links truck or flyaway dish, unable to move more than a few yards. I felt tethered, relying on the reporters to supply the colour and the detail. My main task was to anchor the story, to hold it all together. The latest lightweight transmitting gear has allowed presenters more freedom of movement, but it's still inhibiting. I guess I will always be a roving correspondent at heart.

The dreadful reality was that the terror attacks in Paris and Brussels came more than a decade after the bombing of public transport in Madrid and London. Same horror, just different terror franchises. So-called Islamic State gangs have now replaced al Qaeda. With a death toll of 191, the 2004 Madrid train bombings were the worst land-based attack in Europe in modern times.

I'd been in the studio throughout 9/11. Madrid was my first experience of being at the scene of such an atrocity. The scale of damage and carnage was hard to comprehend. Finding the words to explain it to viewers was tough. How much of what you've seen do you reveal? To an extent you have to self-censor to spare people the grimmest details and images, yet I have always felt that the public have a right to know about the consequences of terrorism. This wasn't a video game; it was for real, designed to scare and terrorise. You can stand up to it only if you're aware of its monstrous intent. We said then that it might be a matter of time before London became a target.

On 7 July 2005, I was presenting Sky News live from the G8 Summit at Gleneagles in Scotland. Global warming was meant to be the big topic of the day. At 8.40 a.m. we were covering a live walkabout in the peaceful gardens by Tony Blair and George Bush. They told us about their plans to tackle climate change, but just moments later the peace was shattered as news came through of explosions on the London Underground, possibly caused by power surges. Within minutes it was clear it was far worse. A code amber alert was declared. The Tube started to shut down. Soon I was linking up live with our correspondents at the scene. They were reporting up to three separate suicide bombings underground. Almost an hour later we heard a double-decker bus had been blown up. The eventual death toll was fifty-two, with over 700 injured.

The Skycopter was in the air within thirty minutes, beaming back live pictures of the chaos in central London. I continued to present from Gleneagles for the next two hours, before getting orders to move to London as soon as possible. My team drove to Edinburgh airport and caught the first plane out. At City airport, I was met by a motorbike courier. I jumped on the pillion seat and we roared through London's grid-locked streets at breakneck speed. I hopped off at Russell Square, one of the affected Tube stations, late that Thursday morning, linked up with a new crew and anchored Sky's programmes for another twelve hours.

My parents had always told me about the 'spirit of the Blitz' in Second World War London. Now I realised what they had meant. The city just pulled together. I watched and reported in admiration as the emergency services worked tirelessly and courageously to save lives and comfort the survivors. And the passers-by who pitched in to help in any way they could. These were people determined never to back down in the face of intimidation.

It was Britain's first exposure to the threat of home-grown terrorists, with three of the four suicide bombers born in England to Pakistani-immigrant parents. A seismic shock, but one Britain dealt with in its stride. Though many of us sensed this was only the start of the domestic terror threat.

My next trip to Pakistan was with Sky correspondents Stuart Ramsay and Alex Crawford for a special series, *Terror's Frontline*. Stuart and cameraman Martin Smith became the first foreign journalists to enter the Swat Valley after the Taliban took control. Their courageous footage showed masked gunmen carrying out public floggings and summary executions, while Alex's reports demonstrated the extent of the Taliban's influence as she and her crew dared to venture deep into Taliban territory.

Armed with their remarkable reports, I confronted the Pakistan President Asif Ali Zardari, widower of the assassinated Benazir Bhutto. Zardari, already mired in sleaze allegations, contemptuously brushed aside my questions, refusing to accept what I was telling him about his own country. In an ill-tempered interview at the presidential palace in Islamabad, he simply got angry when I showed him our emphatic evidence of Taliban gains. His stubborn denials made him look ill-advised and ill-informed. It was soon made clear to us that we were no longer welcome in Pakistan.

It was one of those well-planned and executed pieces of venture journalism that make you proud to be part of the project. It took guts to gather the material, persistence to nail down the interviews and it had a major influence on Western perceptions and policy on Pakistan at the time. It won the Sky News team a rare International Emmy, which we received in New York.

Barely two years later, Alex and I were back in Pakistan after the remarkable news that al Qaeda leader Osama bin Laden had been killed in Abbottabad, 100 miles north of Islamabad. Alex reported from the compound where bin Laden had been gunned down by US Special Forces, while I interviewed local officials who were embarrassed that this secret hit had been carried out right under their noses. Many experts told me Pakistan's intelligence body, the ISI, must have long known of his hideout in a garrison town. Either way, his death didn't end the War on Terror.

A trip to neighbouring Afghanistan to cover the presidential election in 2009 was another chance to witness Taliban violence. On the eve of the ballot, which saw Hamid Karzai returned to power, a suicide bomber drove a car into the NATO HQ in Kabul, before detonating it, killing seven people. Unsurprisingly, just getting to meet the main election candidates involved endless security checks.

There was plenty of armed security at our hotel. The Serena marketed itself as 'an oasis of serenity in the heart of Kabul'. Yet it had come under bomb and gun attack only the year before – six people had been killed. So it wasn't a huge surprise when our Sky security man Martin Vowles warned us that he'd received a very credible threat of a terror attack on the hotel that evening, just as I was about to start anchoring a two-hour election special on Afghanistan from the 'oasis of serenity' gardens.

Martin talked us through his escape plan and showed us the steel-doored cellar, which would be our hiding place. Then Alex Crawford and I got on with the programme, with fingers firmly crossed. It wasn't the easiest show we'd ever done, trying to broadcast while your nerves were jangling just waiting for the sound of gunfire or explosions. In the end, there was no attack. Though that night we were advised to sleep on the floor and put our mattresses against the windows to protect us from bomb blasts. Kabul was menacing and fascinating. It was a city that you were always thankful to leave in one piece as your plane headed home over the rugged Hindu Kush mountains.

It was hard to be certain how much the War on Terror influenced the Arab Spring. The response to 9/11 and the war in Iraq undoubtedly played a larger role in inspiring Arab youth to rise up against oppressive authoritarian regimes. What did become clear was how terror groups exploited the chaos and confusion created by the uprisings in Tunisia, Libya, Egypt and Syria.

My first taste of this Arab revolution was in Libya in March 2011, just as NATO began its campaign of airstrikes to 'protect Libyan civilians'. Though getting into Libya was easier said than done. It mainly involved waiting in Sfax for a fax. For days. Sfax was the Tunisian coastal city where Colonel Gaddafi's government had a small consular office and it was from here they issued visas for journalists wanting to enter Libya to report on the conflict. So me, producer Tom Rayner and our crew filled in numerous forms, attached photos and copies of our passports, handed them to the consul staff and waited to hear whether Tripoli would allow us in. Or, more accurately, whether we would be summoned.

While we waited, our local fixer, an ex-smuggler called Muldi, insisted we tried the Libyan cuisine. He took us on a drive up a desert highway in search of grilled lamb. One village street was lined with freshly slaughtered sheep, dozens of carcasses hanging above little stalls. Muldi got out of the car and started checking the testicles of each animal. 'The smaller the balls the sweeter the meat,' he informed us. He bought the best and we sat down to eat beside the road. The setting was strange but the lamb was delicious.

Several days later the Kafkaesque cadres of the Gaddafi regime finally approved our visas. We were told to get ourselves to the border crossing post at Ra's Ajdir, where we'd be collected by Libyan minders. We were then herded onto a minibus and driven the 120 miles to Tripoli, a dusty, bumpy ride through numerous armed checkpoints and towns already scarred by fighting.

Sinister was the word. Sinister agents on the bus, looking more like prison guards. The Rixos Hotel, which turned out to be little more than a five-star jail for journalists, was certainly sinister. Its corridors were filled with Gaddafi's sons, their cronies, their spooks and an ugly assortment of henchmen and hitmen, who looked at us like they couldn't wait for orders to waste us or take us to the cellars for a good beating. The foreign media was there on sufferance, seen as a necessary evil to be exploited in the propaganda war.

Our minders, most of them educated at British universities, were adamant we were just government mouthpieces. There was always the fear we could become human shields for a regime under attack.

A few months later, as the civil war came to a head, that fear became reality as thirty journalists were held hostage in the Rixos for five days by Gaddafi loyalists before being freed.

It was hard to get out of the Rixos at any time without the say-so of Gaddafi's lieutenants. From our live position on the roof I could literally commentate on the air war as British and French warplanes streaked overhead, raining missiles on strategic targets in Tripoli. The telltale towers of smoke gave away the locations. From time to time, Stuart Ramsay and other Sky correspondents would be taken on government-run trips out of town, essentially to persuade us that Gaddafi's forces were still in control. The intelligence we were receiving from sources around Libya and from our correspondents Emma Hurd and Sam Kiley in the east of the country suggested that this was far from true. There were pitched battles in towns all across Libya. But Tom and I were still subjected to hours of rambling rhetoric and obfuscation from Gaddafi's smooth spokesman Moussa Ibrahim, who turned news conferences into snooze conferences.

We had some interesting spats. Like the night I finally blew a gasket when one particularly nasty minder insisted on labelling all Brits as 'imperial monsters', even though he'd received his education at Glasgow University. And the day Tom lost his cool after yet another early morning summons. When he told the keepers it was a bad start to his birthday, they gave him a massive poster of Gaddafi as a gift.

Sky cameraman Garwen McLuckie had his own solution to the madness, pounding out hundreds of miles on a treadmill, partly to relieve the tension and boredom of being caged in the Rixos, but mainly as part of his training for South Africa's legendary Comrades Marathon. He was probably the only sane one among us and definitely the fittest.

In Syria, the Assad government set out to crush the spring uprising before it could gather momentum, killing or detaining thousands of opponents. But by the time I arrived in Damascus, just as the spring of 2011 was turning into summer, it was clear that all Assad had achieved by his crackdown was to instigate a full-blown civil war.

The reporting problems were similar to those we encountered in Libya. We got into the country only if the government chose to grant us visas. Once in Damascus they watched us like hawks, listened to our phone calls, sent minders with us when we filmed and tried to influence our output.

Sky producer Kelvin O'Shea, who'd learned Arabic and spent years cultivating contacts in the Middle East, did a splendid job of keeping Assad's people at arm's length. With a subtle blend of charm and old-world English courtesy, Kelvin made sure we had plenty of interviews with government ministers to get the 'official' side of the story, while enabling us to slip away quietly to check the mood on the streets.

The big problem was trying to nail down Assad. I got several interviews with his close adviser Dr Bouthaina Shaaban, but the promises of a sit-down with the President didn't materialise. In the early days of the conflict, Shaaban was pushing the line that the government were committed to dialogue aimed at democratic reforms. But while they pushed the softly, softly line, their security forces were getting more and more hardline. We discovered that peaceful protesters we'd interviewed were arrested soon after – and there were increasing reports of mass killings.

Sky correspondent Robert Nisbet and cameraman Pete Milnes, the other half of our four-man team, managed to slip away from their minders and take a train trip to Syria's second-largest city, Aleppo. Their reports confirmed that protests and clashes with police were widespread. The violence was intensifying.

Back in Damascus, Kelvin and I, two technical tyros, managed to keep me on air using a small Panasonic camera, a laptop and hotel broadband. In fact, from our hotel bedroom 'studio' with its backdrop of Damascus, I anchored seventy-five live segments and interviewed over twenty-five local guests in eleven days. And all it cost was $10 a day for hotel Wi-Fi.

By the time we next got a visa to Syria, seventeen months later, the civil war was deeply entrenched. More than 20,000 people had been killed, 1.2 million displaced and twice that number were in need of foreign aid. Kelvin and I, along with Sky's foreign affairs editor Tim Marshall, found Damascus a very different place. As we looked out from the same hotel balcony, we could see that the skyline was now grey with the clouds of battle. Fighting was clawing at the city's suburbs. This time when I interviewed Syria's Information Minister, there was no talk of peace deals, just a warning to the West not to interfere in the conflict. By now Syria was divided. And its problems had divided the region and the rest of the world.

All these stories I followed closely, reporting regularly from the presenter's desk in the Sky studio at Osterley. Much safer, but not nearly as satisfying as seeing events unfold first-hand on the ground.

CHAPTER 37

MICK DEANE

A sniper's bullet. A cold, calculated, cowardly way to end the life of one of the warmest, bravest, kindest and funniest men I ever knew.

IIIIIIIIIIIIIIIIIII

Mick Deane died as he lived – doing his best. Doing his best to open the eyes of the world to injustice. Doing his best for his mates. And he never did less than his best. An indefatigable warrior of the TV news business, he was the ultimate professional, delivering quality pictures and intuitive editorial judgement whatever the place, whatever the pressure. He was a big man in every way. A rock for those around him. The heart of every team he worked with. Mick was full of wicked wit and wonderful wisdom.

Sage, sane and humble, he was the man we all wanted to work with, whatever the assignment. Not just a great cameraman-editor, but a brilliant bloke too. His death sent shock waves through the television news industry.

I was on holiday in Spain when I heard the news. My boss John Ryley rang to tell me Mick had been shot and seriously wounded while working in Cairo. When he called back a couple of hours later to inform me that Mick had died, tears ran down my face. My two young granddaughters, Bella and Sophia, aged thirteen and ten, had never seen me cry before. They looked shocked but, sweet girls that they are, they just gripped my hands a little tighter.

I'd first met Mick in Manila twenty-seven years earlier when we were covering the frantic politics of the Philippines. He was editing for NBC. I was ITN's new Asia correspondent. We hit it off right away. Within a year Mick and his wife, Daniela, a news agency reporter with UPI and then Reuters, moved to Hong Kong. I soon persuaded him to join me at ITN.

He was just the man I needed – an excellent cameraman who could edit too. But he was also a great travelling companion – unflappable, grounded, worldly-wise and above all, funny. You needed a lot of humour to gather news in strange and faraway places.

The third member of our team, Andy Rex, now ITN's cameraman in Africa, remembered the weeks we spent covering the student uprising in Tiananmen Square in 1989: 'Mick called it the Long March or at least the ten-kilometre march' as we filmed the daily walk with the students from the university to the square. Mick soon became a familiar figure among the students and was fascinated by their cause and their courage.

All of the international media in China at the time were stunned and humbled at how the regime could crush this bid for democracy before our very eyes. The cameras of the world had proved to be no protection against a ruthless authoritarian government. And like the rest of us, Mick felt the injustice.

When Mark Austin, who would later become an ITN newscaster, took over the bureau from me, it was his first stint as a foreign correspondent and he was for ever grateful for Mick's experience:

> He was my guiding hand through the forbidding news jungle of Asia. He would know when to go, when not to go. He would know which airline to fly, where to stay, who to talk to, who to

rely on and who to ignore. He would know drivers, local fixers and people you could trust. He was an 'everything will be fine' man and when you're an insecure, uncertain novice trying to make your way in this game he was indispensable.

Austin recalled how they went undercover in North Korea, posing as teachers:

> Mick put geography teacher on his form and maths teacher on mine, knowing full well it was my worst subject at school. And how he laughed when the headmaster of a school in Pyongyang invited me to take a lesson.
>
> On day three of a five-day trip he sensed they'd rumbled us and pushed me to leave. I resisted, but he didn't fancy being banged up in a North Korean jail and found a way to get us out via Beijing. We left and later found out they had discovered we were journalists and had planned to lock us up.

Certainly Mick wouldn't have wanted a North Korean cell or anything else to keep him from his beloved family. Mick was always itching to get home to Hong Kong to be with Daniela and their boys, Patrick and Benny.

Andy Rex recalled Mick telling him: 'Andy take it from me, family first, then the job and you'll always be happy.'

My Sky News colleague Ian Woods told me about a story they'd filmed together of an American father who had lost his soldier son in Iraq and had written to President Bush. 'Mick filmed it all, including shots of the dad tending his son's grave, and when he was finished he just put down his camera and sobbed his heart out because he was thinking of how he'd feel if his sons died.'

Mick made a positive mark wherever he worked. No wonder he was in such high demand – filming for CNN, NBC, ITN, BBC and Sky News. A generation of young cameramen and women learned their trade from Mick, his mentoring all the more meaningful for his integrity, his energy and his boundless sense of humour.

The more any of us worked with Mick, the more we realised how special he was. He had an uncanny knack for seeing the pictures that would make the story and could salvage a news package with the quality of his camerawork.

As we say in the trade, he could turn a shambles into the Shalimar Gardens. Or as Sky correspondent Stuart Ramsay put it even more vividly: 'Mick made shite packages usable on TV. He'd say "Stuart, we just made chicken salad from chicken shit."'

Deano, as he was known to his mates, had more editorial nous than almost anyone I ever met in forty years of TV news. He not only shot the footage and cut the pictures, he could pretty much write the story too. As he sometimes quietly said to me: 'Hey JT, if you could just turn that sentence upside down the pictures would really appreciate it!'

He was also unfailingly funny and resilient, keeping spirits up when others were flagging. Nobody ever had a bad word to say about him. And that was a rare thing in such a cutthroat business.

Another cameraman pal Allen McGreevy, who I worked with in the US, told me how Mick lost the coin toss and became pool camera alone on Capitol Hill during Bill Clinton's impeachment hearings. Not too bad until the ice storm swept in and left Mick frozen in like the abominable snowman. 'When I reached Mick there he was standing next to his camera with a thick layer of ice all over him from head to toe; he had been outside for thirteen hours,' McGreevy told me. 'We chipped free the tripod and camera and left everything else there as it was frozen solid to the ground. On the drive back to the office, Mick said to me, "Hey Al, any chance we can skip the coin toss tomorrow and I could do the editing."'

From freezing to sweating, Mick just kept working. I fondly remember him carrying on filming all covered in ash as we reported live on the volcanic eruption on the Caribbean island of Montserrat in 1997. He handed me his shirt for a piece to camera in Cambodia because mine was wet through from the humidity. When I pointed out that his shirt was just as sweaty as mine, he replied: 'Yes, but my sweat has joined up, so the viewers won't notice!'

Hardly surprising then that Mick had the will, the strength and the stamina to fight cancer and win a few years ago and return to work as keen as ever.

How tragic, how unjust that a man courageous enough to beat cancer should be felled by a remote round fired by someone he never knew, someone who never even looked him in the eye. He was shot on 14 August 2013 by an Egyptian army sniper during the conflict in Cairo. There was no earthly reason why he fired at a man armed only with a camera.

Mick's death was a brutal reminder that reporting from the world's trouble spots has become ever more dangerous. Yet all those who knew and loved Mick were certain that he would never want risk to be a reason for retreat. Like all of us, he went to tough places because he believed the world needed and deserved to know the truth. He died filming. His dramatic footage led the news. The men with guns couldn't stop his pictures exposing the horrible reality of war.

Mick was a man we were all proud to call a friend and a comrade in news. Daniela and her sons asked me to conduct the non-religious funeral service for Mick. It was one of the most daunting yet proudest things that I have ever done.

Mick had been planning to retire the following May to the house he and Daniela had built together, which overlooks the beautiful Lake Bracciano, north of Rome, the city where they'd met.

Peace was so near. It all seemed so unfair.

CHAPTER 38

ROYALS

'So, how did you get it up, on the wall that is?' she asked with considerable interest.

'Well, ma'am,' replied the huddle of excited engineers. 'We loaded the twenty-foot flyaway dish into a rope sling and hooked it underneath one of their local Chinese helicopters.'

ııııııııııııııııı

The Queen seemed intrigued by the technical details of an ambitious ITN effort that had enabled viewers to see her historic walk along the Great Wall of China. It was 1986 and she was on her one and only trip to the People's Republic. It was clearly proving memorable for the Queen and everyone who was involved in the reporting of her epic visit, the first by a British sovereign.

As we talked at a reception at the Diaoyutai State Guesthouse near the Gate of Heavenly Peace, where the Queen and Prince Philip were staying, we could sense that she was genuinely excited at this once in a lifetime adventure.

China had opened the doors to its greatest treasures for the British monarch. She chatted about the thrill of walking on the Great Wall, of touring the Forbidden City and the Ming tombs. Royal reporters had rarely seen her more animated or inquisitive.

What we didn't tell the Queen was just how much it had cost to capture those historic pictures. Nick Pollard ended up more like a bank courier than an ITN executive producer in the days leading up to the Great Wall extravaganza. First he'd had to head up to Beijing airport with a holdall packed with US$26,500 worth of local currency – this was to pay China Airlines for the Antonov cargo plane to fly our satellite dish the length of China. Soon after he was seen parting with another bag of swag, some $19,000 to hire the helicopter that would lift the dish onto the Wall. Quite canny for communists.

A strong wind didn't help as the chopper finally hove into view with its precious load of electronics swinging beneath its belly. It hovered nervously just feet above the Great Wall as links engineer Trevor Davies and rigger Fred Rich heroically unslung a ton of satellite equipment from the net hammock. Somehow they managed to get it all assembled and fired off a test signal to London.

A couple of days later the Queen took her momentous walk along the Wall and the world was able to watch. At the time, it was one of the most enterprising pieces of live TV news ever attempted.

ITN star presenter Leonard Parkin provided the commentary for that big moment and a live half-hour special every night from a Chinese state TV studio that looked like a gloomy coal shed. It wasn't ideal, but it worked and it was history.

Later on the trip, I was unexpectedly asked to anchor an hour of live television when the Queen visited the Huxinting Tea House in Shanghai. Luckily I'd been given just enough time to mug up on Chinese tea varieties and customs. And I needed every fact. For a start the visit began late, which left me sitting in a CCTV voice-over booth frantically filling for ten minutes.

When the Queen eventually arrived she was ushered over the bridge across a small moat in the Yu Yuan Garden and into the Ming Dynasty

Tea House. Unfortunately her Chinese hosts led her into a room where she couldn't be seen by our cameras. As I couldn't spot what she was doing, I was forced to extemporise on the history of what felt like all the tea in China, with over 100 different varieties, tea-drinking customs and even how they made the famous 100-year-old eggs.

I had to go through my full repertoire. I knew the Queen was going to be served Shuang Jing Cha – 'Two Wells' tea. If you were watching you'd have learned that it was a 'delicately smoked brew from the south of China' and served by Leeu Jung Ruay, waiter number 289. Her Majesty was drinking her tea Chinese-style with no milk or sugar out of Jixing pottery. It felt like an eternity as I filled airtime with details of the tea room's famous brass spittoons and swing-door toilets that sounded like very public conveniences.

Thank goodness, Her Majesty was finally guided back into view and had enough sips of cha to give me something more to talk about. Twenty years later I was to end up doing live news broadcasting like that for a living. That endless hour in Shanghai was good training.

It was an amazing tour, a rare chance to see behind the Bamboo Curtain.

We filmed the Queen walking among the terracotta warriors in Xian, sightseeing in Beijing's Forbidden City and watching the cultural delights of Kunming. And we found ourselves reporting on the fallout from Prince Philip's familiar faux pas when he talked about the 'slitty-eyed' Chinese.

Our reporting team, ITN's legendary royal correspondent Anthony Carthew, Paul Davies and I, filmed a host of news features around the country, trying to give a real insight into the Chinese way of life.

I can still recall a medical story I covered in Shanghai. It was a cancer sufferer having a lung tumour removed using only acupuncture as an anaesthetic. The moment filming started in the theatre, our sparks fainted and keeled over. Apparently he wasn't too good around blood and gore. So I found myself wielding the lighting gear for the next two hours as we filmed Zheng Ma Zui having his lung noisily extracted with saws and scalpels, while he looked on, wide awake and seemingly untroubled. Minutes after the operation I was interviewing him in the recovery ward. He told me he felt great. I wasn't sure it would catch on in the NHS.

The logistics of that tour were extraordinary – transporting twenty-two ITN staff and 220 silver boxes of equipment around the country on some very dodgy, old China Airways CAAC planes. On most flights we could hear our gear sliding up and down the cargo bay beneath our seats, clearly not too well secured.

When it came to humping the boxes from aircraft onto ground transport, we didn't get a lot of help. As one colleague remarked: 'It's amazing how quickly 1.2 billion people can make themselves scarce when there's some heavy lifting to be done!'

Most of us found the trip exhausting, but exhilarating – a real voyage of discovery. Though not everyone enjoyed the ride. One lighting man moaned the entire time, mainly about food or the lack of it. Quite simply, he hated Chinese food. And there weren't many options. But about two weeks into the tour we ended up at a hotel in Guangzhou, still known as Canton in those days, where they promised a full English breakfast. There's nothing a news team likes more than a good wind-up and most of us were heartily sick of our colleague's whinging. So the next morning he came down to the breakfast room, looking as happy as Larry, and ordered a big plate of eggs and bacon.

What he didn't know was that we'd persuaded the hotel staff to hide all the Western cutlery. The sight of our grumpy sparks trying to eat his long-anticipated fried eggs with chopsticks was one of the highlights of the entire trip.

I have to admit I was always slightly sceptical about the value of Royal stories. It felt like they were more *Look at Life* documentaries than serious journalism. But ITN had got the hots for the Royals, largely driven by the Princess Diana factor, and they did good business for the network. So sizeable teams were sent on every Royal tour and special programmes produced at the end of each trip.

The doyen of royal correspondents, Anthony Carthew, told me on an earlier tour: 'Just think of them as travelogues, dear boy. We get to go to faraway places, with strange-sounding names and we gather up some lovely pictures. Just use the Royals as cutaways. Easy. Don't sweat it.'

So I took Tony's wise advice and made the most of visiting some unexpected corners of the world. One such trip was with Charles and Diana to Nigeria and Cameroon. Much of the ITN team luggage seemed to comprise of hat boxes for our delightful presenter Fiona Armstrong. She told me she was just covering all eventualities with a hat for every official occasion.

We were taken into rain forests and filmed extraordinary tribal dancers decked in feathers and masks. We even met the 'Fon'. Not exactly *Happy Days*, but maybe the inspiration for Henry Winkler's iconic TV character. This was the real life Fon of Bafut, definitely the inspiration for Gerald Durrell's book, *The Bafut Beagles*. This Fons, dressed in a colourful beaded ceremonial outfit, told us he'd inherited seventy-nine wives and more than 100 children, but he hoped to do better than his dad. Charles and Diana looked a bit overawed at the fecundity of the Fons.

It was one of many occasions when the sweet young Princess blushed as red as the welcome rug.

Royal tours could be a bit like flicking through the pages of *National Geographic* while watching *Comic Relief*. I mean, where else would you get to see a Durbar – a massive tribal horse show, a troupe of dancing hippos, war canoes and a west African pipe band playing 'Scotland the Brave'. Then next day we'd be with the Princess visiting a leper colony and going to Biafra, scene of a bloody civil war not many years before. Only in Nigeria.

Though the abiding memory of the ITN team on that trip was having to stagger up fifty floors of vertiginous steps to the top deck of a communications tower in Lagos just to feed our reports to London. With temperatures over 100°F and 90 per cent humidity, it was the supreme test of loyalty to the crown.

It was almost as hot when we followed Charles and Di Down Under for the Bicentennial, marking 200 years since the First Fleet of British convict ships arrived in Sydney. It was a spectacular sight on Australia Day as a vast flotilla filled the Harbour with 2 million people watching from the water and the foreshore.

The Pom-bashed Prince entered into the spirit of the day wearing an Aussie slouch hat as he reviewed the Parade of Sail. He doffed that hat to the Aborigines, who remembered the day the settlers arrived less fondly. To make their point they tipped three white sympathisers into the Harbour in their own re-enactment.

I remember the day because I was censored by the editor of *News at Ten* for using the phrase: 'Up on the yardarm sailors were jigging in the rigging, as the whole nation was caught up in the party mood.' Apparently he deemed 'jigging' 'too suggestive'. Grudgingly, I re-scripted, while muttering 'frigging editors' under my breath.

Diana's first solo trip to Africa gave me a rare chance to talk to Robert Mugabe. The President of Zimbabwe, still seen in 1993 as more of a benign dictator than the despot he later became, was clearly smitten by the Princess – like most of the world. After their first meeting, he told me: 'She brings light into our lives. You feel elated. You feel good.' As I left he said, perhaps seeing me as a representative of the British nation: 'Take care of her.' He was less keen to talk to me in later years.

She looked radiant, as always, whether comforting an Aids sufferer, holding a leper's hand, serving sudza at a soup kitchen in the bush or touring Great Zimbabwe, the ruined city of the country's first kingdom. I was reminded how photogenic she was and how easy to talk to, as we chatted informally at a reception in Harare. She giggled at our journo jokes and let slip the odd teasing indiscretion about her host, 'Uncle Bob' Mugabe, or backwards, E Ba Gum.

The last time I met her was in Chicago a year before she died. She paid a whirlwind visit to the Windy City and wowed them all. The trip seemed to blow away her royal cares as she tried to redefine herself in the face of her impending divorce. The city couldn't get enough of her. She must have thought of moving there for good. She stunned them on the sidewalks, left Chicago high society starstruck and made a dazzling entrance to a Royal Gala at the Field Museum, sweeping past the resident dinosaurs in a dynamic purple dress. I was inspired to pen the dreadfully pun-packed script line: 'Chicago will always remember the week when Diana came, Diana saw and Diana conquered.' Get it?

I returned to Hong Kong in 1997 to report on its handover to China. It probably wasn't Charles's finest trip. My abiding memory was of the Prince of Wales soaked to the skin as the heavens opened on him at the farewell ceremony. His hat of feathers was drooping, his speech notes turning into pulp and no one could hear him anyway for the drumming of the downpour. He observed later that he'd never before had to 'make a speech underwater'. And he added: 'The things one thinks one's doing for England!'

Many years later I was invited to a reception at Clarence House hosted by Prince Charles. I was never quite sure why I'd been asked. I have a photo of Armando Iannucci and me smiling uncomfortably as the Prince recounts a story. I was looking at Charles and thinking: 'You're the same age as me. How different our lives have been. I wonder if you've enjoyed life as much as I've enjoyed mine.'

The best and worst Royal trip I went on was with Princess Anne. Best because I got to visit countries that were no-go zones for Western reporters at the time, like Burma and Laos. But worst because she really wasn't a bundle of laughs.

Be grateful though. As journalists we would never have got into Laos without the Princess's Save the Children Fund credentials. This was still Communist Indo-China in the aftermath of the Vietnam War. As we entered Vientiane, the capital of this forbidden and forgotten land, we soon got a sense of its secretive brand of socialism. Comrades were sent off to work with a blast of propaganda, the disembodied voice of authority booming out from loudspeakers on every lamppost.

When truckloads of Vietnamese troops trundled by, our government minders shouted at us to stop filming, flapping hands across our camera lens. In Luang Prabang, Buddhist monks in orange robes walked by with bowls to collect their alms, as heavily armed border guards looked on.

Everywhere there were signs of a country battered and broken by thirty years of war. The US dropped more bombs on Laos during the Vietnam War than were dumped on the whole of Europe during the Second World War.

The splendidly named President Phoumi Vongvichit, an old Pathet Lao fighter and revolutionary, wasn't brought up to like royalty. But he did his best with the Princess.

At Si Amphone Temple, the venerable monk bestowed Anne with the highest blessing, cotton wrist charms to ward off evil spirits. Then he showed her his pride and joy – a collection of battered trucks left behind by the US Army. There was even a bullet hole in a Chevrolet's windscreen. He told her he couldn't get it going because there were no spare parts in Laos. This was a landlocked country locked away from the outside world for a dozen years.

Burma felt almost as remote. In Rangoon, it was a barefoot Anne who observed the house rules when viewing the stunning Schwedagon Pagoda, with its great golden stupa, reputedly covered in more gold than is held in the Bank of England.

We saw the Irrawaddy River, took the road to Mandalay and laid eyes on Burma's greatest treasure – the Pagodas of Pagan. The ageless beauty of the 2,000 Buddhist shrines was breathtaking. When I filmed an interview with Princess Anne that evening she told me the legendary pagodas were 'very interesting'. She hardly did them justice. They were of such majesty as should befit a royal tour.

For all of Burma's beauty, it felt isolated and isolationist, a socialist state stuck in a time warp. The Princess met Ne Win, the President, who'd spent twenty-five years sticking rigidly to his vision of creating utopia, only to drag the country into decline. Burma, once Asia's rice bowl, now held out a begging bowl of its own.

The most fun I had with the Royals was at the Queen's Golden Jubilee in 2002.

Buckingham Palace press office had rather carelessly granted me a roving pass to The Mall. And I took it very literally. Thanks to some fast-developing technology we had things called digilinks, which gave us much more freedom of movement. One of our team held a transmitter that looked like a long pole, which he pointed at a receiver on the roof of Buck House. That bounced our pictures on to Sky centre. It allowed the crew and me to roam freely sending back live pictures. And roam we did.

We had a ball dashing around The Mall during the carnival pageant, jumping on and off open-topped buses full of celebrities. I chatted to Cliff Richard, Ronnie Corbett, Barbara Windsor and a host of other personalities. Many seemed a bit surprised when an entire TV news team clambered up to the top deck of a bus to interview them.

I leapt onto a vintage Rolls-Royce carrying four Victoria Cross holders, ran alongside Hells Angels on bikes and sprinted to catch up with sports stars. All of it live on Sky. The BBC, the host broadcaster, were reportedly rather peeved that we'd appeared in a lot of their shots.

I've rarely received so many complimentary emails from viewers all round the world. Usually people write only to complain. But this time they couldn't have been nicer, thanking me for 'taking us to the Jubilee. We felt we were right there with you on The Mall.' Fellow presenter Julie Etchingham emailed to say: 'I thought you were fabulous. You made it fun, gripping and entertaining.'

My much-admired former ITN colleague Mike Brunson, one of the great political correspondents, took the trouble to write: 'You broke every rule in the book and you broke new ground in live coverage of such an event. It was a tour de force. You left the BBC and ITN standing!'

The remainder of the Royal deaths and marriages were less intimate, presented mainly from the comfort and distance of a desk in the studio. As for Royal births, I left those to the grand dame of Sky News, Kay Burley.

CHAPTER 39

PMTs – PRIME MINISTERS' TALES

Picture this scene.

I'm standing between Cherie and an absurdly young-looking Tony Blair.

They're beaming. Blair has just retained his Sedgefield seat and realised he is on the brink of becoming Prime Minister. It's moments after midnight on 2 May 1997. The moment is captured by Alastair Campbell. He snaps the shot on my new camera and promptly drops it, leaving it bent for ever, a lasting reminder of an extraordinary campaign.

|||||||||||||||||||||

Soon after the Blairs left in a chauffeured limo. By the time they reached London it was clear his Labour Party had won a landslide victory ending eighteen years of Conservative power. I followed with my Sky News crew and producer Phil Wardman, driving ourselves back from the count at Newton Aycliffe in County Durham.

After a sleepless night we ended up camped out on the doorstep of the Blairs' house as dawn broke over Islington and, in Tony Blair's words, 'the sun rose over a new Britain'. Around eight in the morning a courier arrived with a bouquet of flowers. Cherie opened the black front door to receive them and was caught in that infamous picture, looking sleepy and tousle-haired in a grey nightie. We couldn't believe our eyes or our luck. A last moment of innocence for the Blair household. By midday Tony Blair had left to meet the Queen and become Britain's new Prime Minister. He was just forty-three years old.

For me it was the end of a two-month journey following Blair throughout Britain on his history-making 'New Labour' crusade. Cherie's doorstep gaffe was almost the only slip in an ultra-slick campaign.

What struck me from the start was that this was an election marking a generational change. After eighteen years of Thatcherite conservatism, Blair, an increasingly popular figure, offered a real change. His freshly minted 'New Labour' brand had widespread appeal. It was surprisingly centrist, offering simple pledges like 'tough on crime and the causes of crime' and 'fiscal responsibility', themes that tempted voters from the Tory centre-right.

Not only was Blair a crowd-pleaser, he was a compelling speaker, an effective campaigner, selling his new brand to a public aching for something different. The student actor from his Oxford days came to the fore as he confidently strutted his stuff on platforms around the country.

It was the first time I'd really been aware of 'spin'. I watched with fascination as Alastair Campbell, whom I'd known since his days as a hack on the *Daily Mirror* in the '80s, tried to control the daily message. He fed the travelling media the party news lines. If they didn't bite, he wasn't afraid to cajole and hector wayward journalists, trying to get them back 'on message'. Like Bill Clinton's campaigns a few years earlier, Campbell had set up a 'rebuttal team' to counter Tory attacks.

The events were more professional than anything I'd experienced before. New Labour's advance guard would set up venues, with camera platforms and easy plug-in sound systems. Blair would arrive to speak already wearing a radio microphone, with a feed readily available to all broadcasters. Most days his campaign slogan, the D:Ream track 'Things Can Only Get Better', was playing as he arrived. An old ITN cameraman colleague Pete Baker was hired by Labour just to provide these facilities for the news media. It was smart new thinking and helped to keep broadcasters happy and onside.

Sky producer Phil Wardman and I had to keep reminding ourselves not to get sucked in by this New Labour media machine. Stay objective, especially when political parties start being nice to you.

As we criss-crossed Britain in buses, trains and planes, visiting over fifty towns in eight weeks, I tried to get to know Blair. He was friendly enough, but quite a distant figure, wary of letting down his guard during such a carefully choreographed campaign. When Cherie joined him on some trips, she happily chatted to the media, mainly small talk, often commenting how much she liked my ties. But Tony was almost aloof. Only once, when we stopped in Southampton, did he agree to come to the pub with us for a pint. We talked more about football than politics. Blair ever the keen Newcastle United fan.

By the end of the campaign we'd seen Tony Blair almost every day over eight frenetic weeks. I'd interviewed him dozens of times. Yet I felt I was still no nearer to knowing this man or what drove him. I was to talk to him on TV many more times over the next twenty years. But I was no closer to understanding him.

Blair's first election brought an end to the Thatcher years. It was the ballot that swept her to power in 1979 that provided my first shot at being on a 'Target Team', as TV news called the crews that followed the party leaders. As a young correspondent on BBC TV News, I was assigned to follow Liberal leader David Steel. Michael Sullivan was to cover Prime Minister Jim Callaghan's campaign and Margaret Thatcher was watched by Michael Cole. The joke in the reporters' room was that the extravagantly coiffured Cole got the Thatcher gig because they shared the same hairdresser. Journos can be pretty cruel.

I spent the month of April on board Britain's first political 'Battle Bus', Steel's own brainchild. It carried the party's bright orange livery along with the words 'Liberal Breakthrough'. Anything but. It proved one of the more attractive features of an unexceptional campaign. As we drove into Truro, I remember faces pressed against the windows to catch a glimpse of its much-publicised interior. 'Ooh, look!' said a young woman with a child in her arms. 'It's got two tellies and big comfy chairs. I wouldn't mind going on holiday in that there bus.'

And a holiday was what it felt like at times. In the age before the internet and mobile phones, when we were still operating on film cameras, nothing was very urgent or very 'live'. We tootled round the country, discovering that Liberal voters mainly inhabited picturesque, rural parts of Britain, like Devon and Cornwall, the Welsh Marches and the Scottish Borders. It was noticeable that we weren't motoring into a lot of metropolises.

In Devon, two weather-beaten old farmers patted the Battle Bus and burred: 'She be a real beauty, real 'ansome.' And added, as an afterthought: 'And 'e be real nice, that Mr Steel.'

David Steel's Scottish reserve didn't serve him well in crowded market places. He wasn't one for walkabouts. He liked scripted, controlled events. But he needn't have worried. He was rarely asked troublesome questions. Most people just wanted to shake his hand and wish him well.

Most weekends we spent in his delightful Borders constituency of Roxburgh, Selkirk and Peebles. There were only three broadcast reporters on the Steel bus, ITN's John Suchet, Nick Jones from BBC Radio and me. Often David and his wife, Judy, would invite us down to their cottage at Ettrick Bridge for tea and biscuits. It was all very civilised. Election rules meant we rarely filmed a story there unless Steel was commenting on national matters. Then we'd have to drive to Edinburgh to process our film and send the story to London.

It rather disturbed our leisurely country weekends.

I learned a good lesson on that campaign: don't get lulled into a false news perspective. Because we spent over a month exclusively with Steel, most of us 'Target Team' reporters started to believe the Liberals were doing really well. We even had a sweepstake on how many more MPs they'd get into Parliament above their current fourteen seats. On election day they lost three seats, including that of the scandal-plagued former leader Jeremy Thorpe and were reduced to eleven.

It wasn't long before I met the new Prime Minister. The Iron Lady came with a fearsome reputation, and I could soon confirm this. She'd come up to Cleckheaton to open an industrial estate. Being a thoughtful lad I got my camera crew to set up in front of an attractive flower garden. I thought she'd appreciate it more than a dull old factory.

Moments later, Mrs Thatcher stormed over and said: 'What ARE you doing? I'll be interviewed in front of this factory.' And added, crushingly: 'Young man, I've come here to promote British industry, not horticulture.' It was a sharp learning curve for a young reporter.

I quickly realised it was a mistake to take on big political beasts, unless you were well equipped and researched. In the BBC studios in Leeds, I watched in drop-jawed fascination as our presenter Michael Cooke tried to grill the indomitable Denis Healey, a former Labour cabinet minister. Instead Healey grilled, griddled, fried and roasted poor Michael. To add to the humiliation, as Healey left the studio he chuckled and said patronisingly: 'You can pull your pants up now Michael.'

Real leaders don't like to be told what to think, where to stand or how to behave. It didn't stop me spending a working lifetime challenging their egos, their ideas, their policies and their decisions. I was never Jeremy Paxman or Sir Robin Day on the political interrogation front. But I like to think I pushed a few politicians into an awkward spot.

When John Reid made his first trip to Afghanistan as Blair's Defence Secretary, he came onto my programme for a two-way with a very upbeat assessment of British military success in Helmand. He insisted: 'We would be perfectly happy to leave in three years and without firing one shot because our job is to protect the reconstruction.'

I said to him: 'Defence Secretary, you're a keen football man.' He later became Chairman of Celtic FC. 'Can I ask you how many away teams have ever won in Afghanistan?'

'A very good question, Jeremy,' he replied. But then he quickly changed the subject. He knew full well. There had been no visiting winners in that country. The viewers got the message.

I've covered eleven British general elections and interviewed every Prime Minister since Heath. But I never got the domestic political bug. As a long-time foreign correspondent, I always found other countries' politics more interesting than our own. Over the years I've reported on elections in ten countries, including six US presidential campaigns.

The first TV leaders' debates in the UK, brokered after a tenacious campaign led by Sky News editor John Ryley, were an intriguing development. From the Bristol quayside, I presented the build-up for the second debate, moderated by Sky News political editor Adam Boulton. It was good viewing, adversarial politics at its best, as David Cameron, Nick Clegg and Gordon Brown clashed over the issues of the election. It certainly gave Clegg a public profile that boosted him into a post-election coalition with Cameron. Though, for me, the first debate was eclipsed by an Icelandic volcano ash cloud. For a few days it brought flights in Europe to a virtual standstill and saw me reporting on a transport crisis.

The first Prime Minister I ever chatted to was Harold Wilson.

He was a reasonably approachable man, with his prominent pipe and Huddersfield accent. Not that we discussed politics. Strangely, it was more about logistics. Wilson was about to give a speech to a huge crowd at Leeds City Hall during the 1974 election campaign.

My worry was getting him recorded. In those days we were still using film.

Like all BBC news crews, cameraman Dave Brierley was using an Arriflex with a magazine on top, loaded with 400 feet of film. That gave us exactly ten minutes of recording. And the crews were never that keen on reloading the mag. It was fiddly and time-consuming and involved rooting about in a black cotton changing bag. That meant we had to tell the entire story of Wilson's speech in ten minutes. Needless to say, most politicians like to speak for at least an hour. Harold Wilson was no exception.

So, I plucked up courage and, as he walked by me on his way to the stage, said: 'Excuse me, Mr Wilson. As we haven't got a copy of your speech, how will we know when you're going to say something important?'

'Aye, good question, young fellow,' he replied. 'I tell you what, when I come to the crucial bit, I'll pause briefly and scratch my nose. Then I'll scratch my nose again when I've finished the key passage. Will that do?'

'Yes, Sir, that's great. Thanks for your help,' I said with relief.

Like a handful of top politicians I've met over the years, Wilson was the consummate pro. He knew what the media game was all about and how to ensure his message came over loud and clear. So Dave recorded Wilson's arrival, some crowd shots – wide and close-up, various angles of Wilson speaking. Then we waited for the nose scratch. And spot on cue, the man who was soon to be voted back into Downing Street, obligingly gave us the signal and we rolled the camera on the key sequence of his speech. A few more shots of the audience applauding, Wilson departing and my piece to camera and our job was done. All on ten minutes of film.

It was all so simple in those far-off analogue days, unlike the no-hiding-place frenzy of live TV, when you sometimes get politics warts and all. Like the time I got stuck between two other big beasts of the Westminster zoo, Labour spinner Alastair Campbell and my Sky News comrade Adam Boulton. They'd known each other for years, but it hadn't always been an easy relationship.

I'd noticed the sparks of friction on election night 2010. I was presenting from David Cameron's Witney constituency count when Boulton and Campbell popped up on a TV screen having a feisty exchange of views.

Four days later, I was anchoring Sky News from a temporary studio opposite the Commons on Abingdon Green. The election had resulted in a hung parliament. The debate was now raging about who would govern.

I was about to talk live to Boulton when a keen young Sky producer spotted Campbell walking by and ushered him onto our platform. The chemistry felt bad from the start. The two old hacks just picked up their row where they'd left off, going toe to toe over what should happen next politically. Boulton argued that the voters had given Gordon Brown no mandate to stay in power.

Campbell began to wind him up: 'Adam, I know you've been spending the last few years saying Gordon Brown is dead meat.'

Boulton snapped back: 'I've not been saying that. Tell me where I've said that once.'

Campbell came back with: 'Adam, you're obviously upset David Cameron isn't Prime Minister.'

Boulton riposted: 'I'm not upset. Don't keep telling me what I think.'

'Calm down, calm down,' Campbell told Boulton, baiting the bull. 'This is live on television. Dignity. Dignity, Adam.'

Looking apoplectic Boulton, now right in Campbell's face, shouted: 'Don't keep telling me what I think. I'm fed up with you telling me what I think.'

Campbell's replied: 'I don't care what you're fed up with. I can tell you my opinion.'

Off camera, I tried to intervene. They drowned me out.

Boulton repeated: 'Don't tell me what I think.'

As the sparring continued, I desperately waved to get the attention of cameraman Martin Ayling. Like everyone else, and this included the Sky gallery who'd gone quiet on me, Martin was transfixed by the bunfight.

At last, I caught his eye and gestured him to swing the camera back onto me. Without being in vision, I knew I'd got no chance of regaining control.

In the end I attempted to get the combatants to calm down. 'Alastair, you're being a bit provocative here and unnecessarily so.'

Campbell told me: 'Sometimes politics is about passionate things.'

As Boulton started to tell Campbell: 'You're unelected, but you've plotted all this,' I managed to get a word in: 'Gentlemen, let this debate continue later.'

Even as I turned to Gordon Brown's earlier statement, I could hear them still bickering beside me.

In hindsight this rumble in the Westminster jungle was seen as six minutes of TV gold, attracting hundreds of thousands of YouTube hits. But at the time I was angry at the disrespect shown by a colleague who'd lost the plot on my programme.

It wasn't something I would ever have done. However, Adam and Alastair have kissed and made up, for now. And I've talked to them both plenty of times since then – separately. It was just another reminder that politics, power and passion can be an explosive mix.

CHAPTER 40

PRESENTERS' TIPS

'Whatever you do, do not wear overlarge earrings on location!'

That was the final line of one boss's imperative style guide for presenters.

I made a promise there and then never to indulge in elaborate pendants, or any other distracting baubles, for that matter.

But, seriously, it did make me evaluate what was required to make a decent news presenter.

|||||||||||||||||||||

An awful lot has been said over the years about presenters who do little more than 'read out loud'. Back in the days when the BBC used actors to host the *Nine O'Clock News*, that might have been a fair point, but for most of my working life, TV news has been presented by journalists who know what they're talking about. Some may be more experienced than others, but they tend to know a news story from a shopping list.

However, there are a few things that can make the difference between doing the job OK and doing it well.

It's probably worth starting with a job description. For instance, what should you call someone who fronts the news?

Newsreader
I've always thought that this sounds far too passive for 24-hour TV news. And it does get back to that whole argument about 'reading out loud'. If that's all you're doing, then you're probably overpaid and in the wrong job.

Presenter
Still a bit laid-back, but heading in the right direction. Let's work on how to present and project.

News Anchor
Very American, but underscores what the job's about – holding it all together, not letting the news drift in an ocean of inconsequence.

News Navigator
A bit fancy, but sums it up – guiding viewers through the news safely, skilfully and assuredly.

Basically, you're trying to engage the viewer, steer them through the main news stories of the moment, make them feel well informed and not annoy them.

Here are a few Dos and Don'ts I found useful:

DO try to look like you're enjoying the job.
DO smile as much as possible – where and when appropriate.
DO try to be yourself, natural, honest and relaxed. The camera spots fakers.
DO respect the viewers.
DO take the viewer into your confidence. Tell them if things go wrong.

DON'T try to be someone you're not.

DON'T patronise the viewer.

DON'T ham it up or overact.

DON'T be a smart-arse or grandstand or try to upstage colleagues.

DON'T bring your cares and woes to work.

DON'T share private studio jokes that exclude your viewers.

Voice

The idea is to speak as clearly and distinctly as possible, while making regular eye contact with the viewer. There's nothing worse than watching a shifty-looking presenter who spends most of the time glancing down at their notes, like they don't know what's next and have forgotten that you're watching. Project your voice enough to gain the audience's attention. Your aim is not to shatter the lens. Imagine telling your news story to a friend or family member just beyond the camera, firmly, confidently and sympathetically. You want them to be interested. So set the right tone.

Interviews

Questions need to be clear and concise. If you make them too long and complicated you've probably lost the viewer and the interviewee.

The vast majority of interviews are exercises in information gathering. So I worked on the idea of teasing the maximum out of people, not bullying or scaring info out of people. There's no good reason to be condescending or confrontational. Conflict rarely works, even with politicians. An angry or overheated presenter invariably loses viewer sympathy. So don't get lippy.

If your subject gets aggressive, stay calm and measured in response.

An interview is not a platform for presenters to show off their knowledge.

Unless you're a lot better informed than your interviewee, you'll rarely win a verbal shoot-out. The chances are you'll just end up looking stupid.

Always try to sound reasonable, however unreasonable the person you're talking to. Always stay in control.

Etiquette

Media training has become the bane of the presenter's life. Every other person you interview these days has been trained, probably by a former broadcasting colleague, to call you by your first name. It makes me even more insistent on calling people, always politely, by their full name and often their title too.

So picture the scene.

I say: 'Joining me now is Theodora Thistlethwaite, Minister for Parliamentary Obfuscation. Minister, your new policy seems shrouded in mystery.'

To which the interviewee replies, no doubt with a lovely smile: 'Well, Jeremy, how nice of you to have me on your programme, and what a good question...' A question that, of course, the politician will fail to answer.

This bit of dissembling tends to leave the impression that the presenter is on first-name terms with the person they're talking to, whether they're a politician, captain of industry or military commander. It suggests we're all big chums in the Media-Westminster-Corporate Village and it probably leaves the viewer feeling rather excluded. I've always countered this by being a little more formal and insisting on calling them by their full names and titles. Don't let them score points. Journalism is like judo: you always try to keep the upper hand.

The other thing I find irritating is overdoing the 'hellos' and 'goodbyes'. Be polite, courteous and friendly, but don't be too effusive.

'Fred Karno from the Slapstick Society, thanks for talking to us,' is quite enough. But how many times have you heard something like this: 'Fred Karno, thank you so, so much for taking the trouble to talk us today and sparing us so much of your valuable time. It's been wonderful, Fred, a truly memorable experience. I know we'll never forget it and I'm sure the viewers won't either.' OK, a bit of an exaggeration, but a reminder we can easily go over the top without thinking.

What's worse is when you hear it during a two-way with your own staff reporters. All too often you get: 'Charlie Farnes-Barnes there, live from Flamborough Head. Charlie, thank you so much for joining us on Sky News today.' For goodness sake! He's a colleague. It's his job. He gets paid to talk to you. 'Thanks Charlie' will do just fine.

When I said try to stay in control, there are still, of course, some moments as a presenter you simply can't plan for. Like being stuck on a hotel rooftop in Kuwait while sirens wail and people start shouting 'Scud attack'. It was the night of 'shock and awe' as the US launched its devastating airstrikes on Baghdad. Saddam Hussein responded with missiles aimed at Kuwait. We were prepared, but it was still a TV news comedy moment as I wrestled to put on my gas mask and then tried to carry on presenting live through a face full of rubber and air filters. Thankfully the threat soon passed. I was able to rip off the mask and take gulps of fresh air.

In 2006, I was broadcasting high on a hill overlooking the Israeli city of Haifa when Hezbollah launched wave after wave of Katyusha rockets from thirty miles north on the Lebanon border. Three years older, but maybe none the wiser, this time I just ducked involuntarily and kept on talking. The old Russian-made missiles were so random and so inaccurate that it was just one of those lottery moments when you cross your fingers and hope you're lucky.

In contrast, the Greek elections in 2012 provided an RPI – a random punter incident. As I came on air at the top of the hour live from Athens's Syntagma Square, a woman ran over to me, grabbed the microphone and started an animated rant, mainly in Greek, with the odd English word. After a few attempts I managed to prise her away from my mic, as politely as possible, and explained to viewers how 'passions are running very high in this election'.

But that wasn't the end of it. Twice more I tried to broadcast from Syntagma with the same result. Wherever I stood in the square the same 'overexcited' woman hijacked my programme, gabbling into the camera. My producer and crew did their best to ease her away without manhandling her. I was sure I heard her say 'Jeremy' a couple of times. Eventually our translator got to the bottom of the manic mystery. It seemed my eccentric news intruder had heard a man called 'Jeremy' being 'very rude about Greece' on British TV. It turned out it was Paxman on BBC *Newsnight*. That's the trouble with having too many Jeremys on television.

CHAPTER 41

BACK TO AFRICA

I rarely got emotional about stories. It was business. Involved yes, but not emotional. I figured the best thing to do with feelings was harness them. Whatever you felt about a news event – sadness, pain, anger, disgust, injustice – you used it to drive home the story, to make it count, to make sure people got the message. But never let emotion cloud your clarity, affect your judgement.

IIIIIIIIIIIIIIIIII

The death of Nelson Mandela was an exception. When he died on 5 December 2013 at the age of ninety-five, it felt like the end of an era, the closing of a major chapter in my career. The poignancy was no doubt more profound because my mother had died less than a month before. She was ninety-nine.

When I told her earlier that year that I was going to South Africa to report on Mandela's declining health, she'd said playfully: 'But he's such a young man, dear.'

It felt strange, almost intrusive, standing outside Pretoria's Mediclinic day after day waiting for medical bulletins. 'He's serious, but stable,' came one report. 'He's under sedation,' said another. 'His health continues to improve,' insisted President Jacob Zuma.

It felt like behind the scenes there was an unholy power struggle going on between the ANC, the President's office and the Mandela family for control of his legacy. On the street outside there was a circus of media trucks, camera crews, drones, well-wishers, prayer vigils and curious tourists. Each hour there were fresh rumours and alarms from way too many unreliable sources.

Sadly, it seemed we were all just waiting for him to die.

I thought back to the last time I'd seen and spoken to him six years earlier. I'd been filming a documentary for Sky on the Mandela years I'd been lucky enough to cover, using my old TV reports to chart his journey from prisoner to President.

I'd wanted an interview with him. But his closest advisers felt he wasn't well enough to go on camera. Instead I was invited to have tea with him in his office at the Mandela Foundation. Just him and me and his remarkable personal assistant Zelda La Grange, the white Afrikaner who became his closest confidante in his final years.

Madiba showed signs that his short-term memory was a little shaky. But he chatted happily and vividly about stories I'd covered a decade or so earlier as he engineered the end of apartheid. He recalled his years in jail, learning Afrikaans so he could better understand his enemy. He talked of his excitement as he finally walked free on that February day in 1990. And his memory of when we returned to Robben Island with him exactly four years later, just before the historic 1994 election. We laughed about my interview with him in his old cell. He told me about his joy on the day of his inauguration as he made his famous 'Rainbow Nation' speech.

He was eighty-nine then, frail enough to need my arm for support as he walked me to the door. But still sharp enough to remember my name was Jeremy. For me it was a special hour or so in the company of a man for whom I had great admiration.

For six months South Africa said its long farewell to the nation's father figure. People worried about how they'd cope without the glue that had held the country united. Some pundits warned of the dangers of deifying Mandela. 'He was no saint,' they said, but he was an icon who'd brought democracy and reconciliation.

In the end, Nelson Rolihlahla Mandela died peacefully at his home in Houghton. South Africans woke up the next morning. And the world kept turning. The eulogies poured in from around the globe. Barack Obama called him a 'hero for the world, whose legacy will last through the ages'. Others called him 'the last great hero on the planet'.

Many feared the impact of his loss. My old friend Francois Pienaar, South Africa's World Cup-winning rugby captain, told me: 'I am worried that our country has lost its moral compass.'

But South Africa had ten days of official mourning to get used to the idea. I joined the crowds braving the rain and the cold to witness Mandela's memorial service at the FNB Stadium on the edge of Soweto. And I saw the huge numbers who waited patiently to file past his body as he lay in state at the Union Buildings, where he'd been inaugurated as President nineteen years before.

The howling gale that nearly swept us and our equipment off a nearby rooftop seemed ominous. And the rain was still falling as the Sky News team slithered into the media encampment overlooking the funeral site at Qunu, Mandela's ancestral home.

The sun broke through as he was laid to rest. Cows grazed on the hill near my camera position, just as they had ninety years earlier when young Nelson helped his father herd the family cattle. These were the roots that he never forgot during his twenty-seven years in prison.

I realised it was the end of a journey for me. I'd first come to South Africa as a young TV reporter thirty-one years earlier to cover the first rebel cricket tour at the height of apartheid. I was soon hooked on the country, the people and their story. I returned as a foreign correspondent based here for four years, reporting the twists and turns, the anguish and the violence, as the nation wrestled over its future. I came close to death on more than one occasion, caught in the crossfire of warring factions. Lying in the dirt, dodging the gunshots, I realised this African soil was under my fingernails, literally and figuratively. I was living and reporting the unfolding drama as the country dragged itself towards democracy.

I witnessed Mandela's powers of persuasion and force of personality that doused the fires of civil war and kept the hope of a fairer future alive. A remarkable man. An amazing story. As a journalist, it had been a privilege to be a messenger.

CHAPTER 42

TRUMP AND OUT

I wanted to go out with a bang, not a whimper.

Certainly not as terminal as T. S. Eliot's poetic words: 'This is the way the world ends.'

Just a good strong story to finish my career.

||||||||||||||||||||

When Sky News chief John Ryley and I met for our annual contract chat over a decent dinner, we'd long ago come up with a civilised formula.

'So the usual deal?' I'd say. 'If I wake up one morning and no longer have the appetite for news, you'll be the first person I ring. And if you wake up, turn on the TV and think "Who's that wrinkly old bugger on my screen?" I'll be the first person you call.' And with that, we'd shake hands and seal it with a good glass of red wine.

Around mid-2015, we agreed one more year would do me fine. John proposed I should bow out at the end of the 2016 US election, which would be my sixth presidential campaign. Neither of us could have imagined it would turn into such a sensational climax to my career at Sky.

By the time I started my election year in the icy flatlands of Iowa,

Donald J. Trump was a candidate, but just one of thirteen Republicans pitching for the nomination. Eight more had already fallen by the wayside. Even then Trump only came second to Senator Ted Cruz. But it gave him lift off. It had a feeling of Snow White, Iowa and the twelve dwarves. Trump was starting to look larger than life and brashly bigger than his rivals.

Though Trump didn't win the Iowa caucus, I wrote an online piece entitled 'Mr Invincible v Mrs Inevitable'. Trump exuded the air of a winner. But then he'd never fought an election in his life, so he'd never lost. While Hillary Clinton looked like a shoo-in for the Democrats – part of the Clinton dynasty, former First Lady and Secretary of State, no one was better qualified.

But I vividly remembered how Obama stole Iowa from under her nose eight years earlier and never looked back. I was surprised she was still stubborn enough and entitled enough to believe she could do better this time around.

The voters seemed angrier and more divided than I'd ever seen before. Across the US, people told me this primary season was 'like no other' and warned me to 'expect the unexpected'.

En route, I tested the chilly political temperature in Port Clinton, Ohio. It seemed an appropriate name and they had an uncanny knack of naming the nation's next President. They were on a winning streak stretching back over seventy years to the election of Harry S. Truman in 1945. It was a journalist's dream. I found a taxidermist called Todd, who told me 'we don't stuff critters, we mount them. And central government mounts us ordinary folk every god dam day.'

Then there was Loria, the popcorn-maker, who normally voted Democrat, but was leaning towards Trump. And Ray, the pilot, who'd 'never vote for Hillary'. Hugh, the new mayor, was a heavy-vehicle mechanic, who thought the new President needed to do a repair job on the nation. He added: 'Above all we need to renew the American Dream and make America great again.' So I was starting to get the picture of who might do well in this election. And it was still only early February.

In one of those amusing quirks of the media game, producer Nina Saada, cameraman Adam Cole and I found ourselves front page news in the local paper. *The Port Clinton News Herald* told its readers that 'international news channel Sky News's had come to the community with its 'finger on the pulse of America's voters'. It was clearly a quiet week for news in northern Ohio.

Next stop New Hampshire and a lucky encounter with Mr Trump. He did lots of rallies, but he didn't like talking to the media much, especially the foreign mob. There were no votes in it. But I waylaid him at a quiet polling station and got a few minutes of his time. I remember the orange and straw-coloured glow emanating from his eminence as I asked about the importance of the US–UK 'special relationship'. 'Sure it'll be special,' he assured me. 'Real special. I own golf courses over there in Britain.'

The election was weird and wacky and turning downright nasty, brimming with bile. I called it the marmite election because it was coming down to two candidates who were either loved or loathed, with way more loathing than loving. It was so polarised, US analysts had dubbed it 'lesser evilism', with voters going for the least worst option.

Trump called his opponent 'crooked Hillary'. She branded him a woman groper, unfit to run the country. It was knockabout, celebrity politics served up for the reality TV age, with a paltry portion of policies on the side. The more Trump fired barbs at the media and tweeted his alternative news, the more it looked like a new version of *The Apprentice*.

He'd certainly ripped up the old campaign playbook and changed the political culture, trampling on the unwritten code of American democracy. It was fascinating to see how his provocative, sometimes outrageous comments, stole the news agenda. Such were the ratings spikes when he appeared on air, it forced the hand of TV news networks, even the more liberal ones. Trump dominated the hourly output. The news channels may not have liked him or what he said, but they were obliged to cover his every move. Quite simply, he was box office.

In the build-up to election day on 8 November, I cantered through some 'battleground states', presenting daily shows from Florida, Ohio, Pennsylvania, North Carolina and Virginia. I was surprised at the depth and breadth of support for 'The Donald'. Many pundits insisted only angry, white, working-class men really backed Trump. But it didn't sound like that to me.

At a sidewalk bar in Tampa, Fred, an IT guy with Puerto Rican roots, explained: 'I simply don't trust Hillary. So I guess Trump gets my vote. He's the lesser of two evils.' In Raleigh, North Carolina, car attendant Tyrone insisted not all African-Americans were Democrats. 'I reckon Trump will get us more jobs.' At Reading Market in Philadelphia, Betsy, a 32-year-old white teacher, wanted me to know that a lot of women backed Trump, though she had reservations. 'It pains me to say I'll vote Trump, but I trust him more than Hillary.' And Sheree, a vivacious accountant in her thirties, was keen to tell me that well-educated whites were behind Trump too. 'I've got three degrees in economics and accounting and I love Trump.'

Trump appealed to the disenchanted, disaffected heart of America. However unlikely it seemed, a self-proclaimed billionaire had sold himself as a Galahad to the grumpy masses. He'd tapped into a protest vote that had echoes of Brexit. He'd channelled the anger of citizens who believed the American dream was slipping over the horizon. Voters who felt abandoned and betrayed by the political classes. They were branded the *disaffectorati*.

But polls still claimed the majority of Americans found Trump toxic. It was Hillary Clinton's to lose and lose it she did. She was the very establishment that The Donald and his 'Trumpstas' were railing against.

At one Clinton rally I covered in Tampa, I was surprised to see an old friend, José Andrés, get up on stage to introduce the candidate. Since I'd first met José in my Washington days, he'd gone on to become one of the best-known celebrity chefs in the US. Even in his Spanish-inflected English, his speech completely outshone Hillary's address, underlining her lack of sparkle and appeal. José told me that Hillary was a good woman, who'd run America well. But she wasn't selling it.

A few days later, watching an Obama rally in North Carolina, I was reminded why he'd won two terms and she hadn't. He had the qualities Bill Clinton possessed, but Hillary never would – charm, charisma, the X factor. The mainly student crowd was in awe. He was an icon, their political inspiration.

The contrast made me wonder if it was more a case of Hillary Clinton losing the 2016 election as much as it was Trump winning it.

It was a great last road trip for me leading up to election day. I had a good crew to keep me company – Andy Portch, a cracking cameraman, who'd filmed some brilliant reports when he was based in China and had lots of creative ideas and gizmos, Chris Curtis, a sound man in every respect, and Kenny Stewart, a bright and very well-informed young producer, whom I'd worked with earlier on the US campaign trail. Hard work, humour and a decent alarm clock are the essence of any trip. Teamwork is about trust and trust comes down to respect. Like any good crew, we believed in each other's abilities. So we worked an awful lot of hours, covered many road miles, flew a load of airlines and filmed a host of people. The mantra: top-notch work, never be late and no complaining. We hit every programme on time, made every flight and never missed an event. And still managed to have a few beers and plenty of laughs.

As the old fella on the crew, I thought the least I could do was pass on a few tips to the lads about life on the road. Like 'whatever you get up to, you've got to be back by breakfast'. In other words, don't tie one on if you can't get up the next morning. That was never a problem with this Sky team. Though Chris admitted he picked up one handy late-night hint: 'Never pick up the bar bill after the presenter has ordered a round of hugely expensive malt whisky.'

They also learned the wisdom of letting the 'talent' pick the restaurant. A substandard dinner can make a presenter very grumpy. And believe in that old nickname 'One Take Thompson' – he really can still do a piece to camera in one go.

I was surprised to discover how many of the team didn't realise the little arrow next to the petrol gauge in the hire car pointed to the side with the fuel cap. Hardly life or death advice, but useful when you're in a hurry. And talking of cars, I reminded them of the words of that fine American satirist, P. J. O'Rourke, whom I'd met in a few dark places: 'The best car in the world? A hire car.'

By the end of our American election adventure I was heartened to see the crew going out for an evening on their own. It looked like the TV news business was ready to manage without me! They were probably thinking: 'Phew! We've finally got rid of granddad.'

Back on the campaign trail, my earlier suspicions that the polls were out of whack and Trump was out to get the media were starting to take shape. In Daytona Beach, we took a taxi ride with driver Nick, who offered me his 'Uber prediction'. He'd spent all year counting campaign posters in Florida. He'd seen hundreds for Trump, but very few for Clinton. He added: 'On that basis alone I reckon Trump will win Florida by a mile.' It turned out Uber man Nick was closer than a lot of pollsters.

I guided viewers through the sanity-defying results from my election night studio high above Times Square, my last major broadcast for Sky. The *Evening Standard* noted somewhat quirkily: 'Sky's Jeremy Thompson resembles a seasoned American anchorman, or even a presidential candidate. For long stretches of the seven-hour broadcast he manned his Starship Enterprise-style desk apparently alone, or chatted lugubriously with handsome political scientist Todd Donovan.'

What an extraordinary election. More than I could ever have

imagined, I went out with a bang. Or, perhaps more accurately, a thump of Trump and a clap of political thunder. As for The Donald's hack bashing, no sooner was he elected than he started branding major networks and newspapers as 'fake news'. He attacked much of the mainstream media, calling journalists 'enemies of the people' and 'among the most dishonest people in the world'. Reporters recoiled.

His supporters applauded.

It was hard to know whether the new President was merely dissing those who dared to question him or damning anything he disagreed with. 'Any negative polls are fake news,' he Trumped.

It looked like a calculated attempt to undermine the traditional media. Trump's use of Twitter to bypass the fourth estate and talk direct to the people showed his determination to manage the message. And that laid down a huge challenge to serious news outlets.

Trump had pledged to 'drain the swamp', referring to the 'entire corrupt Washington establishment'. Now he seemed intent on cleansing America's newsrooms too.

All this against a noisy backdrop of internet chaff. Social media had expedited the growth of fake news sites, spewing out truth-bending propaganda and conspiracy theories, masquerading as authentic news.

Fake headlines went viral, like 'the Pope backs Trump' and 'Hillary sold weapons to ISIS'. Myths and hoaxes jostled for attention with genuine stories. Guerrilla groups of writers in this info war were riding roughshod over the gospel truth, if there is such a thing anymore. Facts were left face down like fresh roadkill on the information superhighway.

The worry was that when Trump called the world's press 'out of control' liars and said 'the public doesn't believe you anymore' a lot of people might really buy it.

This latest misinformation age of so-called 'post-truth' and 'post-factual' politics has created a minefield for the media.

As I retire and retreat from the news frontline, I'll watch with great interest to see how the next generation of news men and women hack their way over the hurdles of the twenty-first century. Brexit, Trump, terrorism, migration, climate, work and poverty all pose great challenges. How journalists report these issues will be vital. As media messengers, there have been too many times when we carrier pigeons have looked more like vultures. I've always felt our role was to ask the difficult questions, to hold leaders to account and to keep society honest.

How do you measure your working life? How do you calibrate a career from the inside? In this celebrity-addicted age, I realised fame meant very little – being fair was far more important. Recognition's fine, but for doing a good story, not just for being on TV. The approval of your peers, your comrades in news, is always appreciated. But the ultimate satisfaction is knowing you've given it your best. For me it was about the job, the journalism, the writing, the being there at big stories.

I've been incredibly lucky. I've survived fifty years in the news business. I've been sent to most corners of the world and reported many of the great events of my time. I've met remarkable people and seen incredible things and I would swap very little, even the most terrifying moments. News has been good to me.

AWARDS

1992 Emmy News Awards Winner Breaking News Story –
Bisho Massacre

1992 New York Festival Winner Best Reporter –
Somali Attack and Bisho

1993 New York Festival Winner Best Special Report –
Somalia Famine

1994 New York Festival Winner Best Reporter –
Africa – Rwanda

1999 RTS TV Journalism Best News Event –
Kosovo Liberation

2001 BAFTA News Coverage Winner –
9/11

2002 RTS TV Journalism Awards Winner News Event –
Holly and Jessica

2002 BAFTA News Coverage Winner –
Soham Murders

2004 TRIC Awards Winner –
Satellite Television Personality of the Year

2004/5 RTS TV Journalism Awards –
Presenter of the Year

2005 International Emmy Breaking News –
7/7 Terror Attack

2009   International Emmy Outstanding News –
        Pakistan: Terror's Frontline
2009   BAFTA News Coverage Winner –
        Pakistan: Terror's Frontline
2012   RTS Journalism Awards Winner: Home News Event –
        UK Riots
        International News Event –
        Libya
2015   BAFTA News Coverage Winner –
        Ebola
2016   RTS TV Journalism Winner –
        Sky News at 5 – Programme of the Year

        RTS News Channel of the Year –
        2001, 2002, 2003, 2004, 2006, 2007, 2009, 2011, 2015

INDEX

Abdi (taxi driver) 178–80
Aidid, General Mohammed Farah 175, 176, 183
Ali, Muhammad 108
Allen, Dominic 59
Andrés, José 373
Angel, Colin 84
Anne, Princess 2, 345–6
Anselme, Gombaniro 231
Appleyard, Ross 253
Aquino, President Corazon 99
Arafat, Yasser 210
Arinze, Francis 316
Arkan (Serbian warlord) 254, 255
Armstrong, Fiona 343
Arnett, Peter 107
Arthy, Sally 305
Assad, Bashar al- 331
Atkinson, Tina 42
Austin, Mark 58, 116, 189, 334–5
Ayling, Martin 357

Bafut, Fons of 343
Baker, Pete 351
Ball, Tony 302
Banks, John 38
Barlow, Eddie 54

Barlow, Eeben 114
Barratt, Nick 32
Barron, Brian 98, 111
Bazalgette, Peter 32
Behrens, Rolf 190, 203, 207, 209–10
Benedict XVI, Pope 316–17
Benn, Tony 108
Bennett, Jon 300, 303, 304
Bhutto, Benazir 83–4, 210
Biko, Ntsiki 141
Biko, Steve 141
Billy (rugby player) 19
Birkett, Chris 306, 307
Bisson, Francois 87–8
Blair, Cherie 350–1
Blair, Tony 238, 326, 349–51
Blakeley, Colin 15
Blakey, Mike 65
Bluff, Peter 103
Blunkett, David 26
Boettcher, Mike 260–1
Border, Allan 57
Boreham, Mr Justice 49
Botham, Ian (Beefy) 37, 57, 58, 60
Botting, Anna 277, 316, 321
Boulton, Adam 354, 356, 357
Boutros-Ghali, Boutros 210

Bowden, David 289
Bowles, Rob 244
Boycott, Geoff 37, 53, 54–5
Bratt, Claes 76
Brattan, Andy 296, 299, 301
Brazier, Colin 300
Bremner, Billy 37
Brierley, Dave 32, 355
Brokaw, Tom 312
Brown, Gordon 354, 356
Brown, Louise 35
Bruno, Frank 240
Brunson, Mike 347
Brunt, Martin 277, 280, 289, 292, 324
Budd, Zola 244
Burley, Kay 263, 271–2, 273–4, 324, 348
Burman, Blake 309
Burrows, Mark 98
Bush, George H. W. 181
Bush, George W. 108, 273, 307–8, 326
Buthelezi, Mangosuthu 200, 202
Byford, Lawrence 47
Byford, Mark 47

Callaghan, Jim 351
Cameron, David 354, 356
Campbell, Alastair 294, 350, 356, 357
Campbell, Eugene 127
'Captain Hawk' 128–9
Carlin, John 219–20
Carlton, Paul 109, 110–11
Carr, Gordon 47
Carr, Maxine 285–92
Carrington, Peter, Lord 8
Carter, Jimmy 306–7
Carthew, Anthony 341, 343
Castro, Fidel 210, 311–12
Cecil (taxi driver) 83
Chapman, Jessica 278, 284–92
Chapman, Leslie and Sharon 287–8
Charles, Prince 2, 343–4, 345
Charlie (pilot) 162–6
Chater, David 128, 189, 253, 294, 300, 308

Che Guevara 312–13
Cheeseman, Ray 99, 120
Chisholm, Sam 191, 192–5
Chissano, Joaquim 169
Chrétien, Jean 88
Christie, Linford 245
Churchill, Winston 215
Clark, William 46
Clegg, Nick 354
Clifford, Michelle 289
Clinton, Bill 183, 234, 238–40, 311
Clinton, Hillary 238, 305, 370, 371, 372–3
Clough, Brian 36–7
Coe, Seb 244
Cole, Adam 371
Cole, Michael 351–2
Collison, Pamela 52
Cook, Ian (Cookie) 193
Cooke, Michael 353
Cooper, Ken 38
Corbett, Ronnie 347
Crabtree, David 289
Crawford, Alex 206, 280, 327, 328
Crow, Sheryl 306
Cruz, Ted 370
Cunningham, Tim 315
Curlewis, Llewellyn 280
Curtis, Chris 373–4

Davies, Paul 341
Davies, Trevor 340
Deane, Daniela 334, 337
Deane, Mick 86–8, 235, 259, 261, 312, 333–7
Decker, Mary 244
Deng Xiaoping 86
Derby-Lewis, Clive 146–7
Dhlakama, Afonso 117, 161–2, 166–8
Diana, Princess of Wales 2, 240, 261–2, 342–5
Dowler, Milly 278
Doyle, Larry 107
Duller, Eddie 15–16, 20

Eales, Maggie 71
Eddie (news editor) 9
Eddie the Eagle 240
Edwards, Jon 305
Edwards, Robert 35
Elizabeth, II, Queen 97, 98, 216–17,
  339–41, 347
Emburey, John 53, 55
Etchingham, Julie 263
Evans, Ken 32, 34
Ewart, Tim 31

Faduma (Somalia) 178
Faku, Nceba 213
Farah, Mo 248
Faulkner, Jackie 251
Fisk, Robert 109, 255
Fitzsimmons, Cait 287
Foley, Mark 139
Forlong, James 206
Fourie, Faan 205
Fowler, Graeme 72
Fraser, Ed 287, 288, 296, 299
Friend, Bob 211
Frost, Bill 103
Frykberg, Ian (Frykers) 187–8, 189,
  190–4, 199

Gaddafi, Colonel Muammar 329–30
Galloway, George 108
Gandhi, Indira 63–4
Gandhi, Rajiv 69, 70, 71, 115
Gatting, Mike 72
Glancy, Bernie 105
Gooch, Graham 53, 55
Gorbachev, Mikhail 88
Gore, Al 210, 307
Gower, David 58, 69
Gqozo, Brig. Joshua 138
Grassrope, Garfield 108
Graves, Keith 253, 255–6, 314
Green, Martin 17
Greengrass, Paul 320
Gregory, Ronald 46–7

Grey QC, Gilbert 52

Habyarimana, Juvénal 221–2
Hale, Nathan 285
Hall, Mervyn 61, 244
Hani, Chris 145–6, 147–8
Hattem (driver) 108
Hattersley, Enid 26
Healey, Denis 353
Heath, Ted 23, 25
Hebb, Andy 288, 290
Heseltine, Michael 37
Hickey, Fred 64, 66
Hickory, Fred 68, 69
Hicks, Zack 17
Hill, David 191
Hill, Jacqueline 45
Honasan, Colonel Gringo 98, 99,
  100
Hookes, David 57
Hoon, Geoff 295
Hope, Bob 240
Hu Yaobang 86
Huddleston, BIshop Trevor 211
Hudson, Jennifer 306
Humble, John ('Wearside Jack') 44
Humphrys, John 53
Hun Sen 81
Hunt, Jonathan 312
Huntley, Ian 285–92
Hurd, Douglas 210
Hurd, Emma 253, 277, 297, 300, 314,
  330
Hurrell, Ron 32, 80
Hussein, Saddam 27, 102, 105, 106,
  108, 363

Ibrahim, Moussa 330
Inglis, Mike 99, 100, 120, 122, 124–5,
  126
Insole, Doug 56
Ironmonger, Ron 26
Isabella (granddaughter) 257, 334
Itoh, Tomoo 75

Jackson, Emily 41
Jackson, John 60
Jeacock, Michael 16–17
Jenkins, Des 300
Jennings, Pat 49
Jennings, Peter 312
Jewell, Richard 246
Jimmy (Tutsi guide) 230–1
John Paul II, Pope 311–12, 313–14,
    315–16
Johnson, Ben 245
Jonah, James 176
Jones, April 279
Jones, Duncan 60
Jones, Joey 324
Jones, Nick 352
Jones, Paula 238
Jones, Ray 97
Jordan, Jean 42
Jordan, Pallo 134
Joubert, Pearlie 190, 203, 205, 207, 226

Kabanda, Celestine 230
Kagame, Paul 222
Kagan, Joseph, Lord 36
Karzai, Hamid 328
Kassell, Allan 28
Kaunda, Kenneth 134
Keating, Frank 59
Kennedy, John F. 12, 311
Kerry, John 308
Khanh, Nguyen 79
Khuroo brothers 69–70
Kiley, Sam 330
Kim Il-sung 245
Kissinger, Henry 61
Kladstrup, Don 181
de Klerk, F. W. 134–7, 139, 147, 200–2,
    204, 210
Krebs, Daniel 134–5
Kunene, Simon 206

La Grange, Zelda 366
Lalani, Dr. Minet 227

Lamb, Allan (Lamby) 57, 58
Lander, Chris (Crash) 56, 57
Leach, Tim 133, 134
Lee, Eunbong (EB Lee) 75–6, 245–6
Lee Jones, Tommy 320
Legend, John 306
Lewinsky, Monica 238, 312
Lewis, Martyn 43
Lilley, Dennis 57
Lloyd, Terry 244, 295–6
Lookinghorse, Orvol 108
Loren, Sophia 12
Luxford, Paul 97

MacArthur, Brian 298
McCain, John 306
McCann, Madeleine 277–8
McCann, Wilma 41
MacDonald, Jayne 42
MacDonald, Pete 252, 255
McGreevy, Allen 236, 237, 240, 241,
    336
MacKenzie, Kelvin 192
McLuckie, Garwen 330
McVeigh, Timothy 235
Major, John 216
Mandela, Nelson (Madiba) 133–41,
    143–8
    death 365–8
    election 202, 206–7, 210–17
    on Obama 304
    Robben Island 199–200
    and Springboks 219–20
Mangope, Lucas 202
Manning, Tim 78, 80, 116, 181
Marsh, Rodney 57
Marshall, Tim 253, 255, 332
Massey, Keith 32, 34, 38
Mates, James 299
Mathope, Aaron 136
Meyer, Christopher 240
Meyer, Roelf 147
Milam, Greg 300
Miller, Geoff 58

Milnes, Pete 296, 331
Milošević, Slobodan 125, 130, 250–1
Mitchell, Waddie 241
Mkiva, Zolani 211
Mlangeni, Maria 136
Mohammed, Ali Mahdi 174, 175, 176, 183
Momoh, Joseph Saidu 153
Morris, Graham (Morro) 56, 57
Muldi (local fixer) 329
Munson, Jim 87
Murdoch, Rupert 188, 189, 191–2

Nathan, 'Boff' 12
Ne Win 346
Neilson, Donald 35–6
Nico (ARD cameraman) 119
Nidal, Abu 66
Nisbet, Robert 331
Nolan, Mike 55, 193, 217
Noone, Kevin 227–8
Norris, Percy 65, 66
Ntaryamira, Cyprien 221–2

Obama, Barack 303, 304, 305–6, 307, 309, 373
O'Flaherty, Michael 16
Ognall QC, Harry 52
Oldfield, George 44
O'Loan, John 191
O'Rourke, Jenny 213
O'Rourke, P. J. 374
Orwell, George 226
O'Ryan-Roeder, Patrick 103, 120
O'Shea, Kelvin 331–2
Ovett, Steve 244

Palin, Sarah 306, 308
Pantich, Pasha 126
Parkin, Leonard 340
Patnick, Irvine 26
Paxman, Jeremy 364
Payne, Sarah 278
Pearson, Yvonne 43

Pegg, Simon 321
Peters, Steve 259
Le Pen, Jean-Marine 108
Philip, Prince 339
Pienaar, Francois 218, 219, 367
Pistorius, Oscar 279–80
Pol Pot 81
Pollard, Nick 194–5, 249–51, 257, 302, 340
Pollock, Graeme 54
Pomfret, Colonel John 300
Ponti, Carlo 12
Portch, Andy 373
Prapanya, Narunart 75
Prebble, Stuart 32
Pretorius, Willy 213
Prime, Dave 306
Proctor, Mike 54
Protheroe, Roger 299
Purnell, Nick 299, 301

Rabuka, Colonel Sitiveni (Steve) 96–8
Radebe, Gugu 138–9, 146, 190
Ramaphosa, Cyril 138, 197
Rameledi, Elizabeth 136
Ramos, General Fidel 99, 100
Ramsay, Stuart 300, 327, 330, 336
Rather, Dan 307, 312
Rayner, Tom 329, 330
Redgrave, Steve 244, 245
Rees, Ken 43
Rees, Norman 306
Reid, John 354
Reid, Peter 103
Rex, Andy 78–80, 82–3, 86, 90, 334, 335
Rich, Fred 340
Rich, Seb 244
Richard, Cliff 347
Richards, Barry 54
Riordan, Joy 175
Robbie, Ian 137–40
    Angola 114
    battlefield training 186

Robbie, Ian *cont.*
  Malawi 162–5
  Mozambique 117–18, 169–71
  Sierra Leone 152, 157
  Sky News 190
  Somalia 173, 177, 181
  South Africa 82–3, 198
  Zaire 223, 226
Roberts, Chris 263
Robin (BBC) 22
Robson, Bryan 60
Rolling Stones, The 61
Romney, Mitt 309
Rudder, Jim 253, 255
Rudolph, Eric 246
Ryley, John 333, 354, 369
Rytka, Helen 43

Saada, Nina 371
Sadler, Brent 52, 107
Saggers, Mark 246
Sankoh, Foday 152–3
Savile, Jimmy 31
Savimbi, Jonas 113
Sayers, Christina 32
Scargill, Arthur 24
Scarratt, Jonathan 265, 269
Schutte, Larry 241
Schwarz, Tim 74–5, 86
Sexwale, Tokyo 145–6
Seymour, Derek 59–60
Shariff, Abdul 198
Sharp, Peter 103, 109, 189, 206, 308
Simon, Bob 103
Simpson, Bob 26–7, 107
Simpson, John 53, 107
Simpson, O. J. 234
Singh, Beant 64
Singh, Karan 71
Singh, Satwant 64
Sisulu, Walter 146
Sivaramakrishnan, Laxman 66
Skekic, Jaksa 255
Skinner, Dennis 26

Slovo, Joe 197
Smartt, Mike 31
Smith, Ian 162
Smith, Martin 327
Smith, Ralph 21–2
Sophia (granddaughter) 6, 334
Sorge, Wayne 236
Spencer, John 17
Spiro, Glenda 190
Springsteen, Bruce 306
Stanford, Martin 263
Staunton, Peter 32, 48, 49
Steel, David 351, 352
Steel, Judy 352
Steenkamp, Reeva 279–80
Steptoe, Patrick 35
Stevens, Siaka 158
Stewart, Alastair 102
Stewart, Kenny 373
Stone, Charles 12
Stone, Mark 9
Strasser, Captain Valentine 153, 154, 156–9
Suchet, John 352
Suk, Yong 76
Sullivan, Michael 351
Sutcliffe, Peter 46, 47–50
Sutcliffe, Sonia (née Szurma) 48–9
Szurma family 48–9

Talreja, Purshotam (Percy) 66, 67, 69, 70, 71–2
Talreja, Sanjiv 67, 68, 69
Tambo, O. R. 146, 148
Tariq (cabbie) 6
Tavaré, Chris 58
Te Kanawa, Dame Kiri 266
Terre'Blanche, Eugène 202, 214
Thatcher, Margaret 37, 64, 108, 135, 215, 351, 353
Thirer, Eric 111
Thompson, Adam (son) 210, 274, 295
Thompson, Daley 244
Thompson, Gordon Alfred (father) 11

Thompson, James (son) 274
Thompson, Lynn (wife)
    family 6, 45, 257
    holidays 69, 70, 78
    Hong Kong 95
    Millennium 265, 269
    phone calls 140
    South Africa 219
    support for JT 122, 188, 302
    yard sale 242
Thomson, Alex 297
Thomson, Jeff 57, 58
Thorpe, Jeremy 353
Thorseth, Ragnar 61–2
Toker, John 72
Toksvig, Nick 259, 265, 269
Troyna, Gerry 32
Trump, Donald J. 370–6
Tucker, Karla Faye 236
Turner, Ted 192
Tyson, Mike 240–1

Uren, Monty 213

Versace, Gianni 236–7
Vickers, Dr Paul 52–3
Viljoen, General Constand 205–6
Virtanen, Rauli 116
von Maltitz, Eddy 203, 213–14
Vowles, Martin 328
Vuknič, Mario 128

Walker, Amanda 277
Waluś, Janusz 146
Wardman, Phil 349, 351
Wells, Holly 278, 284–92
Wells, Kevin and Nicola 285, 287–8
Whetstone, Keith 17, 20
Whiley, Anthony 252
Whiteley, Richard 38
Whittle, Lesley 35
Widener, Jeff 93
Wiener, Robert 107
will.i.am 306, 309

Willis, Bob 56
Wilson, Andrew 252, 253, 255
Wilson, Harold 36, 354–5
Windsor, Barbara 347
Wonder, Stevie 306
Wood, Jamie 304
Woods, Donald 141
Woods, Ian 277, 324, 335
Woodward, Louise 235
Woolmer, Bob 54
Woon, Peter 53
Wright, Edgar 321
Wu'er Kaixi 88
Wyatt, Caroline 297

Young-sam, Kim 78

Zahn, Paula 227
Zardari, Asif Ali 327
Zheng Ma Zui 341–2
Zuma, Jacob 366